Gods, Demons and
Symbols of
Ancient Mesopotamia

Gods, Demons and Symbols of Ancient Mesopotamia

An Illustrated Dictionary

Jeremy Black and Anthony Green

Illustrations by Tessa Rickards

THE BRITISH MUSEUM PRESS

Jeremy Black
The late Dr Black, formerly Director of the British
School of Archaeology in Iraq, was a Fellow of Wolfson
College, Oxford, and University Lecturer in Akkadian.
He was the author of several studies on Sumerian and
Babylonian literature and ancient philology, and headed
the Electronic Text Corpus of Sumerian Literature
project (http://etcsl.orinst.ox.ac.uk)

Anthony Green
Dr Green has formerly held the positions of Fellow of the
British School of Archaeology in Iraq, J. Paul Getty
Postdoctoral Research Fellow in the History of Art at the
University of Pennsylvania, G.A. Wainwright Research
Fellow in Near Eastern Archaeology at Oxford University,
and Alexander von Humboldt Research Fellow at the Free
University of Berlin. He is currently Shinji Shumeikai
Senior Academic Research Fellow in Near Eastern Art and
Archaeology at the Free University of Berlin. He has
conducted extensive archaeological fieldwork in Syria and
Iraq and writes on ancient Mesopotamian art and
archaeology.

Tessa Rickards
Tessa Rickards is a freelance archaeological illustrator
specialising in ancient Mesopotamia. She has worked as an illus-
trator on numerous international excavations in the Middle
East. She is an MA graduate of the Institute of Archaeology,
University College London.

Front cover: Green jasper seal depicting a conflict between two
heroes, a bull-man, a bull and a lion. Dated 2250 BC, origin
unknown.

Frontispiece: A nude winged goddess on a large-scale baked clay
plaque in high relief. The deity portrayed may be an underworld
aspect of Ištar (Inana). Old Babylonian or Isin-Larsa Period.
Ht. 0.49 m.

© 1992 The Trustees of The British Museum
Published by The British Museum Press
A division of The British Museum Company Ltd
46 Bloomsbury Street, London WC1B 3QQ

First published 1992
Second edition 1998
Reprinted 2003, 2004

British Library Cataloguing in Publication Data
A catalogue record for this book is available from the
British Library.

ISBN 0 7141 1705 6

Designed by James Shurmer
Cover design by Andrew Shoolbred

Typeset in Ehrhardt and printed in Great Britain by
The Bath Press, Bath

Authors' note

The names and concepts of Mesopotamian religion are recorded in two languages, Sumerian and Akkadian. Where possible, words have been listed in this dictionary in their Sumerian form, with only a cross-reference under the Akkadian name. Thus the goddess Ištar (Akkadian), for instance, is dealt with under her Sumerian name **Inana**. However, within the entries, the Sumerian or Akkadian name is used as appropriate, depending on the sources or periods referred to. A number of Mesopotamian names are commonly used in modern books (including this one) in Greek or Latin forms (especially place-names, e.g. (Greek) Babylon for Akkadian *Bābili*), or in a form in which they occur in the Authorised Version of the Old Testament (especially the names of Assyrian kings, e.g. Sennacherib for Akkadian Sîn-ahhē-erība). Similarly, archaeological sites are sometimes known by their modern Arabic names, e.g. Abū Shahrain for Sumerian Eridu.

Of course we have no exact information on the pronunciation of the Akkadian or Sumerian languages, but scholars have reconstructed an approximate system based on comparison with other Semitic languages and on ancient transcriptions into Greek. A simplified guide to this is as follows:

All letters are pronounced.

The four vowels **a e i u** are always pronounced as in Italian (i.e. as 'ah', 'ay', 'ee', 'oo').

The signs ⁻ or ˆ over vowels mark them as long.

The letter **g** is always hard, as in 'god', not soft, as in 'gem'.

The symbol **š** indicates the sound *sh*, as in 'shop'.

The symbol **g̃** in Sumerian words indicates the sound *ng*, as in 'sing'.

The letters **ṣ, ṭ** and **q** indicate 'emphatic' forms of the consonants **s, t** and **k** (and can be pronounced as s, t and k).

The letter **h** always indicates the guttural sound *ch*, as in 'loch'. This means that -šh- indicates two sounds – *sh* followed by guttural *ch* – not just *sh*.

Words beginning with **š** are listed separately after those beginning with **s**.

Because our understanding both of the cuneiform writing system and of the languages written in it has improved enormously since the early days of Assyriology (as this study has come to be known), ancient names sometimes appear written differently in early publications. For instance, we now know that in the name of the god Ninurta, the sign IB should be read as URTA, but in older books 'Ninib' will be found. This corresponds to the same group of signs in Sumerian, but is now out of date as a transcription. The books in the reading list on pages 191–2 all use the transcriptions currently favoured by the majority of scholars.

Illustrations have been chosen to accompany many of the entries in this book. Drawings are particularly useful to show iconographic details or scenes, or the occasional relatively simple object. Most have been drawn by Tessa Rickards especially for this work. In other cases photographs have been preferred in order to give a clearer picture of the objects themselves. Although each of these illustrations has been selected with a particular theme in mind, they often contain elements which illustrate aspects covered in other entries. Therefore, each illustration has been numbered in sequence and the numbers of any that are relevant are printed in the margins of the text. Visual representations of some of the supernatural beings and the major symbols of the gods in art are given in illustrations 53 and 76.

Introduction

Ancient Mesopotamia was the home of some of the world's earliest cities, and the place where writing was invented. For these two major developments alone – urban society and literate society – it might justly be titled the 'cradle of civilisation', but in its literature, its religious philosophies and no less in its art it can also be placed firmly as the direct ancestor of the Western world.

Our knowledge of the civilisation of ancient Mesopotamia is constantly expanding. A hundred and fifty years after the first modern excavations, archaeological work in the Near East continues unabated and new dis-coveries are constantly being made which add to, reshape and refine our assessments of some of the most staggering human achievements of anti-quity. At the sites of ancient settlements and in the museums of Iraq and of other countries one can contemplate and wonder at the monuments, arts, handicrafts and utensils of daily life of the Mesopotamians. Thanks to the Mesopotamians' own greatest invention – writing – and modern decipher-

1 Worshippers stare wide-eyed at the heavens. Limestone statues found with numerous others buried in a shrine of an Early Dynastic temple at Ešnunna (modern Tell Asmar). The eyeballs are of inlaid shell. Ht. of each statue 0.34 m.

2 (*below*) A typical ancient mound (or *tell*) site of southern Mesopotamia. A view of Eridu.

3 (*right*) Cuneiform (wedge-shaped) writing. The names and titles of Hammurabi, king of Babylon in the early second millennium BC, from the stone monument inscribed with his Laws.

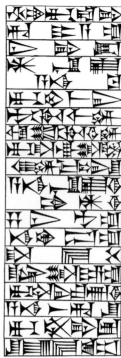

ment of the languages in which they expressed themselves, we can read their literature, reconstruct their history and learn something of their thoughts.

This is not to say that vast amounts of research do not still remain to be done. If some areas of history can be reconstructed down to the smallest detail, there are periods where enormous gaps in our knowledge remain. If numerous copies survive of one poem, there are many others of which only fragments have been recovered. If we can trace the use and meaning of some religious motifs throughout thousands of years, there remain some whose significance still eludes us completely. There is a constant need for skilled archaeologists and scholarly researchers to sift through the great wealth of evidence coming to light. But for the general reader, several reliable accounts of Mesopotamian civilisation, together with the story of how it has been revealed to us, are now available (see pages 191–2). There are lavishly illustrated books showing the full range of ancient art, from temple architecture and palace reliefs to cylinder seals and filigree jewellery. And gradually, accurate and readable modern translations of the extensive Sumerian and Babylonian literatures are appearing, together with explanatory studies.

This book does not attempt to emulate the breadth or detail of such works, but rather to serve as an introductory guidebook for those who are tempted to read for the first time about ancient Mesopotamia, and especially to those whose interest is drawn to the belief systems of ancient peoples as revealed in their art and in their writings. It is not intended to be a complete survey of religion and beliefs, and necessarily reflects the particular interests of the authors. There are a number of extended essays, which are complemented by shorter entries covering the most interesting individual deities, motifs and symbols, and a selection of other topics. Inevitably much has been omitted.

The uses to which cuneiform writing was put in Mesopotamia have ensured that, in addition to administrative, commercial and historical documents, extensive attention was paid to the recording of religious matters. In pre-modern societies, religion had a much more pervasive influence on every aspect of life: government and politics, social relations, education and literature were all dominated by it. Thus in this context we subsume under the term religion a wide sweep of ideas and beliefs ranging from magic at one extreme to philosophy at the other. A very considerable portion of ancient art, too, was produced within this broad religious sphere, or using motifs and images derived from religious traditions. The gods, goddesses and demons, the motifs, symbols and religious beliefs of the several thousand years of Mesopotamian civilisation are bewilderingly complex to the modern reader who stands on the threshold of that world. The authors hope that this dictionary can be used as a first reference book to accompany them on their journey within.

Peoples and places

The cultures of Mesopotamia grew up through the interplay, clash and fusion of different peoples, with their separate social systems, religious beliefs and pantheons, languages and political structures. Uniquely, Mesopotamia was a crossroads and melting-pot for vastly different groups of peoples over thousands of years from the prehistoric periods to the Persian conquest. Moreover, although the potential productivity and prosperity of the region was the impetus for extensive and prolonged immigration, the area has no real geographical unity, nor any obvious or permanent capital, so that it is in marked contrast to civilisations of greater uniformity, such as Egypt. There are, however, a few unifying factors, such as the cuneiform script for writing, the pantheon of gods which through syncretism and assimilation was an evolving tradition, and the highly conservative works of art, especially religious art. In these fields, at least, it is therefore possible to speak of something uniquely 'Mesopotamian'.

The map on page 10 shows the ancient Near East. Mesopotamia – 'the land between two rivers' – was a name given first by the Greeks to the exceptionally fertile river valley of the twin streams Tigris and Euphrates, which both rise in the mountains of Turkey. The Tigris flows faster and deeper, has more

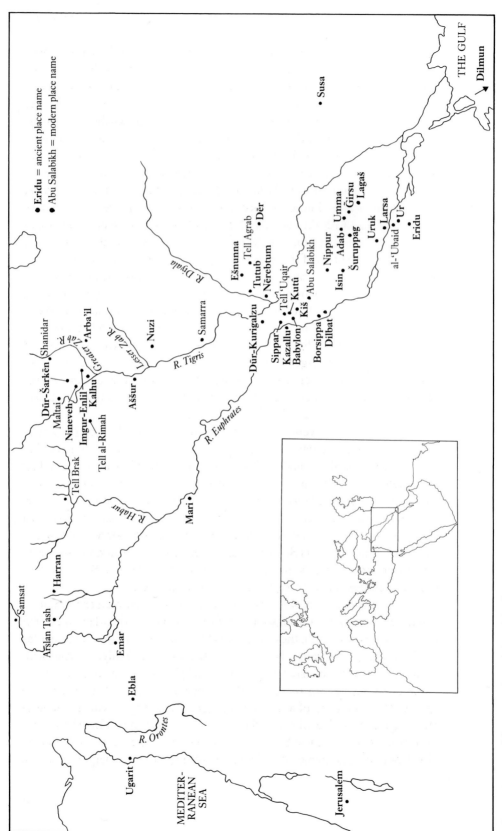

4 Sites of ancient Mesopotamia mentioned in the text.

affluents and is more prone to flood than the Euphrates, which follows a more circuitous course until it joins the Tigris in the very south of Iraq and they flow together as the Shaṭṭ al-ʿArab down to the Gulf (of which the shoreline may have been slightly further north in ancient times). More generally, the term Mesopotamia is used to cover the whole extent of the civilisation associated with this region, so that the term effectively includes an area extending outside the borders of modern Iraq into Syria, and parts of Turkey and Iran. At its greatest extent, the influence of Mesopotamian civilisation could be felt as far away as modern Iran, Lebanon, Jordan, Israel, Egypt, Saudi Arabia and the Gulf States, Turkey, Cyprus and Greece; there were also commercial connections with the Indus Valley (Pakistan). Mesopotamia proper can be divided into two regions, corresponding to two once-great empires and, later, to two provinces of the Persian Empire. The northern area is Assyria, named after its original capital city Aššur; the southern is Babylonia, named after its principal city Babylon: the boundary between the two lay a little north of modern Baghdad. Earlier Babylonia was made up of two regions: a southern area called by modern archaeologists Sumer (anciently Šumerum) and a northern half called Akkad, and it is from these two areas that the principal ancient languages of Mesopotamia take their names: Sumerian, an agglutinative, ergative language of which no related language is preserved, and Akkadian, a member of the Semitic family of languages (including also Arabic, Hebrew, Aramaic, Phoenician and Ugaritic).

The people who invented writing in Sumer in roughly 3400 BC almost certainly spoke Sumerian. They had no traditions of having come to that region from elsewhere and, although the archaeological evidence is not absolutely conclusive, there seems no reason necessarily to assume that they were not the descendants of the earlier, prehistoric peoples of Sumer. Although in time Sumerian spread, as a written language, as far as western Syria, and was widely used as a cultural language throughout Mesopotamian history, its homeland was Sumer, where it was probably spoken as a vernacular until about 2000 BC. None of the other languages related to Sumerian was ever written down and so they remain unknown to us.

The Sumerians, then, were the originators of the early high civilisation of southern Mesopotamia from shortly before 3000 BC. As their language died out as an everyday idiom, they were probably absorbed into the other peoples of the region, who spoke languages of the Semitic family. Scribes with Semitic names are attested in northern Babylonia almost as early as the earliest writing we can read, and they probably spoke Old Akkadian, the earliest recorded form of a Semitic language. Akkadian is used as a general term for this language, of which the later forms Assyrian and Babylonian are also dialects. Other early Semitic languages are Amorite, which we know only from personal names (the Amorites were apparently a largely nomadic people) and the recently discovered language of Ebla in western Syria, which seems to have been very close to Old Akkadian. Akkadian first came to the fore during the period of the Akkadian kingdom (see below), but it was Assyrian and Babylonian, in their respective areas, which gradually took over as Sumerian died out in the south.

A third ethnic group, the Hurrians, were settled in a wide band across northern Mesopotamia, most of Syria and the very south-east of Turkey by at least 2000 BC. These agricultural people spoke a language of their own, of which the only known relative is the later Urartian; the extent to which they possessed a definable civilisation of their own, as opposed to borrowing their religion and art from their neighbours, is still debated. The climax of their history was the formation of the Hurrian kingdom of Mitanni, which reached its high point around 1400 BC. More than a century later, there still seems to have been a considerable number of Hurrians in Assyria and north-eastern Babylonia, but thereafter they must have been absorbed into the general population.

The names of many tribal and nomadic peoples are mentioned throughout Mesopotamian history, especially the often warlike groups who were either attracted down into the fertile river valleys from the inhospitable Zagros Mountains to the east, or were driven into Mesopotamia by the pressure of

5 Assyrian scribes recording the events of the king's campaign. One writes with a stylus in cuneiform Akkadian on a clay tablet, the other writes in alphabetic Aramaic, or perhaps makes sketches, on parchment. From a monumental mural painting in the main reception room of the palace at the provincial capital of Kār–Šulmānu-ašarid (Til Barsip) on the Middle Euphrates, reign of King Tiglath-pileser III (744–727 BC) or slightly later.

other groups behind them. Such a people were the Gutians, whose entry on the Mesopotamian scene coincided with, if it was not actually responsible for, the decline and fall of the Akkadian kingdom. According to some sources, a series of Gutian leaders ruled southern Mesopotamia until a Sumerian dynasty was eventually able to reassert itself.

A similar story can be told about the Kassites, a people who are first mentioned in Syria in the eighteenth century BC but who moved gradually down into Babylonia and eventually controlled it. A dynasty of Kassite kings ruled Babylonia for half a millennium thereafter. We know very little about the origins of the Kassites, and only a few words of their unclassifiable language and the names of some of their gods: despite their position of political control, they appear to have contributed relatively little to the culture of the lands they ruled.

It was inevitable that the stable, urban cultures of Babylonia and Assyria should be infiltrated by nomadic elements who took advantage of the opportunity to gain material benefit, whether peacefully or by raiding. There is good evidence that both the earliest Assyrians (with their 'kings who lived in tents') and the earliest Babylonians were of Amorite origin. During the second millennium a further wave of Semitic nomads entered history, first as troublesome raiders, then as mercenaries and gradually as settled elements in the population. These were the Aramaeans, who may have developed originally out of one particular Amorite tribal clan. By soon after 1000 BC it is likely that their language, Aramaic, was widely used as an everyday vernacular in both Assyria and Babylonia as well as over most of Syria and Palestine (where Hebrew also was still spoken). The Neo-Babylonian Empire founded in 626 BC may also have had its origins in an Aramaic-speaking tribal confederation, the Chaldaeans. In this way, there was throughout Mesopotamian history a constant interference with the settled, traditional civilisation of the great ancient cities by a variety of groups moving into the area from the mountain fastnesses to the east or the rolling plains to the north-west. These new ethnic and cultural infusions were an important factor in reviving and preserving the long-lived culture which they found in the river valleys.

A great power to the north-west of Mesopotamia was the kingdom of the Hittites, with its capital at Hattusas in central Turkey. This people, who spoke the earliest recorded Indo-European language, had become very powerful at a time when Babylonia was weak, and a Hittite king was able to attack Babylon itself during the seventeenth century BC, although their kingdom never made any serious headway with expansion into the Mesopotamian area, and after 1200 BC was no longer a force to be reckoned with. Similarly the kings of Elam, located in south-west Iran to the east of Babylonia, were able at various times to make forays deep into Babylonian territory, on one occasion carrying away the cult statue of the Babylonian national god,

Marduk. For short periods the Elamites (who spoke a language unrelated to any other surviving language) were able to control parts of Babylonia, even to rule it, and some cultural transfer seems to have taken place: certain aspects of Babylonian magic and religion seem to derive from Elam.

Mythology and legends

The myths and legends of ancient Mesopotamia form an exceptionally diverse collection of material. Some are preserved in Sumerian and some in Akkadian, the earliest from 2500 BC and the latest from the first century BC. As might be expected from such a broad field, they display very considerable variety, and in many cases there are several different versions of a narrative, originating from different localities or in different periods, some of which directly contradict other versions. Some myths were created within the historical period; others are of indeterminate antiquity. No doubt they were transmitted orally in many forms and on many occasions: however, the only form in which they survive is of course the written form. It is essential to bear in mind that every myth or legend preserved in written form is preserved as part of a (perhaps fragmentary) work of literature which was created in a specific historical environment and which was intended to serve a specific literary aim. In this way they can be compared to the use of Greek myths by

6 The god Ninurta or Adad pursuing a leonine bird-monster, perhaps the Anzû or Asakku. From a cylinder seal of the Neo-Assyrian Period. See ill. 117.

the Greek tragedians, and the same cautions apply. There is no homogeneous system and it makes no sense to talk of the 'character of Mesopotamian myth', except in the most general terms. The very distinction between myth, legend and history is of course a largely modern one.

A particular problem which must also be mentioned is the evident disparity between those literary versions of the myths which happen to survive and the graphic versions of mythical themes used in various heraldic and iconic ways in Mesopotamian fine art. This has been a source of great difficulty in the interpretation of ancient works of art. It serves to emphasise the extraordinary richness of the Mesopotamian heritage, since it seems to imply that many mythical themes used in art refer to narratives of which no written version has yet been recovered.

Most of the Akkadian works incorporating myths and legends which have been studied and edited so far are now available in English translations, but numbers of Sumerian compositions are available only in foreign language editions or in doctoral dissertations (which may not be readily available), or have not yet been published. Apart from these, there are many that have not yet even been read or studied in modern times.

Interest in the Bible has been an important stimulus to modern research in and about the ancient Near East in general. The very diverse collection of prose and poetry, written down over a considerable period of time in Hebrew, Aramaic and Greek, which makes up the Bible, is the product of a world both alien to that of Mesopotamia and in which nonetheless many echoes of Mesopotamian society, beliefs and history are to be found. This raises the complex question of the existence of various oral traditions throughout the whole Near East, influencing each other. The Mesopotamian evidence happens to be attested in writing at much earlier dates, but this need not lead to the conclusion that it was therefore the origin of all similar themes occurring later on.

Art and iconography

The interpretation of elements in the religious art of ancient Mesopotamia encounters the difficulty that direct 'captions' (that have been so fundamentally useful in the study of Egyptian and Classical art) are extremely rare and hardly ever straightforward. The following examples may help to illustrate this point. The symbols of the gods shown on Babylonian *kudurru*-stones (stones recording royal land grants) occasionally have captions identifying the deities symbolised. All the known examples of these had been looted from Babylonia and taken to the Elamite city of Susa, and the labels were perhaps added there for the benefit of the Elamites. Assyrian and Babylonian figurines of supernatural beings are sometimes inscribed with

7 Symbols carved on a *c.*13th-century BC Babylonian *kudurru*-stone, inscribed with the names of the deities represented. Found at Susa, in south-western Iran, where it had been taken in antiquity as a prize of war.

incantations which name the creature concerned (for example, as Huwawa, Lamaštu or Pazuzu). In the Neo-Assyrian Period, clay figurines of beneficent beings were also often inscribed with magical spells. These do not name the creatures directly, but they are named in ritual texts which give instructions for the figurines' manufacture, the writing to be put on each type and the sites of placement or burial within a building. Furthermore, on stelae and rock reliefs erected by Assyrian kings (or exceptionally governors) to commemorate special events, there is sometimes a one-to-one correlation in both number and order between the gods invoked in the inscription and the symbols depicted. Yet more usually this is not so. For the *kudurrus*, moreover, the gods invoked in the curses of the main text are never those symbolised on the stone.

Sometimes named supernatural beings are described in texts in a way which makes it possible to relate them to extant art. Once again, the Neo-Assyrian rituals concerning the placing of magical figurines, for example, refer to types of creature which can easily be identified even though the figurines of these particular creatures were never inscribed. An example is the Sages (*apkallū*) 'with the faces of birds, and wings, carrying in their right hands a "purifier" (*mullilu*) and in their left a bucket (*banduddû*)', or another set of Sages 'cloaked in the skins of fishes'. Similarly the inscription on one

8 (*below*) The image of the face of the demon
Huwawa or Humbaba, formed from the pattern of
animal entrails, as used in divination. Baked clay
model, inscribed on the reverse: 'If the entrails look
like the face of Huwawa . . .' Probably Old
Babylonian, from Sippar.
Ht. 80 mm.

9 (*right*) Plaque-figurine of sun-dried clay.
Neo-Assyrian, probably 7th-century BC, found in a
brick box buried in the foundations of a building at
Aššur. The piece depicts the protective god Lahmu
('Hairy'), inscribed on his arms: 'Get out, evil
demon!' and 'Come in, good demon!'. Ht. 128 mm.

10 Twelve symbols carved on
the Assyrian rock reliefs at
Bavian (Khinnis) by order of
King Sennacherib (reigned
704–681 BC). The accom-
panying inscription invokes
twelve deities in corres-
ponding order, namely Aššur,
Anu, Enlil, Ea, Sîn, Šamaš,
Adad, Marduk, Nabû,
Nergal (?), Ištar and the
Seven.

11 (*above*) Neo-Assyrian
plaque-figurines of the so-called
griffin-demon, representing the Seven
Sages (*apkallū*) in the guise of birds.
Sun-dried clay. Three from a group
of seven figurines found together in a
brick box buried in the foundations of
royal palace of King Adad-nīrārī III
(reigned 810–783 BC) at Kalhu
(modern Nimrud). Hts. all 140 mm.

12 Neo-Assyrian figurines of
the so-called fish-garbed figures,
representing the Seven Sages
(*apkallū*) in the guise of fish.
Sun-dried clay. (*left*) One of a group
of seven figurines found together in a
brick box buried in the foundations of
the house of a priestly family at Aššur,
probably dating to the reign of King
Sargon II (721–705 BC). (*right*) One
of a group of six (probably originally
seven) figurines found together at
Nineveh and possibly belonging to
the reign of King Sennacherib
(704–681 BC). Hts. 145, 127 mm.

of the *kudurru*-stones refers in clear terms to some of the symbols of the gods (though not the ones carved upon it):

... the seat and horned crown of Anu, king of heaven; the walking bird of Enlil, lord of the lands; the ram's head and goat-fish, the sanctuary of great Ea; ... the sickle, water-trough (and) wide boat of Sîn; the radiant disc of the great judge Šamaš; the star-symbol of Ištar, the mistress of the lands; the fierce young bull of Adad, son of Anu ...

and so on. On the other hand, written descriptions of works of art and descriptions of supernatural beings in works of literature may be too exceptional or too literary or imprecise to correlate with examples of art.

Glyptic art (for the ancient Near East the term refers to the craft of cutting small seals) provides the most spectacular detail of the religious art of any period, including the association of figures and motifs. On the seals were cut, in miniature and in reverse (for sealing), friezes which involve gods, worshippers, symbols and other motifs, often arranged heraldically or in a form which gives the appearance of a mythological scene. The seals are often inscribed with writing (usually also in reverse) which may give the names of particular deities (as part of a person's name, as the name of the seal owner's personal god or within a prayer of incantation). Occasionally it is clear that the deities so named correspond to those depicted. More usually, however, it is not so. Some scholars have argued that while on an individual seal the deity shown may not be the one mentioned, nevertheless in any given period there will be a rough correlation on seals in general between the deities most often depicted and those whose names are most frequently given. However,

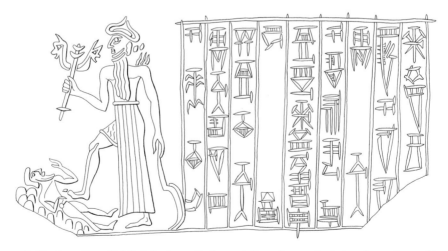

13 Design of an Old Babylonian cylinder seal from Larsa, depicting the underworld god Nergal, holding his distinctive scimitar and the double lion-headed standard. The inscription is a dedication to Nergal by Abisarê, perhaps the king of Larsa of that name.

14 Examples of Mesopotamian glyptic art: (*above*) grey haematite cylinder seal (Ht. 21 mm) of the Old Babylonian Period from Nērebtum (modern Ishchali), with modern rolling; (*middle*) clay tablet of the Old Babylonian Period from Sippar, with impressions from the rollings of a cylinder seal (of Ht. *c.*24 mm); (*below*) blue chalcedony conical stamp seal (Ht. 21 mm) of Neo-Babylonian date, with modern impressions (place of discovery unknown).

the identifications so far suggested appear on other grounds improbable. It may be that the mention of some gods was sometimes an *alternative* to their depiction and that certain gods were known more for their personalities and deeds than for their pictorial forms.

A much-used method has attempted to relate scenes on seals, especially of the Akkadian Period, to later mythology (on the assumption that the scenes reflect earlier, perhaps orally transmitted, versions of the later written narratives). Although fairly plausible in itself, the application of this idea to the question of identification is problematic because it has allowed very imprecise correlations of art and literature. In reaction, some have maintained that one-to-one correspondences of named gods and creatures with elements in art do not exist and that a repertoire of stock figures in art was related only in a very general way to the records of gods, demons and heroes in literature. However, this view has itself led to some very wide and subjective interpretations of artistic themes. Enough identifications can now be made from written sources to suggest that, although they may have developed or even changed their meanings from time to time, the figures and motifs of art do attempt to represent specific gods, beings and well-known symbolic objects.

The identification of specific named gods and demons in Mesopotamian art naturally has implications for our appreciations of the mythological narratives themselves.

Periods

The table on page 22 is intended to give some idea of the chronology of the various political developments and ethnic movements. Writing was invented towards the end of the Late Uruk Period, named after the important city of Uruk in southern Sumer where so much of the monumental architecture of that epoch was excavated. (Uruk is actually the later Akkadian name for Sumerian Unug.) The subsequent series of independent and sometimes warring city-states of Sumer is grouped together as the Early Dynastic Period. This is the period of the earliest literary and religious texts that can effectively be read (for instance the great lists of the names of more than 500 gods and goddesses from the Sumerian town of Šuruppag), so that when the name or cult of a deity is traced back to the Early Dynastic Period, that means in practice to the beginning of written history. Exact dates for these early periods are difficult to calculate, but the Early Dynastic Period (which is sometimes divided into sub-periods for archaeological purposes) is regarded as ending in about 2390 BC, when the first great kingdoms began. Four south Mesopotamian kingdoms follow each other in succession, but the first of these is of special note since, apart from the quite remarkable extent of its rulers' conquests, it was centred on a city of northern Babylonia where a

15 CHRONOLOGICAL TABLE

Date	Southern Mesopotamia	Northern Mesopotamia	World events
7000 BC	Prehistoric cultures		Post-glacial period (Mesolithic culture in NW Europe)
6000			
5000	Ubaid culture (5500–4000)	Northern Ubaid culture (5000–4000)	
4000	Early and Middle Uruk Periods (4000–3500)	Gawra culture	Megalithic cultures of W Europe
3500	Late Uruk Period (3500–3100)	Northern Late Uruk culture	
3000	Early Dynastic Period (Sumerian city states) (3100–2390)	Ninevite 5 culture	Great Pyramid of Cheops beginning of Stonehenge
2500	Akkadian (Sargonic) kingdom (2390–2210)	Taya culture	
	Gutian kings		
	Neo-Sumerian Period		
	Gudea of Lagaš		
	Third Dynasty of Ur (2168–2050)		
2000	Isin and Larsa kingdoms (2073–1819)		
	Old Babylonian Period (1950–1651)	Old Assyrian Period (Šamšī-Adad I, 1869–1837)	
	(Hammurabi of Babylon, 1848–1806)		
1500	Middle Babylonian (Kassite) Period (1651–1157)		completion of Stonehenge
		Mitannian kingdom (1500–1350)	
		Middle Assyrian Period (1350–1000)	Akhenaten/Tutankhamun
1000		Neo-Assyrian Empire (883–612)	Hallstatt/La Tène (Celtic) culture
			First Olympiad 776
			Foundation of Rome c.753
	Neo-Babylonian Empire (625–539)		
500	Persian (Achaemenid) Empire (550–331)		beginning of Maya culture
	Alexander the Great (331–323)		
	Hellenistic Period (Seleucid Empire) (305–64)		
BC/AD	Parthian (Arsacid) Empire (126 BC – 227 AD)		Great Wall of China 214 BC
	Sasanian Empire (226–651 AD)		
	advent of Islam 636		

16 A mural painting from an outer wall of the throne-room of the royal palace of King Zimrī-Lim at Mari, beginning of the second millennium BC. The king is received by the goddess Ištar, while protective deities, animals and hybrids surround the scene.

Semitic language was spoken. The city of Agade, which has still not been located, gave its name to the region of which it was capital (Akkad), to its language and to its kingdom. The period is sometimes known also as the Sargonic period, after Sargon (a Biblical form of the name of the founder of the kingdom, Šarrum-kīn). It was the collapse of this kingdom that the Gutians took advantage of, and a Gutian period of uncertain length marks their control of at least parts of Sumer and Akkad at this date (although the Sumerian city-state of Lagaš seems to have remained independent). The great Sumerian kingdoms of the Third Dynasty of Ur (a city in southern Sumer) and then of Isin and Larsa (partially contemporary with each other) mark the apogee of Sumerian culture, even if the star of a fifth kingdom, that centred on a still insignificant city of Akkad called Babylon, was rising. The kings of this Old Babylonian Period (or First Dynasty of Babylon), including Hammurabi (reigned 1848–1806 BC according to the now preferred chronology), sometimes made their official pronouncements bilingually in Akkadian and Sumerian, but as a living language and culture Sumerian was by now obsolescent. In northern Mesopotamia, the city of Aššur remained a minor city-state in a largely Hurrian area until the fourteenth century BC, with one brilliant and brief exception in the reigns of Šamšī-Adad I (1869–1837 BC) and his son when an 'Old Assyrian' kingdom of enormous proportions suddenly came into being, swept across Syria and was then lost. The collapse of the Old Babylonian kingdom in the south was hastened by the arrival of the Kassites, and their long rule over Babylonia from their capital Dūr-Kurigalzu is termed the Middle Babylonian Period, matched by a Middle Assyrian Period in northern Mesopotamia. The date 1000 BC is then conventionally taken as marking the beginning of the Neo-Assyrian and Neo-Babylonian Periods, although the great days of the most famous Assyrian kings, ruling at successive capitals, Aššur, Kalhu (modern Nimrud), Dūr-Šarkēn (modern Khorsabad) and Ninua (Nineveh) – kings such as Sargon II, Sennacherib, Esarhaddon and Assurbanipal – came to an end with the fall of Nineveh in 612 BC at a time when the Neo-Babylonian Empire, founded in 626 BC, had barely begun. The Neo-Babylonian dynasty – whose territory reached its greatest extent under Nebuchadnezzar II (reigned 605–562 BC) – ruled until 539 BC. This crucial date in Mesopotamian history, the capture of Babylon by Cyrus, king of the Medes and Persians, marks the first point at which the whole of Mesopotamia was to become part of an empire ruled from outside its own borders. The age of 'world empires' had begun. The Persian or Achaemenid Empire (so called from an eponymous ancestor of Cyrus' family) was swept away in 331 BC by Alexander the Great: the Hellenistic Period which followed is often also called Seleucid after the dynasty initiated by the general of Alexander who gained control of Mesopotamia, Iran, Syria and half of Turkey. His son founded Seleucia-on-the-Tigris in 274 BC. The Parthians, an Iranian people, effectively dominated Babylonia from 126 BC, and their dynasty (sometimes called Arsacid, again after an eponymous ancestor) ruled Mesopotamia until they were dispossessed by another great Iranian dynasty, the Sasanians, in AD 227. The very latest texts written in Akkadian in the cuneiform script – reports of astronomical observations – are dated towards the end of the first century AD, and by this time it is very unlikely that there was more than a handful of people – highly educated intellectuals – who were still in touch with the ancient culture of Mesopotamia and able to understand its languages or read its writing. The beginning of the Christian era marks a convenient, if approximate, date for the extinction of the three-thousand-year Mesopotamian literate tradition.

17 At one time the Sumerians believed that, for the highly
privileged, the dismal conditions of life after death could be
alleviated by music. A dancing bear, accompanied by animal
musicians, is shown in a detail from the sound-box of a
bison-headed lyre buried in a tomb of the 'Royal Cemetery' at
Ur. Early Dynastic Period.

abzu (apsû)

Although it can sometimes rain very hard in southern Mesopotamia, it was anciently believed that springs, wells, streams, rivers and lakes drew their water from and were replenished from a freshwater ocean which lay beneath the earth in the *abzu* (*apsû*) or *engur*. (The salt sea, on the other hand, surrounded the earth.) The *abzu* was the particular realm and home of the wise god **Enki** (Ea), his wife **Damgalnuna** (Damkina) and his mother Nammu, and was also inhabited by a number of creatures subordinate to him (see **Enki's creatures**).

18 An *apsû* tank from the extension built for the Assyrian king Sennacherib (reigned 704–681 BC) to the temple of the god Aššur in the city of Aššur. Now in the Vorderasiatisches Museum, Berlin. Ht.1.18m, 3.12m square.

19 The god Ea in the watery *apsû* receives another god, probably Šamaš. From a cylinder seal of the Akkadian Period found at Ur.

Enki was thought to have occupied the *abzu* since before the **creation** of mankind. According to the Babylonian Epic of Creation, Apsû was the name of a primal creature, the lover of **Tiāmat**, and when Ea killed Apsû, he set up his home on the dead creature's body, whose name was henceforth transferred to Ea's residence. **Marduk**, as Ea's son, was called 'firstborn son of the *apsû*'. Enki's temple at **Eridu** was known as **E-abzu**, 'Abzu temple'.

The **underworld** was located even further down, beneath the *abzu*. Since in some traditions it was necessary to cross a river (the Hubur) to reach the underworld, the river may sometimes have been identified with the *abzu* (see **river of the underworld**).

The term *abzu/apsû* was also used to designate a tank for holy water in a temple courtyard.

Adad: see **Iškur**.

Adapa

According to Babylonian legend, Adapa was the ancient 'wise man' or 'sage' (*apkallu*) of **Eridu**, the reputed earliest city of Sumer (see **Seven Sages**). His wisdom and position had been granted him by the god Ea (**Enki**). Having 'broken the wings' of the south wind, Adapa was summoned for punishment by the supreme god Anu (**An**). Ea had told Adapa that he would be offered the bread and water of death. Meanwhile, though, the two **gatekeepers** of heaven, **Dumuzi** and Gišzida (**Ningišzida**), had interceded with Anu on Adapa's behalf, causing a change of heart. Anu instead offered the sage the bread and water of eternal life. Adapa refused, thus losing the chance of immortality. The story is often regarded as an explanatory myth of the mortality of man.

See **food and drink of the gods**.

afterlife

The ancient Mesopotamians appear generally to have believed that after death most human beings survived in the form of a spirit or ghost which lived in the **underworld** (see also **gidim**). One of the duties of the living was to make funerary offerings (of food, drink and oil) to their deceased relatives. A special case is provided by extensive records from G̃irsu from the Early Dynastic Period of offerings made before the prayer statues of deceased rulers and members of the ruling family: these statues were, it is assumed, originally dedicated by the living to stand in temples and pray constantly for them before the gods. After the death of their donors the statues could not be moved and so came to be the recipients of offerings. However, this does not imply ancestor worship. If the living neglected to make *kispū* (funerary offerings), the spirit might wander abroad and return to haunt the upper world.

The conditions of 'life' in the underworld were thought, with few exceptions, to be dismal in the extreme. The Sumerian dead fed on dust and scraps and lived in darkness. This is amply documented in the Sumerian poem 'Gilgameš, Enkidu and the Nether World' (closely paralleled by part of the twelfth tablet of the Standard Babylonian version of the Epic of Gilgameš), where **Gilgameš** asks the ghost (*gidim*) of **Enkidu** about the underworld. Only stillborn children and those who died 'before their time' are envisaged, doubtless as a consolation to parents, as playing at a 'gold and silver table' and feasting. Otherwise, those with most living children are best off, as having the best chance of receiving funerary offerings. The nature of these grave goods, as recovered from excavations, suggests that the dead could perform at least some of the activities of this life in the hereafter. Those who died and did not receive proper burial were in a sorry state; worst of all was the man who died in a fire, who did not even have a body to be buried. 'His spirit is not in the underworld. His smoke went up to the sky.' Another Sumerian poem, 'The Death of Gilgameš', suggests that it was expected, after death, that the deceased would present gifts to the denizens of the underworld. There is reference in a poem of the Third Dynasty of Ur, moreover, to different treatments being accorded to individuals in the afterlife dependent upon their condition of burial (see **death and funerary practices**).

The notion of an underworld peopled by terrifying demonic beings, which foreshadowed the medieval image of Hell, seems to have been a theological invention of the first millennium BC. The dead Enkidu encounters such demons in the Epic of Gilgameš. The clearest literary account of such an underworld, however, is a text recounting the hellish vision of an Assyrian prince (thought by some to be the seventh-century BC crown prince, later king, Assurbanipal) (see **demons and monsters**).

See **Dagan**; **galla**.

akītu ceremony: see **New Year ceremonies**.

alad, aladlammû: see **bulls and lions with human head**; **lama**.

alcohol
Alcoholic beverages probably resulted from an accidental discovery during the early hunter-gatherer stage of human prehistory. Textually attested for Mesopotamia at a later date are beer and wine, probably including date wine. The banquets depicted especially on Sumerian seals and sealings doubtless involved the consumption of intoxicating liquors. Medical texts frequently prescribe the use of beer and wine in the making of potions.

That commercialised social drinking, not for religious or medicinal purposes, was common by at least the early second millennium BC is attested by the laws of Hammurabi of Babylon regulating public houses.

No less than man, the gods were susceptible to drink (see **food and drink of the gods**; **lion**; **Ninmah**; **Utu**). In the Epic of Gilgameš, the hero **Gilgameš**, in search of immortality, meets the barmaid-goddess **Siduri**. She encourages him to abandon his quest and to enjoy the gifts of life, presumably including the pleasures of alcohol.

See **frog**; **libation**.

alim (kusarikku): see **bison**; **bull-man**.

Allatu: see **Ereškigal**.

altars

45,95, An altar is an upright standing object at or upon
158 which **sacrifice and offering** are made, in fact or symbolically. It thereby represents a centrepiece of ritual worship. Prehistoric open-air rituals in Mesopotamia probably employed a natural rock or heap of pebbles or earth, but with the development of temples and shrines, more obvious altars were made of clay, stone or brick. A small shrine of the late fifth millennium BC at **Eridu** already contained an altar set into a niche opposite the doorway, together with an offering table. This axial placement of the altar remained a constant feature except when its displacement to one side was necessitated by the 'portal' arrangement of 'high temples' (see **temples and temple architecture**). Usually the altar would be placed, for offering, before the image of the god (see **cult statues**). In Assyrian temples the altar is occasionally found positioned in front of the statue of the king; in these cases, the king, who was not divine, should be seen as a worshipper before the altar rather than as receiving worship.

Altars could be relatively plain or could be more elaborately decorated. Often they were crafted in an architectural style, as if representing a miniature of the temple itself. At other times scenes of worship or images of protective hybrid figures (**demons and monsters**) would be depicted on the sides. Rarely these religious designs might be accompanied by apparently secular scenes.

In the Middle Assyrian Period, lead figures from the temple of Ištar (**Inana**) at Aššur show scenes of sexual intercourse taking place on top of what looks like an altar (see **fertility; prostitution and ritual sex**). 124

From the way some of the symbols of the 20 gods are depicted on the **kudurrus** and stelae and from designs on seals (especially of the Neo-Babylonian Period) showing a worshipper before an altar, it would seem that emblems, 73,74 such as the **solar disc**, **horned cap**, **spade** 80,158 (**symbol**), 'omega' symbol or wedge, might be placed on the altar to receive worship, or that the altar itself might be placed upon or beside a statue of a deity's animal (see **beasts of the gods**). Sometimes the statue of a god's animal itself seems to have served as an altar, with a symbol placed upon the animal's back.

Ama-ušumgal-ana: see **Dumuzi**.

20 The altar of King Tukultī-Ninurta I of Assyria (13th century BC) from the temple of the goddess Ištar in the city of Aššur, showing the king approaching, then kneeling in worship, before a similar altar supporting a god's symbol (apparently a giant writing tablet). The altar is dedicated to the god Nusku.

amulets

An amulet or talisman is an object – a natural substance or artefact – believed to possess magically protective powers, to bring good fortune or to avert evil (or both). Amulets are carried on the person or placed at the location of the desired magical effect. Usually they are believed to derive their power from a sympathetic magic resulting from their connections with nature, from religious associations or from the propitious time of, or the rituals involved in, their creation.

Although the Sumerian and Akkadian languages appear to possess no word for 'amulet', it is clear that a number of objects were used as 14 amulets, for instance seals. Objects with an apparently amuletic purpose have often been found in graves (see **death and funerary** 21 **practices**).

Neo-Assyrian kings wore a necklace with small metal amulets representing symbols of the gods. In the same period, a small stone or metal head of the god **Pazuzu** would be worn around the neck of a woman in labour as a protection for her child from **Lamaštu**.

In certain cases, amulets (including seals) seem to have served as extensions of an individual's personality, as virtual surrogates for the person.

See **eye and eye-idols; magic and sorcery**.

Amurru: see **Martu**.

An (Anu)

An is the Sumerian word for 'heaven', and is the name of the sky god who is also the prime mover in **creation**, and the distant, supreme leader of the gods. He is regarded as a descendant of the god **Uraš**, with whom he was later even identified; or else as the son of primordial **Anšar and Kišar**. He is father of all the **gods**. His wife is the earth goddess **Uraš**; in a later tradition he is married to **Ki**. As Babylonian Anu he has a wife Antu. It is An who, in Sumerian tradition, took over heaven when it was separated from earth (*ki*), creating the universe as we know it.

In the theory of the three superimposed heavens, Anu occupies the topmost heaven. The 'way of Anu' is the vertical band of the eastern horizon, between the 'ways' of **Enlil** and Ea (**Enki**), which lie to its north and south respectively.

Although in almost all periods one of the most important of Mesopotamian deities, An's nature was ill-defined and, as he is seldom (if ever) represented in art, his specific iconography and attributes are obscure. He has sometimes been thought to be represented among the gods on the Neo-Assyrian rock-relief at Maltai, but this is uncertain. In Kassite 31 and Neo-Assyrian art at least, Anu's symbol is a 80 **horned cap**.

See **Asag; cosmology; Sacred Marriage; zodiac**.

animals, sacred: see **beasts of the gods**.

animal sacrifice

Sacrifice is a religious rite by which an object, animal or person is offered to a divinity in an attempt to establish, maintain or restore a satisfactory relationship of the individual, group of individuals or the community in general to that god. In many cultures, including ancient Mesopotamia, it has commonly taken the form of the ritual slaughter and offering of animal life.

In Mesopotamia it was man's duty and the reason for his **creation** to take care of the material needs of the gods, which included the provision of food (see **food and drink of the gods**). Animal sacrifice, therefore, was regarded as the literal means of satisfying the gods' appetites. Foods were prepared in the temple kitchens and offered to the god's **cult statue**. In practice, the meat of animal offerings probably remained or became the property of the temple, and was used to feed the clergy and their retainers. The sheep seems to have been the primary animal of such sacrifice, although goats and cattle were also sacrificed. Excava- 23,68 tions of rooms in prehistoric and early historic temples, however, have at times uncovered enormous quantities of **fish** bones, believed to be sacrificial deposits.

21 (*above*) A gold necklace with amulets in the form of *lama* goddesses and divine symbols such as a crescent, lightning symbol and solar disc. Babylonian *c*.19th-18th centuries BC, found at Dilbat. l.430mm. (*right*) Detail of stone stela of the Assyrian king Assurnasirpal II (reigned 883–859 BC), found in his royal palace at Kalhu (modern Nimrud). The king, pointing to the symbols of his gods, wears a necklace with similar pendant symbols as amulets.

22 King Assurbanipal of
Assyria (reigned
668–*c.*627 BC) personally
dispatches a lion. Detail of
a carved stone monumental
wall relief from the king's
royal palace at Nineveh.

23 A Sumerian worshipper or priest with
sacrificial kid. Early Dynastic Period. From a
shell inlay found in the temple of the goddess
Ninhursaǧa at Mari.

A rather different form of animal sacrifice is
attested by the animals commonly found in all
periods in Mesopotamian and Near Eastern
burials (see **death and funerary practices**).
For the most part these probably represented
food for the deceased. In Sumerian burials,
however, equids and oxen, sometimes harnessed to carts, must have been part of the great
ceremonial of the funeral. Possibly their purpose was also to continue their tasks as working
animals in the service of the deceased beyond
the grave. 83,84

The sacrifice of a goat (called 'man-
substitute') was used in some rituals to divert
sickness or portended evil from individual
persons. However, the sacrifice of a sheep during the **New Year ceremonies** at Babylon is
not, as has been suggested, connected with
the idea of the scapegoat, an animal sacrificed
or killed to bear the sins of the whole people
(e.g. Leviticus 16:8, 10, 21), a concept alien to
Mesopotamian thought.

There is occasional evidence of animal
sacrifice in connection with **building rites**. In
excavations at Kalhu (modern Nimrud), for
example, an animal, perhaps a gazelle, was discovered buried beneath the floor of a royal

building. At **Ur**, the bones of small **birds** were occasionally found together with **figurines** in clay boxes set into the foundations of a Neo-Assyrian building.

At least in the Neo-Assyrian Period, the royal hunt seems to have been, in some respects, a form of animal sacrifice, since King Assurbanipal (reigned 668–*c*.627 BC) is shown on one of his palace reliefs standing beside the slain lions and pouring a **libation**. Except for these hunting scenes of dying animals, the depiction in Mesopotamian art of sacrificial animals in all their gory detail (so commonly shown in Classical works) is extremely rare.

Sometimes ritual burning was an element in animal sacrifice, and oblations were conveyed to the gods by one of the fire gods **Gibil** or **Nusku**.

See **animal skins**; **bull and 'winged gate'**, **divination**; **figurines**; **human sacrifice**; **purification**; **sacrifice and offering**.

animal skins

An interesting deposit has been discovered in excavations at the site of Zawi Chemi Shanidar in northern Mesopotamia, a small settlement dating to the late tenth or early ninth millennium BC. In a heap lying just outside a stone structure were at least fifteen skulls of goats and the articulated wing bones of at least seventeen huge predator birds, vultures, eagles and a bustard. Knife marks on the bird bones indicated that they had been carefully cut from the birds. The archaeologists interpreted these wings as part of ritual costumes. The goat skulls were thought to be part of the paraphernalia of the ritual.

In the Babylonian epic, **Gilgameš**, in mourning for **Enkidu**, roams the desert clad in a lion's skin.

Some Neo-Assyrian art seems to depict human figures dressed in animal skins. The figure in a lion's pelt on a palace relief of King

24 Figures dressed in the pelts of lions, perhaps in imitation of the god La-tarāk, carved on a monumental stone relief from the throne-room of the royal palace of the Assyrian king Assurnasirpal II (reigned 883–859 BC) at Kalhu (modern Nimrud).

Tiglath-pileser III (reigned 744–727 BC) may possibly be dressed in imitation of the god **La-tarāk**, but it does not appear very likely, given his appearance and context (in a line of human figures, perhaps **priests**) that this could be the god himself. A pair of such figures, apparently dressed-up men, is earlier to be seen on a relief of King Assurnasirpal II (reigned 883–849 BC). Similarly, while figures of the **fish-garbed figure** may represent the **Seven Sages**, certain contexts in which we see such figures, for example flanking the bed of a sick man, may suggest that they could sometimes be human figures dressed as the ancient sages. In this case, however, it seems unlikely that the ritual garb consisted of the full skin of an actual **fish**, reaching from the man's head down to his waist, upper leg or even to the ground, and it has been suggested that cloth costumes were created in precise imitation of a living fish.

Margin numbers: 24 / 65, 108, 151 / 104

anointing

The symbolic custom of anointing has its origin in the habit of rubbing the body with fine quality oil (usually sesame oil) for medical or cosmetic purposes. Oil might also be symbolically poured over the head, e.g. of a bride, of persons involved in property transactions, or at the manumission of a slave. 'Anointed' **priests** (*pašīšū*) were one particular class of the clergy.

An extension of this custom, from the Old Babylonian Period on, was the duty of anointing the stone inscription or monument of a past king if it were exposed during building work, clearly a substitute for anointing the ruler himself.

In **magic and sorcery** and medicine (see **diseases and medicine**) ointments of all sorts were frequently used, prepared both from symbolic (and to us revolting) ingredients and also from genuinely curative herbs and simples.

Anšar and Kišar

In Mesopotamian myth, Anšar and Kišar were a pair of primordials, respectively male and female, and perhaps representing the heaven (**An**) and earth (**Ki**). According to the Babylonian Epic of Creation they were the second pair (after **Lahmu** and Lahamu) of offspring of Apsû (**abzu**) and **Tiāmat**. (An alternative interpretation of the passage makes them the children of Lahmu and Lahamu.) Anšar and Kišar in turn bore Anu (**An**), the supreme god of heaven.

See **Aššur**.

anthropomorphism: see **gods and goddesses**.

Antu: see **An**.

Anu: see **An**.

Anuna (Anunnakkū)

The Anuna (Anunnakkū), which possibly means 'princely offspring', is used in earlier, especially Sumerian, texts as a general word for the **gods**, in particular the early gods who were born first and were not differentiated with individual names. They are put to work to help build the temple at Ĝirsu in a Sumerian hymn, and are linked with the benign **lama**-deities. There are fifty Anuna of **Eridu**. The sky god Anu (**An**) is described as king of the Anunnakkū. In the Epic of Creation the multitude of gods are called the 'Anunnakkū of heaven and earth'.

Possibly following the use from Middle Babylonian times of the name **Igigū** to refer especially to the gods of heaven, the term Anunnakkū came to be used more for the gods of earth (**Ki**) and **underworld**. **Marduk** and Damkina (**Damgalnuna**), **Nergal** and Madānu – associated with the underworld – are said to be powerful among them. There are 600 Anunnakkū of the underworld, but only 300 of heaven, according to one text. This implies the gradual development of a detailed imagery of the underworld.

Anunītu

Anunītu (earlier Annunītum) was a Babylonian goddess especially associated with childbirth. Annunītum and Ulmašītum were two aspects of **Inana** worshipped at Agade. Annunītum was also worshipped at Sippar. Later, as the name of a constellation, Anunītu referred to the north-eastern part of Pisces.

See **zodiac**.

Anunnakkū: see **Anuna**.

Anzû: see **Imdugud**.

apkallū: see **Adapa; Seven Sages**.

apotropaic figures: see **building rites and deposits; demons and monsters; magic and sorcery**.

apsasû: see **lama**.

apsû: see **abzu**.

Arabian gods

A number of Arab kingdoms are known to have existed in the Arabian peninsula from at least the first millennium BC. The generic name 'Arabs' and a kingdom called 'Aribi' appear in the inscriptions of the Assyrian kings.

Little is known about the religion and pantheon of the region before the coming of Islam in the seventh century AD. In northern Arabia the chief deity seems to have been known as El or Ilah, meaning 'God'. A number of astral and local deities are also known. At the Arab city of Palmyra, in the third century AD, a triad of gods is attested, headed by Bel (originally Bol, probably equivalent to Baal 'Lord') or Belshamin ('Lord of the heavens'), together with a solar deity Yarhibol or Malakbel and a lunar deity Aglibol.

In the southern Arabian kingdoms the cult seems to have centred around a triad of astral deities. The most important was the moon god, who was usually also the local protector of each individual city, and was therefore referred to under a variety of names, including that of the Babylonian god Sîn (**Nanna-Suen**). Next was the god 'Athtar, related to the Mesopotamian goddess Ištar (**Inana**), the planet Venus. Third in rank was the sun god, usually known as Shams, clearly related to the Babylonian name Šamaš (**Utu**). The remaining southern Arabian gods known to us are numerous and seem to have had more specific functions, which sometimes gave them their names.

In the sixth and fifth centuries BC there was a cult centre of the moon god at Tayma in north-west Arabia. The Babylonian king Nabonidus (reigned 556–539 BC), a devotee of Sîn, spent some twelve years of his reign there away from Babylon (see **Nanna-Suen**).

In the fifth century BC, the Greek historian Herodotus mentions as the gods of the Arabs Orotalt and Alilat ('The Goddess'). In the Islamic Qur'an, al-Lat together with al-'Uzza and Manat are mentioned as daughters of Allah. They are also attested as divine names in earlier north Arabian inscriptions.

There were also direct borrowings from Mesopotamia and Syria. The pantheon at Palmyra included **Nergal** (assimilated to the Greek Herakles), **Nabû** or Nebo (assimilated to Apollo), the Syrian goddess Atargatis, and possibly Astarte, that is Ištar (**Inana**), and Beltis (Bēlet-ilī).

arali: see **underworld**.

arrow

An upright arrow is depicted on Kassite **kudurrus** as a symbol of the star Sirius (known in Sumerian and Akkadian as 'The Arrow').

25 An arrow. Detail from the carving on a Babylonian *kudurru*.

Aruru: see **mother goddesses and birth goddesses**.

Asag (Asakku)

In the Sumerian poem *Lugale*, the Asag is a monstrous demon who is defeated by the god **Ninurta/Ningirsu** (in another version by Adad (**Iškur**)). The Asag was hideously repulsive in appearance and his power caused fish to boil alive in the rivers. He was born from the mating of **An** and **Ki**, and the Asag himself mated with the **kur** (mountains) to produce offspring. He was accompanied by an army of stone allies (the stones of the mountains). On one level the defeat of Ninurta in this myth of the Asag and the stones expresses the unease felt by the inhabitants of the Mesopotamian plain about the inhabitants of the Zagros mountains.

The defeat of Asag by Ninurta may be depicted in relief on the large slabs erected by the ninth-century BC Assyrian king Assurnasirpal II on either side of the main entrance to the temple of Ninurta at Kalhu (modern Nimrud). Here a god carrying thunderbolts attacks a **lion-dragon**. A related scene is found on Neo-Assyrian seals.

In magical theory the *asag/asakku* is a **demon** who attacks and kills human beings, especially by means of head fevers, and who is mentioned in poetical enumerations of **diseases**.

In another tradition, the Seven (or Eight) *Asakkū* are a specific group of demons, the offspring of Anu (**An**), who are said to have been defeated by Ninurta, in a clear reminiscence of the Sumerian poem.

Asarluhi

Originally the god of Kuara, a village near **Eridu**, Asarluhi came to be associated with **Enki** (the god of Eridu), and with magical knowledge, the special preserve of Enki. Asarluhi was regarded as the son of Enki and **Damgalnuna**, and when **Marduk** was also accorded the title of son of Ea (the Akkadian name of Enki) it was natural for Asarluhi to be absorbed in the personality of Marduk. A hymn of the Old Babylonian Period addresses Asarluhi as the river of ordeal (see **river ordeal**), as the first-born son of Enki and as Marduk. In the Standard Babylonian magical tradition Asarluhi is used as an alternative name for Marduk in incantations and prayers.

assembly of the gods

In a number of Sumerian and Babylonian myths the **gods** are depicted discussing their own affairs, or those of mankind, in an assembly (*ukkin/puhrum*) of which An/Anu is the leader and which met at the *ub-šu-ukkina* in the **E-kur**, **Enlil**'s temple at Nippur. In some narrative poems, men also debate questions of policy in an assembly of elders or adult men. Probably these both reflect some social reality at the time when the poems were taking shape, whether at national or village level, but it seems impossible to relate this securely to any theoretical reconstruction of the political system of early Sumer.

See **dreams and visions**.

astrology and astronomy

Strictly speaking, astrology refers to observation of the movements of astral bodies with a view to **divination** of the future thereby, as opposed to astronomy (disinterested scientific observation). From the movement and appearance of the moon, stars and planets, the Babylonians believed that it was possible to predict future events in the world, especially in the political and military spheres. 'The signs in the sky, just as those on earth, give us signals': the Babylonian view was that portents gave indications – clues – about the gods' intentions. By contrast, Hellenistic (and modern) astrology views the planets themselves as exerting influences over human destinies. It was only from the fifth century BC that Babylonian astrologers began to cast horoscopes to foretell the fortunes of ordinary individuals. However, although many ancient astronomical texts are expressed in a form which allows for their astrological application (for example, they include associations of deities with the constellations where appropriate), the basic facts and procedures are of astronomical or chronological interest, and there is some evidence that the main reason for the development of astronomy was the wish to be able to control the calendar, rather than to interpret celestial events astrologically. Although some deities have connections with stars or planets, many do not, and the idea that Mesopotamian religion was astral in origin is untenable.

Babylonian observation of the night skies

can be documented from at least 750 BC in daily records (only a small part of which survive), and by about 400 BC had reached a remarkably accurate level given the pre-Galilean **cosmology** with which they worked. Lunar eclipses could be predicted with considerable accuracy. Halley's comet was observed and recorded in 164 BC and again in 87 BC. The 157 **ziggurats** (temple towers) may have been used in the later periods as suitable observation platforms, although that was not their original function. Babylon and Uruk were important centres of astronomy during the fourth to first centuries BC.

In Babylonian astronomy the eastern horizon was divided into three vertical bands, the 'ways' of **Enlil**, Anu (**An**) and Ea (**Enki**), which were used for locating the position of the 159 eighteen zodiacal constellations recognised from about 1000 BC. Later these eighteen constellations were assigned singly or in pairs to the twelve months, foreshadowing the later **zodiac**. Five planets were recognised: Mercury (called 'Jumping'), Venus, Mars, Jupiter (called 'the Ferry') and Saturn (called 'Constant'). Many of the names for the constellations were the same as or similar to those transmitted to the modern world by the Greek astronomer Ptolemy (*c.* AD 150).

Ašimbabbar: see **Nanna-Suen**.

Ašratu: see **Martu**.

Aššur

Aššur was the god of the Assyrian nation. Originally he may have been the local deity of the city of the same name, or rather – since it is 26 unusual in Mesopotamia for the god and city to bear the same name (see **local gods**) – a personification of the city itself. (**Oaths** were sworn by the name of the city as if it were itself a god). As, therefore, the extent and power of Assyria spread, Aššur became the supreme god of the emergent state and empire. Details of the origins and development of the god, however, are lacking.

Eventually, with the growth of Assyria and the increase in cultural contacts with southern Mesopotamia, there was a tendency to

26 A view of the Assyrian city of Aššur, as it appears today. In the foreground is the partly restored Temple of Ištar; behind are the remains of one of the ziggurats or temple-towers.

assimilate Aššur to certain of the major deities of the Sumerian and Babylonian pantheons. From about 1300 BC we can trace some attempts to identify him with Sumerian **Enlil**. This probably represents an effort to cast him as the chief of gods. **Ninlil** was thus regarded as Aššur's wife, though worshipped in Assyria under the name Mullissu. Then, under Sargon II of Assyria (reigned 721–705 BC) Aššur tended to be identified with **Anšar**, the father of Anu (**An**) in the Babylonian Epic of Creation. The process thus represented Aššur as a god of long-standing, present from the **creation** of the universe. The particular identification may have been suggested by nothing more than the similarity of the names. Under Sargon's successor Sennacherib (reigned 704–681 BC), an attempt was made, at an official level, to reattribute to Aššur the

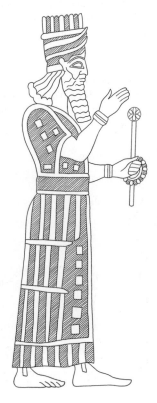

27 The god Aššur. From a glazed brick panel found in a private house in Aššur. 9th–7th centuries BC.

mythology of the Babylonian national god **Marduk**, as well as the rituals of the **New Year ceremonies** at Babylon itself. The underlying reasons behind this action were clearly the current political and military struggle between Assyria and Babylonia. This culminated in Sennacherib's nine-month siege, conquest and systematic sacking of Babylon in 691 BC, and his subsequent imposition of direct rule and personal assumption of the Babylonian throne.

Even the emblems of Aššur were adopted from Babylonian gods. His animal, the **snake-dragon** (which even on Sennacherib's rock reliefs at Maltai is not exclusive to him) was taken 31 over from **Marduk**. In collections of symbols of the gods, moreover, Aššur seems to be represented by a **horned cap**, inherited from Anu 10 (**An**) and Enlil.

The modern attribution to Aššur of the **solar** 140 **disc** is certainly incorrect. Some scholars, however, believe that the **winged disc**, very common in Assyrian art and often on Assyrian sculptures with the image of a god above it, and 155 placed over scenes of battle, ritual and the chase, must represent Aššur. The evidence, however, points strongly to this emblem as a symbol of the sun god Šamaš (**Utu**). Again, there may be some borrowing of an image proper to another god.

In spite of (or possibly because of) the tendencies to transfer to him the attributes and mythology of other gods, Aššur remains an indistinct deity with no clear character or tradition (or iconography) of his own. It was 27 said to be solely within his power to grant (or to remove) kingship over Assyria, and the Assyrian king was his chief priest and lieutenant on earth. It was particularly common for the names of Assyrian kings to contain the god's name as an element (e.g. Assurnasirpal, Assurbanipal, Esarhaddon (Aššur-ahhē-iddina)). The god supported and encouraged the armies of Assyria. The god's seals were used to endorse documents of the utmost political importance, such as King Esarhaddon's (reigned 132 680–669 BC) treaty providing for the succession (see **seals of the gods**). In these contexts, however, Aššur appears as a mere personification of the country, people and power of Assyria as a political entity.

See **letters to gods**.

Atra-hasīs: see **Ziusura**.

augury: see **divination**.

Aya: see **Šerida**.

Baba: see **Bau**.

ball-staff

A symbol sometimes called by modern writers a 'ball-staff' or 'ball-and-staff' appears on cylinder seals of the Isin-Larsa Period. It looks like a staff with a large bulge on one side. A motif looking like a pot is almost invariably placed above it. It has been suggested that the 'ball-staff' depicts a type of vessel, balance, rod or loom. Which deity (if any) it represents is unknown.

barley stalk

With possible antecedents reaching back into the Uruk Period, the motif of a barley stalk or ear of corn first occurs as a divine attribute in the Akkadian Period, and as an independent religious symbol in Kassite and Mitannian art. It is captioned on one **kudurru** as a symbol of the goddess **Šala**, and is later, in the Hellen-

istic Period, shown as an attribute held by this goddess.

See **zodiac**.

bašmu: see **snakes**.

Bau

Bau was a goddess worshipped almost exclusively at Lagaš, where she was regarded as the spouse of the god **Ninĝirsu**, or else of **Zababa**. Numerous records survive of the offerings made in the E-tarsirsir, her temples at Lagaš and Ĝirsu, where oracles were given in Early Dynastic times. Bau was a daughter of **An**, and had two sons by Ninĝirsu, the deities Ig-alima and Šul-šagana, as well as seven daughters (minor goddesses of Lagaš) for whom Ninĝirsu's paternity was not claimed.

Formerly the goose was thought to be the bird associated with Bau, but this is now known to be erroneous. On Babylonian **kudurrus** Bau is represented by an object which has been thought to be a winnowing fan.

It is possible that the correct form of the name is Baba.

See **Ĝatumdug**.

beasts of the gods

As well as their distinctive attributes, weapons and inanimate or astral symbols, many Mesopotamian deities had their familiar beasts,

28 The so-called 'ball-staff' with vessel above. Detail from a cylinder seal of the Isin-Larsa Period.

29 (*centre*) A barley stalk or ear of corn, symbol of the goddess Šala. One of the emblems carved on a *kudurru* of the Kassite Period.

30 (*far right*) A god walking his human-headed lion. Detail from a cylinder seal of the Akkadian Period.

31 The best preserved of four similar panels of rock reliefs at Maltai, carved on the cliff-face on the southern side of the Dehok valley, by the road leading from Assyria to the Upper Zab valley. The Assyrian king, probably Sennacherib (reigned 704–681 BC), flanks a procession of seven deities on their animals, probably (left to right) Aššur on snake-dragon and lion-dragon, his consort Mullissu enthroned on a lion, Enlil or Sîn on lion-dragon, Nabû on a snake-dragon, Šamaš on a horse, Adad on lion-dragons and bull, and Ištar on a lion.

45, 79, sometimes natural animals but more usually
87, 105, elaborate hybrid combinations. Sometimes representations of such beasts in art served the function of symbolising the various gods, or
31, 89, else individual deities are shown standing on
110, 132, their respective beasts; sometimes large-scale
151 statues of the creatures guarded the entrance to their masters' shrines, or served, in effect, as
75 **altars**, with other symbols placed upon their backs. Among these beasts were:

the **snake-dragon**, with snake-like body, horns, lion's forelegs and bird's hindlegs, which was transferred from and to a number of different high-ranking gods, including **Marduk** and **Nabû** in Babylonia and **Aššur** in Assyria;

the **lion-dragon**, also with lion's forelegs, bird's hindlegs, tail and wings, perhaps originally the beast of the god **Iškur**, later transferred (as a second associated animal) to a number of Assyrian gods;

the **bull**, usually the animal of a god whose forked **lightning (symbol)** identifies him as a weather deity (see **Iškur**);

the **lion**, associated at different times with a number of different deities, including **Ninğirsu** and the goddesses **Ninlil**, **Ištar** (**Inana**) and Damkina (**Damgalnuna**);

the **horse**, at least by the seventh century BC the beast of the sun god **Šamaš** (**Utu**);

the **dog**, sacred animal of the goddess **Gula**;

the **turtle** and **goat-fish** of the water god **Enki**/Ea;

various types of natural and hybrid **snakes** and **birds**, associated with a variety of deities.

See **Asag**; **Imdugud**; **Lamaštu**.

beer: see **alcohol**; **libation**.

Bēl: see **Marduk**.

Bēlet-ilī: see **mother goddesses and birth goddesses**; **Nergal**; **Ninhursağa**.

Bēlet-ṣēri: see under **Martu**.

bells

It has been suggested that the 'Strong copper', one of the trophies of the god **Ninurta** (see **Slain Heroes**), may be a personified clanger or bell. However, the earliest bells found in Mesopotamia are Assyrian, dating to the first millennium BC. Magical texts refer to the ringing of a bell as a means of driving away evil spirits. One example of an Assyrian bell has protective supernatural figures (see **demons and monsters**) depicted on it.

32 A Neo-Assyrian copper or bronze bell, cast with figures of magically protective demons. It was probably used in rituals of exorcism. Ht. 97 mm.

Berossos

Berossos (a Greek form of a Babylonian name, perhaps Bēl-uṣur) was a priest of Bēl (**Marduk**) at Babylon in the late fourth to early third centuries BC. He wrote a three-volume work in Greek, now lost, on the culture and history of Babylonia. An abridgement was made in the first century BC by Alexander Polyhistor.

Although also now lost, this served as a source for the Jewish historian Joseph ben Matthias ('Josephus', AD 37/38–*c*.100) and the church father Eusebius (died AD 342). Berossos was thus the ultimate source for authoritative knowledge of Babylonia by the ancient Greeks.

He is said to have emigrated in old age to the Aegean island of Cos, where he founded a school of astrology. There is no absolute certainty, however, that Berossos of Babylon and Berossos of Cos were one and the same. It is also possible that certain ideas attributed to Berossos in Classical sources were later in origin (so-called 'Pseudo-Berossos'), along with certain other traditions concerning his life, including that he was the father of the Sibyl!

The first book of his work *Babyloniaka* opened with an account of the beginnings of the world and the myth of Oannes and other fish-monsters, who, emerging from the sea, first brought the arts of civilisation to mankind (see **Seven Sages**). It continued with the Babylonian **creation** story and an account of Babylonian astrology.

The second book recounted the history of Babylonia from the 'ten kings before the Flood', through the story of the **Flood** itself (see **Ziusura**), followed by the restored kingship with its six dynasties down to the reign of Nabonassar (Nabû-nāṣir, reigned 747–734 BC).

The third book dealt with the history of Babylonia down to Berossos' own time, including the reigns of Tiglath–pileser III, Sennacherib and Nebuchadnezzar II.

Akkadian mythological and historical texts found in modern excavations have largely confirmed the authenticity of the tradition represented by Berossos.

Bes

Bes or Bisu was the Egyptian god of play and recreation, represented as a full-faced bow-legged **dwarf**, with oversized head, goggle eyes, protruding tongue, bushy tail and usually a large feathered crown as head-dress. He was a magically protective deity who averted the power of evil, and was especially associated with the protection of children and of women in childbirth. Some Egyptologists believe him to be of non-Egyptian origin, since he is said to come 'from the holy land' (the east, interpreted as Arabia or Babylonia) and called 'Lord of Puoni' (Punt, on the African coast of the Red Sea).

Representations of a very similar figure are
33 found widely in Syria, Palestine, Assyria and Babylonia in the first millenium BC. In Assyria and Babylonia the god may have been known as Pessû.

Bilulu: see **Inana**.

bird gods
Some fragmentary stelae of Gudea, ruler of Lagaš, show shaven-headed **priests** carrying standards surmounted by the figure of a bearded god 'wearing' the head and splayed wings of a bird of prey as if they were an
76 elaborate head-dress. It has been suggested that since **Ninĝirsu** was symbolised by the lion-headed bird **Imdugud**, this deity associated with a natural-headed eagle might rather be identifiable as **Ninurta**. However, Ninĝirsu seems to have been nothing more than the local form (in the city-state of Lagaš) of Ninurta at this time. Perhaps the distinction is between the god Ninĝirsu/Ninurta himself and his familiar animal the Imdugud bird.

In some ninth-century BC Assyrian representations of the god in the **winged disc**, a bird-tail is shown beneath the disc as if it were
144 one with the body of the god above. According to one idea, this is a bird god who can, again, be identified as Ninurta. The winged disc, however, appears to be a symbol of the sun-god Šamaš (**Utu**).

bird-men: see **animal skins; griffin-demon; Imdugud**.

birds
76 A number of different birds occur in Mesopotamian art as deities' symbols. One type, a long-necked species, first occurs in the Uruk Period, as a type of standard, with the bird

33 A Neo-Assyrian cast copper figurine of a dwarf god, of a type known in Egypt as Bes. It has a hollowed back and probably was originally fitted to a timber pole or item of furniture. From a room in the residential area of the royal palace arsenal at Kalhu (modern Nimrud), 8th–7th centuries BC. Ht. 122 mm.

shown on top of a small rod mounted on the back of a **snake-dragon**. The bird recurs on a Neo-Sumerian seal, associated with a seated goddess, and on Old Babylonian seals, after which it disappears from art. Representations of a goose-like bird perched on a tall pole, shown on Parthian stamp-seals, are probably unrelated.

34 Depictions of a walking bird are naturally common in all periods, but only on the Kassite **kudurrus** and in Neo-Babylonian glyptic art does the motif stand definitely as a religious

7,76 symbol. *Kudurru* captions characterise it as a symbol of the minister god Papsukkal (**Ninšubur**). A bird with back-turned head is found frequently in Kassite-Period art as a divine symbol and attribute. The accompanying inscription on one *kudurru* is partially broken but probably named the Kassite god

90 Harbe. The symbol of a bird on a high perch, probably in fact representing a bird-standard, is common on the Kassite *kudurru*s, and is identified from the inscriptions on two of them as a symbol of the obscure dual gods Šuqamuna (and) Šumalia (see **Kassite gods**).

The motif of a bird on a low perch is found as a divine symbol on the rock stelae of the Assyrian king Sennacherib at Judi Dagh, where the inscription characterises it as symbolising the avian war god **Ninurta**.

34 A walking bird. Detail from the carving on a Babylonian *kudurru*.

An Old Babylonian clay plaque shows a man riding an ostrich. However, the ostrich appears only rarely before the glyptic art of the Middle and Neo-Assyrian Periods. Often the bird is under attack from, or being throttled by, a pur- 14 suing god. The mythological or religious basis of these scenes is unknown. The early existence of the ostrich in Mesopotamia is proved by the presence in Sumerian graves of ostrich eggs. The top of the egg was severed and to the open shell were attached a rim and base of pottery decorated with inlays.

A lion-headed bird depicted in works of art 86 from the Early Dynastic to the Neo-Sumerian Periods appears to represent **Imdugud/Anzû**, associated with the god **Ninĝirsu/Ninurta**.

A common scene on cylinder seals of the 61 Akkadian Period shows a large bird carrying the figure of a man, which has usually, and fairly plausibly, been interpreted as depicting the flight episode in the myth of **Etana**.

See **animal skins**; **Bau**; **Enmešarra**; **griffin**; **Ziusura**. For the eagle-headed staff, see **standards, staves and sceptres of the gods**. For augury, see **divination**.

bird talons and wings

According to one suggestion, the presence of *fr.*, 6, bird talons and wings as part of the combina- 45,89, tion of various Mesopotamian **demons and** 100,117, **monsters** suggests an association with death 120 and the **underworld**. Some Babylonian poems describe the dead as clothed with bird-like plumage. The main literary basis for the idea, however, is a poetic account of a **dream** of an Assyrian prince, possibly the later King Assurbanipal (reigned 668–*c.*627 BC). In the dream, the prince descends to the underworld, which is peopled by a horde of unpleasant demons, described in graphic detail. In almost all cases these hellish demons are said to have been winged and to have had the talons of birds (or the feet of **Imdugud**, which amounts to the same thing).

The content of this poem, however, is unique as the first known description of the 'medieval' image of a hell peopled by demonic figures. While this may represent a new and powerful element in theological thinking, in descriptive terms it takes over elements already familiar in Assyrian iconography. Even in the Assyrian Period these iconographic elements were not confined to underworld denizens, since they are shared by beneficent and magically protective figures. Moreover, the suggestion of an association of wings and talons with creatures of the underworld cannot be applied to the art of earlier periods.

birth goddesses: see mother goddesses and birth goddesses.

bison

The bison survives today in Europe and North America. The Mesopotamian bison seems to have become extinct in pre-Sumerian times. The Sumerian term *gud-alim* (Akkadian *kusarikku*) was used, however, for the super-

35 The gold head of a bison with affixed lapis lazuli beard. The ornament on the sound-box of a lyre from the 'Royal Cemetery' at Ur. Early Dynastic Period.

natural figure of the **bull-man**, possibly also 40 for the **bull with human head**. In Sumerian 42 art, the bull-heads of the lyres from the Royal Graves at Ur, for example, have beards (made of lapis lazuli) that are reminiscent of the bison. 35

Astronomically, the constellation *gud-alim/kusarikku* corresponds to part of Centaurus.

See **Slain Heroes**.

bīt akīti: see **New Year ceremonies**.

boats

In Mesopotamia, the importance of the Tigris and Euphrates rivers, their tributaries and the canals dug from them made boats essential for many commercial, state and ritual activities. Even deities had their own barges (see **boats of the gods**).

A common theme on cylinder seals, especially in the Early Dynastic and Akkadian Periods, involves human-looking figures sitting or standing in a boat. This has been interpreted as **Gilgameš** and Ūt-napišti (**Ziusura**) in the Epic of Gilgameš, but the suggestion is dubious, especially as the two heroes never actually travel by boat together in the surviving versions of the story, while the number of figures in the boat in artistic representations is not always limited to two. Gilgameš does cross the waters with Ūt-napišti's pilot Uršanabi, but it seems more likely that these boating scenes refer to various different ritual excursions of men and perhaps sometimes of gods (see **journeys and processions of the gods**). In scenes of the presentation of offerings to a temple, common on seals of the Late Uruk Period, the procession of devotees, usually on foot, is sometimes shown approaching the temple by boat (or else on foot and by boat), as some temples were sited on the water-front. Occasionally a small shrine is mounted on a boat, while people standing on the same vessel approach from one side.

The Babylonians recognised a constellation called the Barge.

boats of the gods

Just as the **gods**, or the **cult statues** which rep-

36 Šamaš, the sun god, in his anthropomorphised deified boat. Detail from a cylinder seal of the Akkadian Period from Ešnunna (modern Tell Asmar).

resented them, had houses (see **temples and temple architecture**), tables to eat from (see **food and drink of the gods**), beds to sleep in and clothes and jewellery to adorn them, so they also had full-sized barges – usually propelled by rowers – in which to travel by river or canal. These boats were actually used when the statutes of the gods made ritual journeys to visit one another at festival times (see **journeys and processions of the gods**). Individual boats had names. During that period of Mesopotamian history when each year was named after an important event of the preceding year (about 2300–1650 BC), the refitting and caulking of the boat of a god was a sufficiently grand and expensive undertaking to serve as a year-name.

The god's boat would be stored in the temple and it seems that the **cult statue** of the god and some of the god's or goddess's treasure might be exhibited in the boat.

The boats of the gods are a favourite theme in Sumerian literature, especially in the various poems celebrating divine journeys. In the poem *Lugale*, the god **Ninurta** travels home in his barge Ma-kar-nunta-ea and the boatmen (rowers) serenade him with a hymn of praise. The Assyrian king Sennacherib (reigned 704–681 BC) made an offering of a ship of gold to the god Ea (**Enki**).

See **Lamaštu**; **'omega' symbol**.

boat with human head
On seal designs of the Early Dynastic and Akkadian Periods, the boats which are shown conveying people or deities by river or canal are on occasion rendered with a prominent prow terminating in a human head, occasionally also with human torso and arms, with which the man-boat might actually row himself. Since 36 the human head is sometimes crowned by a **horned cap**, it seems likely that the rendering is of a boat god (perhaps the minor deity Sirsir), or in effect, perhaps, an animation and personification of the boat of a god.

Among the group of mythological characters known as the **Slain Heroes**, defeated and killed by the god **Ninĝirsu** (or in an alternative version **Ninurta**), is one referred to as the *Magillum*-boat. Nothing is known of the form in which this creature was envisaged.

boundary stones: see **kudurrus**.

bow-legged dwarf: see **dwarf**.

bucket and cone

In Neo-Assyrian art, objects resembling a pine cone and a bucket (or occasionally a bucket alone) are held as attributes by a number of different **genies**, often in association with the stylised tree; the 'cone' is held up in the right hand, the bucket held down in the left. Only very rarely are these objects held by figures which might be interpreted as entirely human; almost always they are held by genies or human-animal hybrids (see **demons and monsters**). As well as in front of the stylised tree, the bucket and cone are seen held before floral decorative elements, guardian supernatural figures, the king or his attendants, or open doorways. The cone has been interpreted as a fir cone (*Pinus brutia*), as the male flower of the date palm or as a clay object in imitation of such. The bucket has been thought to have been of metal or wicker, and to have contained

18,37,
49,65,
78,82,
108,144,
155

either water or pollen (see **stylised tree and its 'rituals'**). Written sources on the matter are few, but it seems clear that the bucket and cone were associated with **purification**, for they are known respectively as *banduddû* (bucket) and, significantly, *mullilu* (purifier), and **figurines** of genies holding these attributes were among the types placed within buildings for protection from malevolent demons and **disease** (see **building rites and deposits; magic and sorcery**).

11

building rites and deposits

In ancient Mesopotamia, building activities seem generally to have been accompanied by certain appropriate rites. During the construction of new buildings, especially **temples**, there were usually some religious ceremonies and magical practices associated with the consecration of the edifice, its **purification**, **dedication** and protection from demonic forces. The residents of private houses might employ

related rituals to safeguard themselves and their property from **demons** and **diseases**, at the completion of the building or at the outbreak of a particular illness. Such rituals are generally treated together in modern literature as foundation or building rites. They often involved the use of deposits of various kinds placed in the foundations, or installed at the time of the foundation, of a building.

9,11,
12,38,
40,57,
70,116,
136

See **figurines**; **g̃ipar**.

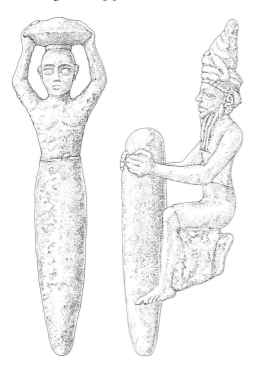

bull

A bull's head on early historic painted pottery has been thought to symbolise a storm god, but without definite proof. From the Old Babylonian Period onwards, however, the bull is usually associated with a god whose attribute of **lightning** confirms his identity as a storm god. Thunderclouds are referred to as the 'bull-calves' of the storm god Adad (**Iškur**). In the Old Babylonian Period, the bull can also be an attribute of the moon god **Nanna-Suen**, since it is associated with the **crescent** on seals. On astronomical tablets, the depiction of a bull represents the constellation Taurus.

31,89

159

See **crescent**; **horned cap**; **wedge**; **zodiac**.

bull and 'winged gate'

Occurring prominently on cylinder seals of the Akkadian Period is a motif of a tripartite rectangular structure with sealed central portion and multiple projections emanating from the upper part. Carrying the construction on its back, or perhaps simply lying in front of it, is a recumbent bull. A god or goddess sits in front of the animal. Either the deity gestures to the

39

38 (*left*) Copper 'peg figurines', which were driven into the foundations of buildings: (*left*) from the temple of the goddess Inana at Nippur, depicting King Šulgi of the Third Dynasty of Ur ceremonially carrying a builder's basket; (*right*) a deity securing the peg, from the time of Ur-Ninĝirsu of Lagaš, son of Gudea.

39 (*right*) Goddess, bull and so-called 'winged gate'. Detail from a cylinder seal of the Akkadian Period.

37 (*left*) Details of bucket and cone held by genies on monumental stone reliefs from the Royal Palace of the Assyrian king Assurnasirpal II (reigned 883–859 BC) at Kalhu (modern Nimrud).

beast with raised hands, offers a small bowl, or else holds the animal's horns or the end of a halter fastened to a ring piercing its nostrils. Alternatively, or in addition, the deity holds a rope fastened to one side of the main construction, while a second rope attached to the other side is held by an attendant.

Some modern commentators have regarded the construction as a partly closed doorway, and have thought that the projections resemble wings, hence the term 'winged gate'. These projections have alternatively been regarded as rays of light, either of the morning sun (with the 'ropes' regarded as streams of water), or of the moon, the 'gate of night', shutting in the moon god in his aspect as the 'young bull of heaven'. Since the **bull** was also an animal of the storm god, a possible interpretation of the projections might be as flashes of **lightning**. A related theory sees in the subject a case of **animal sacrifice** to a conquering sky god. When the deity is a goddess, the scene has also been explained as a depiction of the myth of Ištar (**Inana**) and the **Bull of Heaven**. Probably, however, the scene represents an episode of some myth of the Akkadian Period which is

now lost to us. That the iconography is very rarely attested after that time may suggest that the myth was no longer current, which would render its chances of recovery extremely slim.

bull-man
Bulls and lions in quasi-human pose figure among the fabulous beasts of the so-called 'proto-Elamite' (early third millennium BC) glyptic art of south-western Iran. They have been interpreted as personifying the elementary principles of world order.

The figure of the 'bull-man', with human head and torso but taurine horns, lower body and legs, first appears in the second phase of the Early Dynastic Period, when the creature is to be seen very commonly on cylinder seals. He is usually shown in profile, with a single visible horn projecting forward, although we know from those rarer occasions when either the head only or the whole body above the waist (but not below it) is shown in frontal view, that he was intended to be double-horned. He appears singly, in pairs or even in triplicate, in contest scenes with rampant animals. Sometimes he is associated in his struggle with a

40 The bull-man on clay reliefs. (*left*) Example from the Old Babylonian Period, place of discovery unknown. Ht.127 mm. (*right*) Example from the Neo-Assyrian Period, found in a brick box buried in the foundations of a building at Aššur. Ht.141 mm.

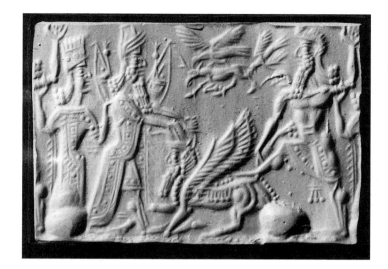

41 The heroes Gilgameš and Enkidu slay the Bull of Heaven sent by the goddess Ištar. Blue chalcedony cylinder seal of the Neo–Assyrian Period, with modern impression. Ht. 28 mm.

human figure, from the later (Third) Early Dynastic Period usually with another stock figure, the 'hero' with curls (see **Lahmu**). Contest scenes involving this pair of figures become the most common of all themes in the glyptic art of the Akkadian Period.

73 In the art of the Old Babylonian and Kassite Periods, the bull-man appears, as well as in contests, as an attendant of the sun god Šamaš (**Utu**). In the scene on a Neo–Babylonian foundation tablet, a pair of bull-men support the throne of this god.

From the Kassite Period, perhaps, the figure becomes a magically protective demon, and by Neo-Assyrian times it seems that his specific association with Šamaš has been weakened; he might still hold the god's symbol, and is also

82 seen as a supporter of Šamaš's **winged disc**, but the bull-man also appears as one of a repertoire of generally beneficent creatures, monumental and small-scale images of whom were placed

40 within buildings as a barrier to evil (see **building rites and deposits; demons and monsters**). The bull-man is also found in the art of the Achaemenid Period.

Kusarikku (Sumerian *gud-alim*), probably the name for the extinct **bison**, became the term for the bull-man (and possibly also for the bull with human head – see **bulls and lions with human head**). There is no basis for the suggestion that the figure of the bull-man in art represents the legendary hero **Enkidu**.

See **Tiāmat's creatures; Slain Heroes; ring-staff**.

Bull of Heaven

53 The Bull of Heaven was a mythical beast demanded by Ištar (**Inana**) from her father Anu (**An**) so as to destroy the city of Uruk when her amorous advances toward **Gilgameš** were repudiated by the hero. The bull caused wide-spread destruction but was eventually killed by

41 Gilgameš with the assistance of **Enkidu**. As a taunt, Gilgameš dedicated the animal's horns to his personal god **Lugalbanda**. The story is told both in the Sumerian poem 'Gilgameš and the Bull of Heaven' and in tablet VI of the Babylonian Epic of Gilgameš.

As a constellation, the Bull of Heaven is Taurus (see **zodiac**), and it has been suggested that the story of Enkidu throwing the thigh of the bull at Ištar attempts to account for the apparent lack of the bull's hind quarters in the outline of the constellation.

See **bull and 'winged gate'**.

49

42 A colossal stone gateway guardian in the form of a human-headed winged bull, one of a pair that originally flanked one of the entrances to the royal palace of the Assyrian king Sargon II (reigned 721–705 BC) at Dūr-Šarkēn (modern Khorsabad). The creature was designed to be viewed from either the front or side, hence its five legs. Ht. 4.42 m.

bulls and lions with human head

53
30,36 A human-headed winged or wingless bull is a common motif in Mesopotamian art from the Early Dynastic Period through to Neo-Babylonian times, and was taken over also into the art of the Achaemenid Empire. Monumental sculptures of man-headed bulls and lions carved in the round were particularly
42 common in the Neo-Assyrian Period (and similarly in Achaemenid times) as gateway guardians. Such figures adorned the palaces of the more important Assyrian kings from Assurnasirpal II (reigned 883–859 BC) until Esarhaddon (reigned 680–669 BC); their absence from the palace of King Assurbanipal (reigned 668–c.627 BC) was perhaps due to the lack of availability of large enough blocks of stone at that time; some of Esarhaddon's bull-colossi were made from separate blocks fitted together. Male and female human-headed lions (often
16,53 referred to as 'sphinxes') occur.

It is possible, but not certain, that the bull with human head was, like the **bull-man**, known in Akkadian as *kusarikku* (see **bison**). The more usual identification with figures called by the Assyrians *aladlammû* (or *lamassu* and *šēdu*) is also possible (see **lama**).

Bunene: see **Utu**.

burials: see **death and funerary practices**.

canal gods: see **Enbilulu**; **Ennugi**; **Enkimdu**; **Ninĝirsu**.

Cedar Forest: see **Gilgameš**; **Huwawa**.

centaur

A figure human above the waist with, below, the 53 body and all four legs of a **horse**, is known in the Kassite and Middle Assyrian Periods on 43 seals and sealings and on **kudurrus**. It also occurs on Babylonian stamp-seals of Hellenistic date. Sometimes it has the tail of a **scorpion**. The human part is often shown armed with a bow or club, hunting other animals. In the Hellenistic Period the creature represents the god **Pabilsaĝ**.

See **bison**; **lion-centaur**; **merman and mermaid**.

chaplet

A so-called 'chaplet', or string of beads, is carried as an attribute by a goddess who appears on the palace sculpture of King Assur- 44 nasirpal II of Assyria (reigned 883–859 BC). On Neo-Assyrian seals, the goddess carrying the 87 chaplet is sometimes Ištar (**Inana**). Sometimes the ring of the '**rod and ring**' attribute, often

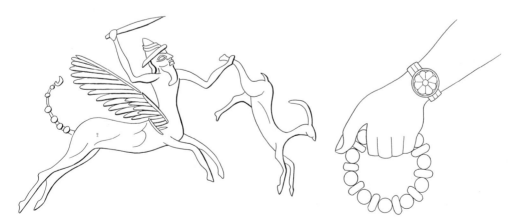

43 (*left*) A centaur catching an antelope. Detail from a cylinder seal of the Middle Assyrian Period.

44 (*right*) A 'chaplet' of beads, held in the hand of a goddess. Detail of a carved stone monumental relief from the royal palace of the Assyrian king Assurnasirpal II (reigned 883–859 BC).

27 held by the more important gods, resembles
such a chaplet. On the reliefs probably of King
31 Sennacherib (reigned 704–681 BC) at Maltai,
male deities carry a 'rod and ring', goddesses
just a ring, probably a similar chaplet.

chariots of the gods

Just as there were **boats of the gods**, so the
45 gods also had chariots for use in travel and
battle. They are often depicted standing in
their chariots, especially the storm god **Iškur/
Adad**. In actuality, the **cult statues** of the gods
were transported by land in chariots and wagons. Perhaps on occasion, when documentary
accounts describe a god as overseeing or actually involved in a battle, the statue of the god
was conveyed to the battlefield.

Bunene is said to have been the charioteer
(and in some accounts the son) of **Utu**. At least
in seventh-century BC theology, Utu was
thought to ride his chariot across the sky by day,
and through the 'interior of heaven' by night.

See **horse**; **journeys and processions of
the gods**.

charms: see **amulets**; **magic and sorcery**.

'cone-smearing' ceremony: see **bucket and
cone**; **stylised tree and its 'rituals'**.

cosmology

A variety of cosmological ideas were current at
different periods of Mesopotamian history.
The earlier, Sumerian, view of cosmology
seems to have been one of a dipartite universe
consisting of **an** (heaven) and **ki** (earth,
including the **underworld**) (see **Du-ku**).
Originally united and inhabited only by gods,
they were at a primordial time separated from
each other. This separation may have been
connected with the need to have a place for
mankind to inhabit. The earth was viewed as a
rectangular field with four corners, an image
which persisted, at least as a formulaic expression, until much later times.

The Babylonians, on the other hand,
according to one tablet showing a map of the
world, regarded the earth as a flat disc, with the
salt sea surrounding it. Beyond the sea lay eight
nagû (regions), one of which was the home of
Ūt-napišti (**Ziusura**), survivor of the **Flood**.
Under the world, according to other sources,
was the *apsû* (**abzu**) and below that the underworld, entered by a pair of bolted gates at the
extreme eastern and western horizons, down to
which the approach was by staircase. Through
these the sun passed each day, entering at the
west side and emerging at the east. A staircase
also led up to heaven. According to one tra-

45 A worshipper pours a libation over an altar before a god (probably Iškur) riding in his chariot, drawn
by a winged lion-dragon. A naked goddess stands on the back of the beast. From a cylinder seal of the
Akkadian Period.

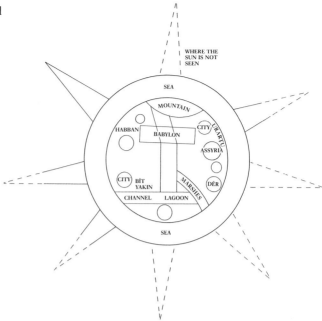

46 A bird's-eye view of the world according to the Babylonians, as sketched on a clay tablet of later Babylonian times now in the British Museum.

dition, there were three superimposed heavens, the lowest of which contained the stars, the middle being the home of the **Igigū** and the topmost that of Anu (**An**). In a separate, astronomical, tradition the eastern horizon was divided into three vertical bands (see **astrology and astronomy**).

The Babylonian Epic of Creation adapts this system, reflecting both the dipartite universe of heaven and earth (when **Tiāmat** is split in two), and a four-part universe of heaven, lower heaven (home of **Enlil**), earth (home of **Marduk**) and *apsû*.

Reflecting the old Sumerian idea of the separation of heaven and earth, an important cosmological image is that of the 'mooring-rope' or 'mooring-pole' of heaven and earth (also called the 'nose-rope', as used for cattle, or the 'boundary post'). A temple thought to be a channel of communication between earth and heaven might be so described.

See **creation**.

cow and calf

With apparent antecedents in early historic and Sumerian art, a group consisting of a cow and her calf is a common motif from the Old Baby-

lonian to the Neo-Assyrian Period, and recurs even in the Parthian era. The motif often appears to be a divine symbol, and has been interpreted as an emblem of Ištar (**Inana**) or, perhaps with more probability, of **Ninhursaĝa**. That the group was represented in apotropaic monumental sculpture, at least in Urarṭu, is proved by the record of the pieces plundered by Sargon II of Assyria from the temple of Haldi (see **Urarṭian gods**) at Muṣaṣir in 714 BC, which included 'one bull; one cow together with her calf'. The cow and calf motif was depicted on the Assyrian palace relief showing the sacking of the temple.

creation

Mesopotamian accounts of the beginning of the world vary according to which **cosmology** is followed. Generally, however, it is assumed that the **gods** have existed for a very long time, but not forever, and that man is a later arrival on the scene. **Nammu** was the mother who gave birth to **An** (heaven), **Ki** (earth) and the other '**great gods**'. (See also **Anšar and Kišar**.)

To express the idea of creation various images were used. First, the idea of sexual intercourse between gods: the god **Nanna** was the offspring of **Enlil** and **Ninlil**. **Enki** and **Ninhursaġa** produced a series of eight deities. An and Ki produced natural vegetation. Enlil and **Kur** produced Summer and Winter, personified in a Sumerian poem.

Second, the image of modelling by hand a **figurine** of clay was used, particularly for the creation of mankind. Either a **mother goddess** such as Nammu or Aruru, or else Enki, moulds the creature (sometimes with another goddess standing by as 'midwife'). In the Epic of Atra-hasīs, the clay is mixed with the blood of a slain god. In the Epic of Creation, man is apparently created solely from the blood of a slain god, **Qingu**.

Finally, the quickening power of the divine utterance is seen as responsible for creation. Especially Enki is described as undertaking the organisation of the universe, and as accomplishing this solely by the creative power of his **word**.

Personal gods are sometimes described as being responsible for the creation of the individual under their protection.

See **Berossos**; **Igigū**; **Sacred Marriage**.

crescent

7,10, 14,21, 49,82, 87,88, 95

74

47,73

111

The recumbent crescent moon occurs as a motif in Mesopotamian art from prehistoric times down to the Neo-Babylonian Period, and at least from the Old Babylonian Period is known from inscriptions to have been a symbol of the moon god Sîn (**Nanna-Suen**). Its Akkadian name was *uškaru*. In all periods a common variant placed the emblem on a post, sometimes with elaborate trimmings, when it appears as an independent motif or is held by gods, goddesses, or animal or hybrid figures. Probably it was then considered to have a magically protective power. From the Old Babylonian Period onwards, and especially from Kassite times, Sîn's crescent was often depicted within a disc; sometimes this appears to be a fusion of the crescent and **solar disc**, as if symbolic of an eclipse. In Neo-Assyrian and Neo-Babylonian art, the upper body of a god, presumably Sîn, may appear emerging from the crescent. On at least one Neo-Assyrian cylinder seal we find a winged crescent with centrally placed god, who wears a crescent-headed cap, and smaller inward-facing deities on the ends of the wings, in apparent imitation of the common symbol of the gods on the **winged disc**.

See **'omega' symbol**; **star (symbol)**.

crook

The crook-headed stick is an element mainly occurring in Old Babylonian glyptic art. It occurs as an isolated motif, held by a god, or set above a goat or sitting **dog**. It is often placed close to the 'figure with **mace**', with whom it may, therefore, have been associated. It is a symbol of the god Amurru (**Martu**).

On a Kassite seal the crook is held by the **fish-garbed figure**, who is associated with Ea (**Enki**). On Neo-Assyrian seals a god who stands upon a **goat-fish**, probably Ea, sometimes carries the crook; here it may serve simply as a crude representation of the god's staff with ram's head (see **standards, staves and sceptres of the gods**).

The constellation called the Crook corresponds to Auriga (see **zodiac**).

76

106

76

cross

Apart from the **swastika**, the only cruciform motif attested as a distinct element in Mesopotamian art is the 'cross formée', a form approximating to that today known as the Maltese cross. In prehistoric and early historic art, the form occurs only as part of geometric and floral designs, or in isolated contexts to which it is difficult to attach with any certainty a religious meaning. After the Early Dynastic Period the motif disappears from art until the mid-second millennium BC.

Appearing frequently on Kassite Period cylinder seals (with a rarer variant on Middle Assyrian), the 'Kassite' cross, as it has been called, probably had an independent origin. It may have been a symbol of the Kassite sun deity. It appears in contexts which strongly suggest that it is a sun symbol, substituting for the **solar disc**, or in positions later occupied by

48

76

the **winged disc**. These include, most commonly, positioning between a god with raised hand and a worshipper (the latter sometimes, in fact, omitted), above scenes of hunting, or in association with the **stylised tree**. The cross does not, however, appear on the **kudurrus**, where the **solar disc** represents the sun god.

In Middle Assyrian and Neo-Assyrian art, the cross was apparently normally replaced by the winged disc. Sculptures of Assyrian kings, however, can show them wearing divine symbols as earrings or as pendants strung upon a necklace, and in these cases it is the cross

rather than the winged disc which is invariably to be seen. It is only rarely that the cross stands in place of the winged disc on Assyrian seals, but here in some cases it is shown with four undulating projections, probably solar rays, emerging diagonally from its intersections. These are strong indications for the cross as a further symbol (together with the solar disc and winged disc) of the sun god Šamaš (**Utu**).

cult statues

The **gods** manifested themselves on earth through the vehicle of their cult statues. Without exactly *being* the god, the statue was

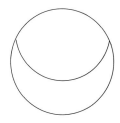

47 A crescent (here, as often, enclosed within a disc), symbol of the moon god Sîn (Nanna-Suen).

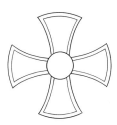

48 A Neo-Assyrian version of a cross, probably a symbol of the sun god Šamaš.

49 (*right*) Scenes of worship before the cult statue of the goddess Ištar standing in her shrine. From cylinder seals of the Neo-Assyrian Period, of a modelled style attributable to the 8th–7th centuries BC.

regarded as much more than his or her image, since it was imbued with (but did not in any way restrict) the divine presence. The closest parallel in modern religions, perhaps, is the rôle of the icon in Eastern Orthodoxy, while in the secular field it may be as well to remember that the eye of a child will see life and personality in a doll which, on another level, the mind recognises as an inanimate toy.

Cult statues were made at least as early as the Third Dynasty of Ur, usually carved in an expensive imported wood, overlaid with gold. In the Babylonian periods, at least, the newly dedicated image was imbued with the presence of the deity by the performance of rituals, known as 'Washing the mouth' and 'Opening the mouth'. Since the deity needed to eat and drink (see **food and drink of the gods**), the temple kitchens would prepare daily meals. Animals and plants were raised and grown in the temple's fields or were contributed by local fishermen and farmers. The **sacrifices and offerings** of devotees supplemented the stocks of food, which, in practice, were eaten by the clergy and temple staff. The cult statue was not only fed, but also dressed in the finest garments, constantly bathed, taken to bed in the god's richly adorned bedchamber, and treated to festivities and entertainments, such as music. Diversions from the routine were provided by the great monthly festivals and other special occasions, such as visits by land or river to other cities (see **boats of the gods; chariots of the gods; journeys and processions of the gods**).

See **nude woman; Sacred Marriage; temples and temple architecture**.

Dagan

Dagan (Hebrew Dagon) was a West Semitic corn god who came to be worshipped extensively throughout the Near East, including Mesopotamia. The original meaning of the name is unknown, but *dagan* is a common word in Hebrew and Ugaritic for 'grain', and according to one tradition the god Dagan was the inventor of the **plough**.

Dagan's cult is known at Mari from about 2500 BC, at Ebla about 2300 BC and at Ugarit over a thousand years later. Sargon of Agade and his grandson Narām-Suen attributed many of their conquests to the power of Dagan. At some point Dagan became the principal god of the Philistines.

At Ugarit, on the Mediterranean coast, Dagan was regarded as the father of the god Baal (Hadad) and second only in rank to the supreme god El. However, he is not an important figure in Ugaritic myths. His rôle as vegetation god seems to have been largely usurped by Baal by about 1500 BC.

At an early date Dagan was assimilated into the Sumerian **pantheon**, but only as a minor deity, attendant upon **Enlil**. The goddess **Šala** became his spouse; in a different tradition, Dagan's wife was **Išhara**. It was said to be by the might of 'his creator' Dagan that Hammurabi of Babylon was able to conquer the city of Mari, while the contemporary Assyrian king Šamšī-Adad I, 'worshipper of Dagan', built a temple to the god at Terqa, which he named E-kisiga, the 'House of Funerary Offerings'. In an Assyrian poem, Dagan sits, along with **Nergal** and Mīšaru (see **good and evil**), as judge of the dead when they reached the **underworld**. In Babylonian belief Dagan kept with him in the underworld, in everlasting bondage, the seven children of the god **Enmešarra** (see **Seven (gods)**).

A tradition dating back at least to the fourth century AD of Dagan as a fish deity is erroneous.

Damgalnuna (Damkina)

Damgalnuna is the earlier Sumerian name of the goddess Damkina. **Fish** offerings were made to her in Lagaš and Umma in early times, but her principal cult centre was the city of Malgûm. Perhaps originally one of a number of **mother goddesses**, she achieved an independent personality as the wife of **Enki**. In the Babylonian Epic of Creation, Ea (Enki) and Damkina are the parents of the god **Marduk**. Assurnasirpal II, king of Assyria (883–859 BC), built a temple to them at Kalhu (modern Nimrud).

The animal associated with Damkina was the **lion**; astrologically she was associated with the constellation called the Wagon of Heaven (Ursa Minor).

Damkina: see **Damgalnuna**.

Damu

A god of healing, who drives away demons and 'binds the torn sinew', Damu was honoured especially at Isin, and also at Larsa, Ur and perhaps Ĝirsu. He is usually regarded as a son of the goddess **Ninisina** and as a son of, or else identical with, the god **Ningišzida** (although one Akkadian translation of a Sumerian poem erroneously describes him as a 'daughter' of Ninisina). But these details vary, and sometimes he seems to be more closely linked with the circle of **Nanše**. It is unclear whether the Damu worshipped at Ebla and Emar in Syria was the same deity or a local hero. The official cult of Damu seems to have died out after the Old Babylonian Period.

Astrologically, Damu was associated with the constellation called the Pig (possibly Delphinus).

In some Sumerian poems, **Dumuzi** is addressed as 'my Damu', but it is possible that a different word, perhaps meaning 'child', is involved here.

Dayyānu: see **good and evil**.

dead gods

In Mesopotamia, although immortality was reserved for the **gods** (see **Siduri**), not all gods were immortal. A number of deities were regarded as dead. Nor were 'heroes' exempt from death. Only **Ziusura/Ūt-napišti** was granted eternal life, while others (including the partly divine **Gilgameš**) would perish.

Unlike mortal men, gods do not seem ever to have died of **diseases**, nor generally of the activities of **demons** (although **Dumuzi** was seized by **gallas**). Dead gods were usually those who had been slain. Seals of the Akkadian Period show deities in battle, sometimes one slaying another.

The idea that gods could be killed as well as created is met with near the beginning of the Babylonian Epic of Creation, when Apsû (see **abzu**), having engendered a line of deities by his union with **Tiāmat**, almost immediately decides to destroy them again because of the nuisance they have caused him. In fact, the tables are turned, and Apsû himself falls victim at the hands of Ea (**Enki**). The subsequent death of Tiāmat is presented as playing a crucial part in the **creation** of the universe, since heaven and earth (**Ki**) are made from the two separated halves of the monster's body (see **cosmology**). Furthermore, humankind is created, in part, from the blood of Tiāmat's consort, the god **Qingu**, who meets his death, following Tiāmat's defeat, by a kind of judicial execution. Apparently, the eleven monstrous creations of Tiāmat who have fought at her side (**Tiāmat's creatures**) are killed by **Marduk** in the great battle, but statues of them are placed by Marduk in the *apsû* (**abzu**).

Nothing in detail is known of the myth or myths concerning the killing of the **Slain Heroes**, but it seems clear that they were gods who were believed to be long dead, yet who

50 One god cuts the throat of another. Both figures wear the horned cap of divinity. From a cylinder seal of the Akkadian Period.

continued to receive offerings (see **sacrifice and offering**) and worship just as living gods. Their slaying by **Ningirsu** or **Ninurta** is 135 paralleled by Marduk's defeat and killing of the creatures of Tiāmat. Since in both cases images of these slain monsters were made (statues of Tiāmat's creatures, at least, were in the first millennium BC regarded as magically protective demons), it seems that, in spite of being dead, these gods were thought still to possess some effective powers. Similarly the magical power and wisdom of ancient (and 9, probably dead) gods such as **Lahmu** and even 11,12 the **Seven Sages** could be harnessed by the modelling of a **figurine** in the image of the creature and by the recital of incantations to imbue the figure with the dead entity's presence (see **magic and sorcery**). Huwawa/Humbaba, 69 slain by **Gilgameš** and **Enkidu**, is a further 85 case in point: probably his image was believed to be effective as a magical force against evil.

For men, 'death' usually meant journeying to the **underworld** (see **afterlife**; **death and funerary practices**), but for a god who was not dismembered (as Tiāmat or Qingu were) the precise meaning of his or her 'death' is unclear. Huwawa seems simply to disappear from the scene, as if into oblivion: we do not hear of his doings or sufferings after death. Some 'dead gods', however, seem to have had underworld associations.

The most famous 'dead god' of ancient Mesopotamia is **Dumuzi**. Since he was a shepherd god, the tradition of his death and rebirth was possibly an aetiological myth related to the passage of the seasons. The god's 'death' seems to have involved his forced abduction to the underworld. (See **Ningišzida**.)

Another god described as 'dead' is Gugalana, the first spouse and consort of the underworld queen **Ereškigal**. In the Sumerian poem 'Inana's Descent to the Nether World', in order to gain admission to the underworld, **Inana** says that she has come to attend the 'funeral' of Gugal-ana, her brother-in-law. Whether Gugal-ana's 'funeral' merely commemorated his removal to the infernal regions (in a certain sense, his 'death') or whether it

followed a 'second' death in the underworld – whatever might be understood by that – is unknown. (Inana herself, on her visit to the nether regions, is described in terms that sug- *frontis.* gest her 'death').

Some baked clay figurines possibly of the Isin-Larsa or Old Babylonian Period show a god who seems to be lying in a coffin. This has 112 been interpreted as **Nergal**, lord of the underworld, at rest.

death and funerary practices

It was believed in ancient Mesopotamia that immortality was reserved for gods; death was the inevitable lot of man (see **Siduri**). Nor was the **afterlife** considered very palatable: in the Sumerian **underworld** the dead consumed dust, while the Assyro-Babylonian hell was peopled by a plethora of intimidating **demons and monsters**. This is in marked contrast to Egyptian concepts of the glorious life to come, which gave rise to the practice of embalming and mummification. Mesopotamian pessimism in this regard probably arose from the comparatively harsh conditions of almost every aspect of life, the alluvial plain of Sumer being well suited to agricultural production but lacking virtually all raw materials, except for natural clays.

It has been suggested that the practice of burial in the prehistoric societies of Mesopotamia sought either to maintain close communication with the deceased, by means of a cult of the dead, or, conversely, to restrain the dead from haunting the living, as they would do if left unburied and free to wander (see **gidim**). The Sumerian rite of pouring **libations** into the ground by means of a clay pipe, probably intended to give the deceased a drink, may be evidence that the dead were believed to remain in their graves. In the time of the Third Dynasty of Ur, however, as illustrated by a funerary poem, there was a belief in different treatments of the dead on arrival in the underworld dependent upon the nature of their burials. The proper burial of the deceased was therefore of crucial importance to his or her future 'life'.

The most usual practice throughout the ancient Near East seems to have been inhumation (interment of the body in the earth or in a container), although the almost complete absence of adult burials of the Uruk Period may possibly suggest the practice of exposing corpses at that time. Cremation (the burning of the bodily remains) does not seem to have been practised in any period: there is no evidence in excavated graves in Mesopotamia for the use of fire and a Sumerian text suggests that to be burned to death accidentally was regarded as a sorry plight indeed (see **afterlife**).

The earliest known human remains in Mesopotamia have been excavated at Shanidar Cave in the Zagros mountains. The nine skeletons (seven adults and two infants) do not all belong to a single period, but date from perhaps about 60,000 to 45,000 years ago.

The majority of burials known from archaeological excavations have been found in cemeteries. These involve the graves of male and female adults and children. Young children were sometimes buried in the same graves as (male or female) adults, and in certain periods there is evidence for a blood relationship in such cases. Babies, however, were normally not buried in the cemeteries but either under the floors of private houses, often in cooking pots (sometimes with a hint of

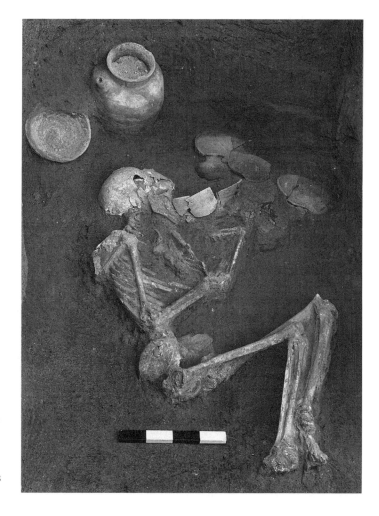

51 A Sumerian burial of the Early Dynastic Period, excavated by archaeologists at the site of Abu Salabikh (perhaps ancient Ereš).

human sacrifice), or simply tossed onto rubbish dumps as if they were regarded as sub-human. Adults were also buried beneath the floors of houses, but only rarely on rubbish tips.

The relative wealth and degree of elaboration in the construction of graves varies considerably according to time, place and, in some periods, the social status of the individuals involved. Sumerian burials can show a very high level of effort and expenditure, most notably with the so-called 'Royal Tombs' at Ur, but also in the richly furnished graves in cemeteries at some urban sites. At less wealthy

35,52, 83,84

sites, however, burials can have comparatively little in the way of grave goods. By the first millennium BC, an exaggerated social differentiation is apparent within given cultures. Neo-Assyrian burials, for example, range from simple pit burials with few or no funerary goods, through wealthier interments often in 'bath-tub' coffins of terracotta or copper/bronze, to fantastically wealthy graves such as those of the Assyrian queens very recently discovered at Kalhu (modern Nimrud).

The construction of graves ranges from simple pits, through slightly more elaborate burials with burial chambers bricked off from

52 An elaborate object used for supporting some grave furnishing. A he-goat made of shell, lapis lazuli and gold on a wooden core. One of a pair found in one of the fantastically rich 'Royal Tombs' at Ur. Early Dynastic Period. Ht. 470 mm.

the access shaft and rock-cut or stone-capped tombs, to brick or stone mausolea involving considerable cost and effort in construction. Often the burial chamber, even in the poorest graves, seems to have been lined with reeds or palm leaves, loose or in the form of woven mats. The body was often covered in a similar manner.

In Early Dynastic, contemporary northern Mesopotamian ('Ninevite 5') and early Babylonian burials the body has usually been found in the flexed or so-called 'sleeping' position (with the legs together, bent and raised), though not often in the crouched or so-called 'foetal' posture (with legs tightly flexed and close to the chin). Later the preferred position seems to have been the 'stretched' posture (with the body laid out full length, legs straight, and lying on the side or back).

The orientation of burials was often by the points of the compass, and can sometimes be shown to be related to other factors such as the sex or age of the deceased. Preferred orientation, or avoidance of certain orientations, varied according to period and location.

Except in the case of very wealthy individuals, adorned with a mass of jewellery, evidence of the clothing worn by the deceased is slim, since in the arid conditions of the Mesopotamian plain textiles rarely survive. A few fragments have, however, been found. Those from one Ninevite 5 Period burial have been identified as silk (!) and linen. The fairly common occurrence of copper or bronze pins, often found on the chest or at the shoulders, does suggest that the body was usually dressed. Beads have often been found in large numbers as necklaces (or more rarely strung around the waist) or in smaller numbers or individually at the wrists (on occasion close to the ankles). Numbers of cylinder seals have also on rare occasions been found strung around the wrist, perhaps worn as beads; more usually a single seal was placed separately in the grave.

Burials without grave goods were not uncommon, but even an impoverished burial would often contain a pot or two, even a broken one. Pottery is the most common of objects found in graves, although it is difficult at times to distinguish between those vessels which were themselves funerary offerings and those which served merely as carriers for food, drink, washing water or cosmetics. There is only occasional, and equivocal, evidence for vessels made purposefully for the grave. 'Sets' of vessels of differing sizes, placed one inside another, and apparently to be used together, are common, however, in Sumerian and Ninevite 5 burials. The position of the vessels within the graves may – almost accidentally – give us some indication of their intended purpose, for even if no rules governed the positioning, it would be natural to locate the more important and personal items close to the body, with other objects piled into the remaining space. In Early Dynastic and Ninevite 5 burials the deceased often holds a small bowl in front of the face as if to eat: even when no vessel is present, the hands are normally held in this position and perhaps originally held some food, long since perished. The bones of a small animal have in one case been retrieved from the bowl in this position. The bones of larger animals and the carbonised remains of cereals, probably the remains of food or sacrificial offerings (see **animal sacrifice**), have sometimes been found in the graves. A large vessel often placed close to the head, regularly with a smaller pot sitting within its rim, was perhaps a provision of drinking water, complete with scoop. Another large vessel is sometimes found together with a large natural stone slab (the so-called 'gravestone'): these have been interpreted as a container for washing water and an ablution slab.

Smaller stones and pebbles, sometimes of differing colours and carefully placed on the body, have been interpreted as having a symbolic or magical function.

Tools and weapons are not very common in Mesopotamian burials of any period.

The grave goods seem to have served a variety of purposes. Some objects were so personal to the deceased that their inclusion in the grave was natural, since they would not be used by others. Except in the richest graves, this

51

category of goods probably comprised only items of clothing or children's toys. A second category of items was included for the use of the dead person in or on their way to the after-life, or as gifts for the denizens of the under-world (referred to in texts of the Early Dynastic Period and Third Dynasty of Ur). Finally, goods eventually assigned to the grave could represent a public display of wealth by the de-ceased's family and friends during the funeral ceremonies. Probably in the case of high-ranking or wealthy individuals an elaborate ceremony accompanied the procession from the house to the site of burial, although for Mesopotamia we have little in the way of evi-dence for the rites involved (in contrast to the depictions on Egyptian murals).

It is this aspect, the apparent relationship between the wealth of an individual in death and his or her wealth and/or status in life, which has stimulated a renewed interest by archaeologists in burial practices during the last quarter century. Once considered only a basis for (often imaginative) speculations on religious beliefs, burial data are today widely studied as evidence of social stratification. Specialists in the archaeology of ancient Mesopotamia have on the whole been slow to make use of mortuary evidence in this way, but a number of recent studies have laid the groundwork for what may be a fruitful area of research in the near future.

See **Adapa; animal sacrifice; dead gods; Dilmun; diseases and medicine; galla; Gil-gameš; human sacrifice**.

dedication

At every period it was considered proper for a victor in battle to dedicate some of his spoils to his or his city's special protective deity. Such objects usually carry inscriptions to this effect and became part of the temple's treasure. Valu-able ceremonial objects, often of precious materials, might also be dedicated to a god in peace time for the 'life' of an individual, especially a ruler, by the individual himself or by one of his 'servants', possibly as a thanks-giving following illness or some other crisis.

There is not much evidence that objects were dedicated in connection with vows or pledges (votive offerings), but small models of e.g. beds or genitalia, feet or other limbs were probably 124,12 dedicated either as thank offerings by those who believed the solution of their sexual prob-lems or bodily illnesses to be due to a particular deity, or as promptings by those hopeful of achieving cures.

Ancient Mesopotamian society always took slavery for granted, and an extension of this was the dedication of certain human beings as 'belonging' to the gods. At different periods this took different forms, with varying social effects. The dedication in the Old Babylonian Period of the daughters of wealthy families to a god and their confinement within a 'cloister' did not stop these women engaging in com-plicated financial transactions, but at least ensured that their property reverted to their family on their death (since they were forbid-den to marry) and so prevented dissipation of the inheritance. In later Babylonian times the temple *širkūtu* (dedicated slaves) was an order of male and female persons dedicated to **Mar-duk, Nabû**, Šamaš **(Utu)**, **Nergal** or Ištar **(Inana)**. Parents dedicated their children and freemen their slaves. They were branded with a **star, spade** or **wedge**.

See **priests and priestesses**.

deification of kings

The deification of kings during their own life-time was confined to a limited period of Meso-potamian history. The first king to become a living god was Narām-Suen, king of Agade (reigned 2310–2274 BC) and the practice con- 75 tinued with the subsequent kings of Agade, of the Third Dynasty of Ur, and with those of the dynasties of Isin, Larsa and Babylon down to Samsu-ditāna (reigned 1681–1651 BC). Kings who were deified claimed to be sons or brothers of major gods (see **Lugalbanda**). A cult was offered to deified kings in temples throughout their kingdoms, and praise poetry was com-posed in their honour.

See **Sacred Marriage; temples and temple architecture**.

deities: see **gods and goddesses**.

demons and monsters

53 In most religions there is a belief in various kinds of supernatural beings ranking between the level of **gods** and men. 'Demon', in its original Greek sense (*daimōn* 'supernatural being', 'spirit') serves as an approximate translation of Akkadian terms like *rābiṣu* (Sumerian *maškim*), which can refer to, and be qualified as, a good or bad 'demon'. In spells of the Neo-
9 Assyrian Period, we read 'Get out, evil *rābiṣu*! Come in, good *rābiṣu*!'

In modern studies of ancient Mesopotamian art and iconography, however, the term 'demon' has generally been applied to any upright human-bodied hybrid creature, while 'monster' has been applied to an animal combination on all fours.

Demons only rarely figure in mythology. The scores of demons whose names are known to us are mentioned mainly in magical incantations. Generally, 'evil' demons seem to have been conceived as mere agents and executors of the will of gods; their rôle was to implement divinely ordained punishment for **sin**. Such 'evil' demons were often imagined as weather spirits, of the wind or storms. Their usual method of attacking humans was by inflicting **diseases** (but not all illness was thought to be due to them); there is no evidence for a general belief in demonic possession. Evil gods and demons are only very rarely depicted in art, perhaps because it was thought that their images might endanger people; in some cases descriptions of their appearances are so vague and inconsistent as to suggest they were not well established. By the first millennium BC, however, **Lamaštu** is commonly represented, usually in connection with incantations against
151 her, while **Pazuzu** is even turned to good purpose, being shown forcing Lamaštu back to the **underworld**. This change may be related to a new concept in the first millennium BC of an underworld populated by demonic beings.

A greatly simplified but plausible chronology for the development of demons and monsters in ancient Mesopotamian art has adopted a division into five main phases, namely:

(1) a formative phase, in the late Ubaid and Uruk Periods, when the features of different animals were first combined into unnatural composite beings;

(2) an optimistic phase, in the Akkadian Period, when glyptic scenes show the capture and punishment of nefarious demons;

(3) a balanced phase, in the Old Babylonian Period, when cylinder seal designs often mix images (gods, symbols and other motifs) of good and bad associations with respect to mankind;

(4) a transformative phase, with Mitannian, Kassite and Middle Assyrian art of the fourteenth to eleventh centuries BC, when the human-centred imagery of the Old Babylonian Period gave way to a preponderance of animal-headed hybrids;

(5) a demonic phase, represented by Neo-Assyrian and Neo-Babylonian art, when individual evil demons were depicted in their full horror.

This last phase of development accords well with the new theology of a demonically populated underworld in the first millennium BC. The change happens, moreover, at the same time as the advent of the practice of erecting in palaces and temples monumental statues and reliefs of magically protective beings, and of burying small clay images of them in the foundations. Diverse in cultural background and original significance, the various gods, demons and monsters involved were brought together into a fairly restricted visual series at this time, and for the first time they came to be treated as a group in mythological narratives.
65, 78, 99, 101, 107, 117, 134

9, 11, 12, 40, 70, 136

See **galla**; **good and evil**; **lama**; **'omega' symbol**; **udug**.

destiny and fate: see **divination**; **divine intervention**; **diseases and medicine**; **me**; **Namtar**; **tablet of destinies**.

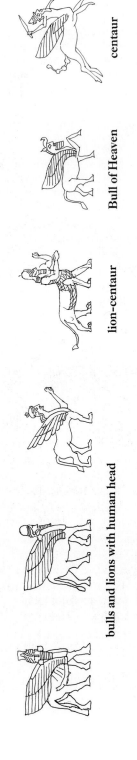
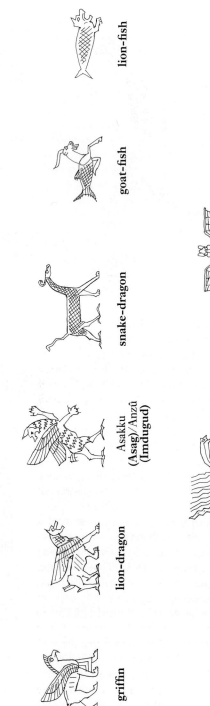

53 Demons, monsters and minor protective deities.

centaur

lion-fish

Bull of Heaven

goat-fish

lion-centaur

snake-dragon

Imdugud

bulls and lions with human head

Asakku
(Asag)/Anzû
(Imdugud)

snakes

griffin

lion-dragon

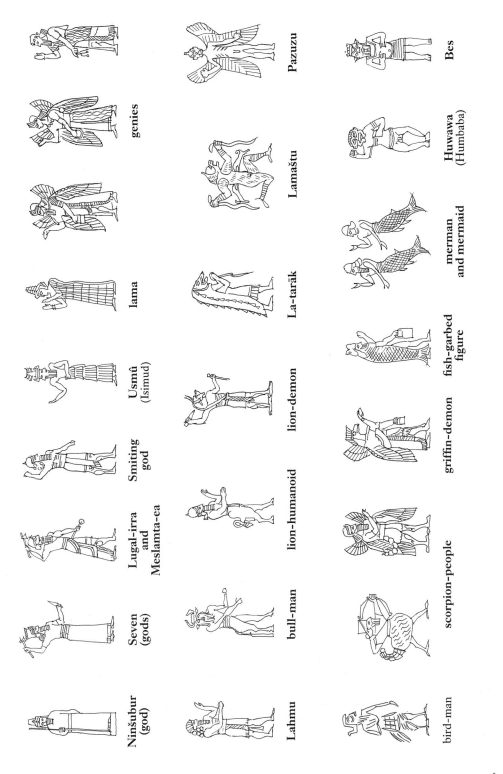

genies

Pazuzu

Bes

Lamaštu

Huwawa (Humbaba)

lama

La-tarāk

merman and mermaid

Ušmû (Isimud)

lion-demon

fish-garbed figure

Smiting god

griffin-demon

Lugal-irra and Meslamta-ea

lion-humanoid

scorpion-people

Seven (gods)

bull-man

Ninšubur (god)

Lahmu

bird-man

Dilmun

Dilmun (or Telmun) was a Mesopotamian name for Bahrain and an area of the western coast of the Gulf (the latter area apparently called Agaru by the inhabitants of Dilmun themselves), possibly also including Failaka and other islands. It became increasingly important in Mesopotamian trade from the end of the Early Dynastic Period on.

In the poem 'Enki and Ninhursaǧa', Dilmun is described as a 'holy', 'virgin' and 'pure' land without any normal civilisation, human or animal, or even water supplies. At the request of his wife-daughter, the goddess Ninsikila (**Ninhursaǧa**), Enki first arranges for Dilmun to be provided with fresh water and abundant produce. Then in a series of incestuous unions a number of gods and goddesses are born, among them the 'Lord of Dilmun' and the 'Lord of Magan'. Recent work on the geography of the Gulf suggests that a number of low islands may have gradually risen from the water towards the end of the third millennium, and it is possible that the myth is connected with this. The fuller text of the poem now available shows that Dilmun was not, as was earlier thought, described as a 'paradise' land.

According to another Sumerian poem, after the **Flood** the gods settled **Ziusura** in 'a foreign land, the land of Dilmun in the east'.

The idea in some modern literature that Bahrain was a 'sepulchral island' where the bodies of the wealthy or eminent would be shipped for burial from the Mesopotamian or Arabian mainlands has no reliable basis. It derives from a consideration of the numbers of Bronze Age burial mounds present on the island, the apparent lack of corresponding settlement sites, and the suggestion that certain tombs, recorded as 'empty' by their excavators, were prepurchased sites awaiting their occupants. In fact, although the low levels of soil above bedrock necessitated the construction of above-ground tombs, which makes them abnormally visible, the numbers involved (most recently estimated at some 172,000) are not excessive for a local population, especially given the increasing numbers of Bronze Age settlements now identifiable on the ground, though little investigated. The supposed 'empty' graves can for the most part be explained by lack of archaeological technique in the excavation of often disturbed or poorly preserved burials.

Dilmunite gods

The two principal gods of **Dilmun**, the god Inzak and the goddess Meskilak, are referred to in both Mesopotamian and Dilmunite sources. Inzak was regarded by the Sumerians (by whom he was called **Enzag**) as the chief god of Dilmun, but in Dilmun itself he was characterised as a god of Agaru (eastern Arabia). He probably also had a cult centre on Failaka island, where the temple seems to have been dedicated to him. In the Neo-Babylonian Period he was identified with **Nabû**. A god called Inzak was also worshipped in Elam, as one of a trinity with Ea (**Enki**) and the **Elamite god** Inšušinak.

The name Meskilak, goddess of the city of Dilmun, must be related to Ninsikila, another name for **Ninhursaǧa**. Nin-Dilmun, 'lady of Dilmun', was probably a title of the same goddess. She may have been regarded as either the wife or mother of Inzak. A Babylonian hymn refers to a goddess called Šuluhītu as wife of Enzag.

Another goddess was Lahamun, described as the 'Ṣarpānītu of Dilmun'.

Some Mesopotamian gods are referred to in texts found in Bahrain, including Enki, **Damgalnuna**, Adad (**Iškur**) and **Marduk**. However, despite Enki's relationship with Dilmun in Sumerian myth (probably a result of trading connections between Sumer and Dilmun from the time of the Third Dynasty of Ur onwards), Enki is not explicitly mentioned as a deity of Dilmun and there are no grounds for supposing that his cult was established there or that the temple at Barbar on Bahrain was dedicated to him (as is commonly assumed).

Dingirmah: see **mother goddesses and birth goddesses**.

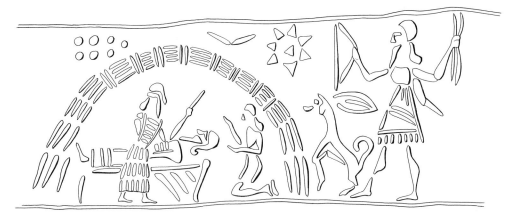

diseases and medicine

Although a practical knowledge of many herbal remedies, as well as some surgical knowledge, existed in ancient Mesopotamia, the causes (as we mean the word) of disease were not understood. They were often ascribed to the work of **gods** or of **demons** acting as the agents of gods for the punishment of **sin**. Particular demons were thought likely to cause specific diseases. Some diseases were described as, for example, 'the hand of god', 'the hand of a ghost (**gidim**)', 'the hand of Ištar (**Inana**)', 'the hand

55 Nergal, god of the underworld, instructs a lion-demon in the punishment of a sinner, a graphic rendering of seizure by disease. Detail from a cylinder seal of the Old Babylonian Period.

54 Within a reed shelter a priest ministers to a sick man, while a man and dog stand guard outside. From a cylinder seal of the Neo-Assyrian Period.

of Šamaš (**Utu**)', indicating the deity or demon thought responsible for them. The god or demon is said to 'seize' the victim. In art, a demon holds a man upside down, or a god tramples someone under foot. In a Neo-Assyrian prayer, a sufferer pleads forgiveness for his unwitting offence of a god or goddess 'whom I know or whom I do not know'. Such diseases were treated by the exorcist (see **priests and priestesses**). Some illnesses which we should regard as psychological were referred to as the work of demons; psychological illness could also be caused by sorcery (see **magic and sorcery**). 14,54

In some cases a distinction seems to have been made between such divine or demonically originating illness and more 'naturally' occurring conditions (although the causes were not known). For the treatment of the latter type of diseases a different priest was usually involved, who practised a primitive form of medicine. However, the functions of this 'general practitioner' and the exorcist overlapped and were to some extent interchangeable. If the type of disease was unclear, both priests would be called in, and a common complaint was that neither had been able to effect a cure. 55

Collections of diagnostic omens give copi-

67

ously detailed descriptions of medical symptoms, with explanations and prognoses for the course of the disease. However, these also include, for instance, omens observed by the exorcist on his way to treat the patient at his house.

A degree of primitive surgery was known in Mesopotamia from a very early period. Among the skeletons from Shanidar Cave in the Zagros (dating from perhaps 60,000 to 45,000 years ago) was one of a forty-year-old man with an atrophied right arm, the lower part of which had been successfully amputated before his death in a rock-fall.

Herbal and other mixtures concocted by the Babylonians included ingredients such as honey and syrup of dates, as well as varied and apparently secret substances. These potions were often given quaint names, such as 'Šamaš's remedy', 'pigeon droppings' or 'snake-skin'. Other medicinal agents included warm and cold baths, the rubbing of oils into the body and blood-letting. Mesopotamian measures of public health control included the use of parasols for shading from the sun and of fly-whisks against insects, the provision of toilet and washing facilities and the construction of drains for the proper disposal of sewage, and in battle the use of large trenches for mass burial. Models of the liver, used for instruction in **divination**, were anatomically superior to later (five-lobed) medieval European models. One achievement of the Babylonians in the field of medicine was their recognition of the transmissibility of leprosy: sufferers were exiled from the community.

The laws of Hammurabi of Babylon regulating standards of professional conduct and fixing medical fees certainly suggest some sharp practice, but equally confirm the existence of a profession of medicine, well attested throughout Mesopotamian history. This refutes the claim of the Greek historian Herodotus in the fifth century BC that the Babylonians had no doctors.

See **dogs**; **galla**; '**hands-of-Ištar**'; **Nergal**. For gods and goddesses of healing, see **Damu**; **Gula**; **Ninisina**.

divination

Divination was widely used in Mesopotamia. It is based on the idea that to some extent the future is pre-determined; but that the gods, especially Šamaš (**Utu**) and Adad (**Iškur**), have made available to man certain indications of the future (omens or portents) in the world around him, which can be interpreted (divined) by experts with specialist knowledge.

Some forms of divination required special rituals. Particularly important from Sumerian times was extispicy, in which the liver, lungs or colon spiral of a specially slaughtered young ram were inspected for peculiarities during a nocturnal rite. By the Old Babylonian Period, extispicy was highly developed and had a complex technical vocabulary. Also used were lecanomancy (in which the behaviour of oil on water was observed) and libanomancy (the behaviour of smoke from **incense**). Necromancy (calling up the spirits of the dead) was used only rarely and considered to be dangerous.

Other forms of divination involved the observation of chance natural occurrences and these forms gradually became more widespread. The study of celestial omens (astrological and meteorological) came to surpass even extispicy in popularity and survived until after the end of Mesopotamian civilisation. Also important were teratological omens (from monstrous births among animals), terrestrial omens (from a whole range of everyday occurrences), hemerological and menological omens (based on the idea of favourable and unfavourable days), prognostic omens (predicting the course and outcome of diseases), physiognomic omens (from the appearance and behaviour of individual people), augury (the observation of birds, only in later periods) and oneiromancy (the interpretation of **dreams**), a branch of the subject with its own specialised practitioners.

Diviners had to be descendants of free men and perfect in body and limb. They were considered to be as important as physicians and practitioners of **magic**. Often they accompanied troops on campaign or were attached to

56 An anatomically detailed model in baked clay of a sheep's liver, probably of Old Babylonian date. It is covered with writing giving the prognostications derived from signs observed in the various parts of the organ, and was probably used as an aid in teaching divination. 145 × 145 mm.

the palace as state functionaries.

Divination could be used to control the behaviour of kings and important persons. Extispicy was resorted to by many ordinary people to investigate the future (often in connection with specific questions). Before military campaigns, before building a temple, when appointing civil servants, in weather forecasting, to ensure the king's wellbeing and safety – and also on a much more homely level as a form of personal fortune-telling – divination played an important part in decision-making.

See **astrology and astronomy; gidim; priests and priestesses; right and left; river ordeal**.

divine intervention

Although it is a commonplace of certain types of Sumerian religious literature that the mind of a god was unfathomable –'like a sealed beer-barrel, who knows what is going on inside?' – it was generally accepted that the gods did intervene to some extent in human life. The idea

of a god determining the 'destiny' or 'fate' (Sumerian *nam-tar*, Akkadian *šimtu*) of an individual was more a settling of certain potentialities than an absolute predestination of the future. There were certain 'plans' or 'designs' behind the world, and it was up to gods, kings and humanity at large to do their part to ensure the harmonious functioning of civilisation. Human misfortune and **diseases** were often regarded as an indication of divine displeasure. Behind the theory of **divination**, which gradually became more and more complex, lay a desire to extract rather more specific information in advance about what gods had in store for mankind. In the myths and legends, gods and goddesses mingle with heroes and even mortals, giving them explicit advice (sometimes even involving them in their interdivine disputes) and wielding supernatural power on their behalf. Rulers were careful to give credit, where due, to their divine protectors for assistance in battle. Offerings (see **sacrifice and offering**) accompanied by re-

155

quests or thanks, and parents' choices of names for their children, testify to a wide belief in the power and willingness of the gods to alter the course of individual human destinies. Indeed one can say that religious belief in ancient Mesopotamia would have had no meaning unless it was accompanied by at least the possibility of divine intervention in mortals' affairs.

See **dreams and visions**.

dogs

The sitting dog first occurs as a divine symbol in the Old Babylonian Period and continues through to the Neo-Babylonian. Inscriptions on **kudurrus** identify it as the symbol of **Gula**, goddess of healing. An Old Babylonian dog figurine from Ğirsu (modern Tello) is dedicated (see **dedication**) to **Ninisina** (Gula) and many dog **figurines** were discovered in the temple of Gula at Isin, confirming that the association dates back to that time. That it continued down to the Neo-Babylonian Period is shown by another figurine from Sippar dedicated to Meme (another name for Gula), while King Nebuchadnezzar II (reigned 604–562 BC) records the placing of statuettes of gold, silver and bronze dogs as deposits in the gates of Gula's temple at Babylon. A dog is commonly seen on seal designs of this period, sometimes sitting by an enthroned goddess, presumably Gula, but also sometimes without the goddess, sitting and supporting the symbol of the **crook**.

In the Neo-Assyrian and Neo-Babylonian Periods, the dog, sitting or standing, was also used as a magically protective figure, not attached specifically to any individual deity. Groups of five clay figurines of dogs painted different colours were prescribed as foundation deposits for either side of a gateway. They were inscribed with such gems as 'Don't stop to think, bite!' Bronze dog figurines are in the same period usually found in groups of seven (see **numbers**). Whether they were magically protective or dedicatory or served some other purpose is unclear.

It has been suggested that the disease of rabies was present in Mesopotamia by the beginning of the second millennium BC and more widespread during the first millennium BC.

The dog family to the Mesopotamians meant not only wolves, hyenas, jackals and dogs, but also **lions**.

donkey: see **Lamaštu**.

donkey ears

Mesopotamian **demons and monsters** with lion's heads were very often depicted also with long upright ears, probably those of a donkey. The **lion-dragon** is shown with such ears from the time of its invention in the Akkadian Period. The **lion-demon** is depicted with leonine ears in the Akkadian Period, but thereafter also acquires the upright ears. The evil

57 Five little clay models of dogs. They had been placed in a hollow at the base of a monumental stone relief on one side of a doorway in the royal palace of the Assyrian king Assurbanipal (reigned 668–c.627 BC) at Nineveh. They are painted in different colours and inscribed in exact conformity to the prescription of written rituals, which denote their purpose as one of protective magic. Hts. 45–56 mm.

151 goddess **Lamaštu** also has such ears when she is represented in the first millennium BC. Her special beast is the donkey. When such creatures were copied in arts outside Mesopotamia the ears were generally altered to those of a lion, an interesting example of lack of 'understanding' of the Mesopotamian convention. However, in Greek art the griffin retained its long ears, and these passed into the iconography of medieval and modern European griffins and dragons.

The inclusion of an element of the swift-footed wild ass along with aspects of the fierce lion in such demonic hybrids might have seemed an appropriate combination of wild animals. They frequently also have bird talons (see **bird talons and wings**).

See **griffin; standards, staves and sceptres of the gods**.

dragons

Dragon (Greek *drakōn*, 'serpent') is the word usually used in English for a terrifying mythical monster with a scaly snake-like or lizard-like body. Belief in such creatures arose in antiquity without any knowledge of the monstrous reptiles and birds that had actually existed in remote prehistory. Mesopotamian art includes a number of such dragon-like creatures, of malevolent and beneficent natures. Most closely corresponding to the general image is the so-called **snake-dragon**, but other hybrids such as the **lion-dragon** might also be regarded as dragon-like images.

6,117, 135

138 100

In Sumerian poetry, *ušumgal*, a serpentine monster, can be a metaphor for a god or king; it is a term of praise and not necessarily evil or unpleasant.

See **demons and monsters**.

dreams and visions

Since Freud and his successors in psychoanalysis, dreams have usually been regarded as the direct or more oblique references of the subconscious mind to events of the immediate or more distant past. Throughout antiquity, however, and indeed until the late nineteenth century AD, dreams were normally regarded as portents of *future* events, and thus were studied as a branch of **divination**.

The importance attached to dreams can be seen, for example, in the number of dream episodes related in the stories of **Gilgameš**, in both the Sumerian and Akkadian versions. Here they are used as a literary device to open a window upon subsequent events and, by their consequent effects upon the protagonists, as a catalyst for moving the story on. In the Standard Babylonian version of the epic, Gilgameš has two dreams presaging, through symbolism, the arrival of **Enkidu** (see **Ninsun**). He has a series of three dreams concerning the projected campaign against Humbaba (**Huwawa**). Then there is Enkidu's 'death-dream' and a dream of Ūt-napišti (**Ziusura**). For Enkidu's 'death-dream', the Hittite version apparently substituted a dream of his visiting the **assembly of the gods**. The Anatolian version of the epic also recounts a dream of Gilgameš presaging his struggle with the **Bull of Heaven**.

As a means of glimpsing the future, rulers took their dreams very seriously. Gudea, ruler of Lagaš, recounts a dream in which he was instructed to rebuild the temple of **Ningirsu**. The Assyrian king Assurbanipal (reigned 668–*c.*627 BC), when apparently in a desperate military position, tells of a dream in which the goddess Ištar (**Inana**) appeared to encourage him and to assure him that she would defeat the enemy on his behalf. The appearance of the goddess before the king was also seen in a dream of a priest of Ištar's temple. No dream episodes are related in the Assyrian royal annals before Assurbanipal's reign. Yet is seems that their portents were earlier considered significant, because at Imgur-Enlil (modern Balawat) Assurnasirpal II (reigned 883–859 BC) had built a temple to **Mamu**, possibly identical with the god of dreams. Archaeological excavations have unearthed a set of doors of the temple, which were decorated with bands of bronze depicting scenes from the king's campaigns. (Other similar sets of doors, of Assurnasirpal and his son and successor Shalmaneser III, were found in the neighbouring palaces.) Imgur-Enlil was close to the capital city Kalhu (modern Nimrud), and may have been the usual place of the first night's rest at the start of a campaign. Here, we guess, the king would hope for dreams portending the outcome of the coming battles. From another site (ancient Huzirina, in Turkey) we have a fragment of a poem, rather in the epic style, which relates a dream of Shalmaneser III (reigned 858–824 BC) about the course of one of his campaigns.

If they were related in some way to the revelation of future events, dreams could also be a means of seeing into other worlds. Since **death** is the future for all men, there were dreams of the **afterlife**. Enkidu's death-dream is an example. There is also an account of a dream of an Assyrian prince (thought by some to be Assurbanipal at a time before he became king) in which he visits the **underworld** and contemplates the horrors of the demonic creatures residing there. That Enkidu was able to have a dream of the gods resolving his fate shows that heaven as well as hell could be seen through dreams.

A compilation of dream omens has survived. In it are collected a host of dream scenarios, together with prognostications. The predictions seem to be based upon precedent. That is to say that the recorded subjects of the dreams represent actual dreams reported by individuals, while the prognostications record the events that subsequently took place in the lives of the respective dreamers. Occasionally alternative predictions are offered, presumably based upon the reports of similar dreams with differing sequels. The array of dream subjects listed is itself of interest: they include episodes of daily work, of journeys near and far, of family matters and sexual acts, encounters with other people, animals and deities.

There were specialised dream-interpreters (see **priests and priestesses**).

See **Ĝatumdug**; **Ĝeštinana**; **Nanše**; **'plant of life'**.

Du-ku

In Sumerian mythology, the Du-ku ('holy hill' or 'holy mound') is a cosmic locality situated 'on the mountain of heaven and earth'. It is where the gods determined the destinies, and has therefore been interpreted as a 'world mountain' where the **Anuna** gods lived in primordial times and where elements of human culture (agriculture, animal husbandry, weaving, etc.) first came into being. It is described as the home of sheep and grain, and is punningly referred to as the 'holy lap' (*du ku*) of **Enlil**. An alternative interpretation sees it, more prosaically, as the foothills of the Zagros mountains, whose fertile climate may in a very real sense have contributed to the development of human civilisation. Most likely the phrase 'mountain of heaven and earth' is intended to imply the world at the time before heaven and earth were separated from each other (see cosmology).

Du-ku was also the name of shrines at Ĝirsu, Nippur and **Eridu**, earthly counterparts of the cosmic Du-ku.

Dumuzi

The god Dumuzi is a shepherd god. In a disputation with **Enkimdu**, the god of irrigation and cultivation, Dumuzi represents the conflicting interests of the pastoralist. When **Inana** visits the **underworld**, and cannot return without a substitute to take her place, **demons** come to fetch her beloved young husband Dumuzi to replace her. In this way Dumuzi died and became a god of the underworld. In the **Sacred Marriage**, in which Sumerian kings were ritually married to Inana, the king was identified with Dumuzi. In another tradition, Dumuzi and **Ningišzida** are represented as the gatekeepers of the Heaven of Anu (**An**).

The early history of the various local cults of Dumuzi and related deities is complex and bewildering. The Dumuzi worshipped at Badtibira was later thought to have been an antediluvian king of the town (described as 'a shepherd'). The Dumuzi worshipped at Uruk as the husband of Inana was connected with nearby Kuara and was also, in one account, thought to have been an early king of Uruk. The god Ama-ušumgal-ana, later identified with

Dumuzi, was originally worshipped at a village near Lagaš and in one cult song is described as a warrior hero. In some Sumerian poetry, Dumuzi is also referred to as 'my **Damu**'.

Tammuz, mentioned in the Biblical book of Ezekiel (8:14), is a Hebrew form of the name.

Ritual lamentation for the death of Dumuzi seems to have been widespread. In Early Dynastic Lagaš the sixth month of the year was named after the festival of Dumuzi, and in a later north Mesopotamian calendar one of the months is called Dumuzi. The fourth month of the Standard Babylonian calendar was called *Du'ūzu* or *Dûzu*, and *Tammuz* is still used in Iraqi Arabic as the name for July.

The god Dumuzi and the stories concerning him do not seem to be depicted in Mesopotamian art.

See **dead gods; galla; G̃eštinana; stylised tree and its 'rituals'**.

Dumu-zi-abzu

A local goddess of the village Kinunir near Lagaš. Although her name (which possibly means 'good child of the **abzu**') was sometimes abbreviated to Dumu-zi, she has no obvious connection with the god **Dumuzi**.

Duttur: see **G̃eštinana**.

dwarf

Persons of arrested growth have in many societies been the butt of humour, often employed as entertainers and fools. We know that dwarfs were kept as curiosities in Egyptian households. For Mesopotamia there is no evidence of such a practice, but on southern Mesopotamian

58 The bow-legged dwarf as depicted on cylinder seals of the Isin-Larsa Period.

seals of the nineteenth century BC a dwarfish figure with bow legs is a common motif. He has 58 variously been interpreted as a dancer in rituals or entertainments, or as a type of **demon**, perhaps a prankster or a protective spirit. The figure may be related to the grotesque Egyptian dwarf god **Bes**, whose form was known in 33 Mesopotamia and other areas of the ancient Near East.

Ea: see **Enki**.

E-abzu

E-abzu ('**Abzu** House') was the temple of **Enki** 97 at **Eridu**. According to Sumerian tradition, Eridu was the first city and the E-abzu the oldest shrine. Excavations conducted at the site, Abu Shahrain in southern Iraq, have uncovered a long sequence of superimposed temples beginning probably in the fifth millennium BC and demonstrating gradual elaboration of temple construction.

See **temples and temple architecture**.

E-ana

E-ana ('House of Heaven') is the name given to the temple at Uruk dedicated to the goddess **Inana**. The city had been built, according to tradition, by the **Seven Sages** and **Gilgameš**. The temenos or sacred enclosure of E-ana, as known from excavations, was constructed over a long period of time by a number of different rulers, including Ur-Nammu (reigned 2168–2151 BC), first king of the Third Dynasty of Ur. Subsequently, Assyrian, Neo-Babylonian and Achaemenid Persian rulers (including Cyrus and Darius) had building programmes in this area.

See **sacrifice and offering; temples and temple architecture**.

ear of corn: see **barley stalk**.

earth: see **Ki**.

E-gal-mah: see **Gula**.

Egyptian gods and symbols
Egyptian religious concepts and the pantheon seem to have penetrated Mesopotamian culture remarkably little given the geographical proximity. Egyptian ideas about death and the afterlife, cosmology and the nature and form of the gods (in Egypt often in animal form) were so alien to Mesopotamian concepts that they could not easily be assimilated, nor did political or cultural circumstances ever require such assimilation. Of Egyptian gods, only the dwarf 33 god **Bes** – or at least his physical form – was adopted widely throughout the ancient Near East.

155   The symbol of the **winged disc** derives originally, in all probability, from Egypt, but appears to have arrived in Mesopotamia indirectly, and to have been assimilated because of its close similarity to the pre-existing **solar disc**.

Only two other Egyptian symbols appear before the Neo-Assyrian Period. The *djed-*
59 pillar, Egyptian sign for 'duration', is found on a few Syrian cylinder seals of the eighteenth and seventeenth centuries BC. The motif appears to be used as a decorative element, devoid of its original meaning.

More common on Syrian seals from about 1800 BC onwards, but very rare in Mesopotamia proper, is the *ankh* symbol, in Egypt the emblem of life. Usually it is used as a '**filling motif**', but it can be carried by a goddess, or

59 The Egyptian symbols *ankh* and *djed*, as known from the designs of some Syrian seals.

used in sequence to create a composite element, such as an arch composed of rows of *ankh*s, in a superficially Egyptian but inauthentic style.

In the ninth to seventh centuries BC, the Assyrian aristocracy seems to have cultivated some taste for Egyptian artwork, and palaces might contain furniture carved, panelled or inlaid with Egyptian or Egyptianising designs.

E-kiš-nu-ğal: see **Nanna-Suen**.

E-kur
The E-kur ('Mountain House': see **kur**) was the name of **Enlil**'s temple at Nippur, also incorporating the E-ki-ur, the shrine of **Ninlil**. According to a Sumerian poem, it was founded and built by the god Enlil himself. The E-kur was sometimes described as having a cosmological rôle as the 'mooring-rope' of heaven and earth. Adjacent to it stood the **ziggurat** Dur-an-ki ('Bond of heaven and earth': see **cosmology**), which was originally built by Ur-Nammu (reigned 2168–2151 BC), founder of the Third Dynasty of Ur. It is described in some detail in a hymn from the reign of Ur-Nammu, in which the mythological scenes on its gates are enumerated: **Imdugud** kills a lion, while an eagle seizes a wrongdoer.

See **assembly of the gods**; **Nungal**; **snake gods**; **temples and temple architecture**.

Elamite gods
A number of gods belonging to the pantheon of Elam, a country lying to the south-east of Babylonia (in modern Iran), are mentioned in Mesopotamian texts. These include:

Pienenkir, later called Kiririša ('Great Goddess'), a mother goddess;

Humban, later called Napiriša ('Great God'), a sky god (see **Huwawa**);

Hutran, son of Kiririša and Napiriša;

Inšušinak, god of the city of Susa, later a god of the underworld;

Lagamal and Išmekarab, goddesses, judges of the dead;

Nahhunte, sun god and god of justice;

Ruhurater, Kilahšupir, Tirutir, local gods;

Napir (?), moon god;

Siyašum, Narunte, Niarzina, goddesses and sisters of Kiririša, also called sisters of the Sebittu (the **Seven (gods)**);

Simut, a herald god, and his wife Manzât (see **rainbow**).

Most of the Mesopotamian gods were also honoured in Elam.

E-mah: see **Ninhursaǧa**; **Šara**.

E-meslam: see **Nergal**.

E-mete-ursaǧ: see **Zababa**.

Enbilulu: see **Enkimdu**.

engur: see **abzu**; **Enki's creatures**.

E-ninnu: see **Ninǧirsu**.

Enki (Ea)

Enki (Akkadian Ea) was god of the subterranean freshwater ocean (**abzu**), and was especially associated with wisdom, **magic** and incantations, and with the arts and crafts of civilisation. He is sometimes called by the names Nudimmud or Ninšiku or by the title 'Stag of the **abzu**', i.e. the giant fallow deer *Dama dama mesopotamica*. Enki/Ea was a son of **An**/Anu, or else of the goddess **Nammu**, and a twin brother of the god **Iškur**/Adad. His wife was **Damgalnuna**/Damkina, and their offspring included the gods **Marduk, Asarluhi, Enbilulu**, the sage **Adapa** and the goddess **Nanše**. His minister was the two-faced god **Isimud**/Usmû. This Enki (whose name is Enkig in full) is not the same as **Enlil**'s ancestor Enki ('Lord Earth').

Enki's most important cult centre was the **E-abzu** ('Abzu House') at **Eridu**. As a provider of fresh water and a creator god (see **creation**) and determiner of destinies, Enki was always seen as favourable to mankind. In the epics of Atra-hasīs and **Gilgameš**, especially, he takes the part of man against the gods and helps mankind to escape the **Flood** sent by the decision of the other gods. In the Sumerian poem 'Inana and Enki' he controls the **me** concerned with every aspect of human life, and in 'Enki and the World Order' he has the rôle of organising in detail every feature of the civilised world.

In art Enki is represented as a seated god with long beard, wearing a cap with many horns and a long, pleated robe. Streams of 60 water flow from his arms to the ground, sometimes with little **fish** swimming along the flow. Often the god is shown receiving worshippers or bearers of offerings, or else he receives the 115 **bird-man**, brought before him as a prisoner 88 under guard, or the **lion-demon**. These might be introduced by other gods, most commonly by Enki's minister Isimud. Sometimes Enki is 19 shown seated within a structure, the *abzu*, or else his E-abzu shrine, surrounded by channels of water.

In the symbolism of the Kassite, Babylonian and Assyrian Periods, Ea's beast was the **goat-** 70 **fish**. The god's other symbols were a curved stick terminating in a ram's head (see **stan-** 76 **dards, staves and sceptres of the gods**) and a turtle. 150

See **Enki's creatures**; **horned cap**; **Ninhursaǧa**; **ring-post**; **river ordeal**; **wedge**.

60 The water god Ea and his two-faced minister god Usmû. Detail from the cylinder seal of a scribe named Adda, Akkadian Period.

Enkidu
In Sumerian poems, Enkidu is usually the servant and fellow-traveller of Gilgameš. In the Akkadian epic he is the hero's friend and equal companion.

41,69   For the tales of his life, exploits and death, and for representations in art, see **Gilgameš**.

See **afterlife**; **Bull of Heaven**; **Huwawa**; **underworld**.

Enkimdu
The god Enkimdu is 'lord of dike and canal' or, in the disputation between him and the shepherd god **Dumuzi**, 'of dike, canal and furrow; cultivator'. A son of **Enki**, he is closely identified with the god Enbilulu, the 'canal inspector', regarded as a form of Adad (**Iškur**) or, in the Babylonian Epic of Creation, as one of the names of **Marduk**. A third god, **Ennugi**, is also 'lord of dike and canal' and 'canal inspector of the **great gods**', but has extra associations with the **underworld**.

Enki's creatures
As well as by his minister **Isimud**, the god **Enki** is served by a number of creatures who inhabit the watery depths of the **abzu**. First come the *enkum* (male) and *ninkum* (female). Enki sends them after **Inana**'s boat when he realises that she has stolen the **me** from him. Next are the 'fifty giants of **Eridu**', then the 'fifty **lahama** of the *engur*'. (*Engur* is a synonym of *abzu*.) In the poem 'The Cursing of Agade', the *lahama* are protective figures standing in the great gateway of a temple. Then come the 'great fishes ...' and the 'guardians of Uruk', difficult to understand in the context of Enki and Eridu. Finally in the hymn addressed to the temple of **Asarluhi** at Kuara, the 'seven *abgal* (**Seven Sages**)' are also included.

The terms *enkum* and *ninkum* are also the names of temple dignitaries at Eridu, purificatory **priests** on the temple staff. Similarly *abgal* is also the name of a temple official among the clergy of Eridu.

In the Sumerian poem 'Enki and Ninmah', another group of creatures, the *sig-en-sig-du*, help **Ninmah** to create mankind by preparing pieces of clay from 'above the *abzu*' (see **creation**).

Enlil (Ellil)
Enlil (Akkadian Ellil) is one of the most important gods in the Mesopotamian **pantheon**. According to one Sumerian poem, the other gods might not even look upon his splendour. Sometimes he is said to be the offspring of **An**, and brother of the goddess Aruru (see **mother goddesses and birth goddesses**). He is also described as a descendant of Enki and Ninki ('Lord and Lady Earth'), not connected with the god **Enki**. His wife is **Ninlil** (or Sud). Among the children of Enlil are the goddess **Inana** and the gods Adad (**Iškur**), **Nanna-Suen**, **Nergal**, **Ninurta/Ninĝirsu**, **Pabilsaĝ**, **Nusku**, **Utu** (**Šamaš**), **Uraš**, **Zababa** and **Ennugi**. Nusku is Enlil's minister.

The great centre of the cult of Enlil was the temple **E-kur** (the 'Mountain House') at Nippur, at the northern edge of Sumer, and Enlil is often called the 'Great Mountain' and 'King of the Foreign Lands', which may suggest a connection with the Zagros mountains. Other images used to describe his personality are king, supreme lord, father and creator; 'raging storm' and 'wild bull'; and, interestingly, 'merchant'. He is also called sometimes by the name Nunamnir. Although he is in one text referred to as East Wind and North Wind, there is no evidence to connect the name Ellil with the *lila/lilû* or desert wind demon (see **Lilītu**). The Kassites worshipped Ellil at their capital Dūr-Kurigalzu (modern 'Aqar Quf).

Astrologically, Ellil was associated with the constellation Boötes.

In Neo-Assyrian art Ellil is symbolised by a **horned cap.**   10,80

See **Aššur**; **Nusku**; **snake-dragon**; **tablet of destinies**.

Enmešarra
Enmešarra is a god connected with the **underworld**. The *suššuru* (a type of pigeon) was associated with him. Seven (or sometimes eight) minor deities were regarded as his children.

In an incantation Enmešarra and Nin-mešarra, his female counterpart, are described as ancestors of the god **Enlil**, and they were apparently regarded as primeval deities.

See **Seven (gods)**.

Ennugi

Ennugi is the god who has special care over dikes and canals, and he is called the 'canal inspector of the **great gods**'. He is regarded as a son of **Enlil**, or else of **Enmešarra**; and his wife is the goddess Nanibgal. He may be identical to Gugal-ana, first husband of **Ereškigal**.

He is also associated with the **underworld**.

See **Enkimdu**.

Enzag

Enzag is one of the gods created by the union of **Enki** and **Ninhursaĝa**. In the Sumerian poem 'Enki and Ninhursaĝa', Enki has eaten eight plants which grew from his semen spilt on the thighs of his daughter **Uttu**, and has become ill in various parts of his body. As a result of their union, Ninhursaĝa gives birth one after another to eight divinities. One of these is Enzag, 'lord of **Dilmun**'. In a later text, Enzag is called the '**Nabû** of Dilmun'.

See **Dilmunite gods**.

Ereškigal

Ereškigal, whose name can be translated 'Queen of the Great Below', is also known in Akkadian as Allatu. She is the goddess who rules the **underworld**, mother of the goddess **Nungal** and, by **Enlil**, of the god **Namtar**, who serves as her messenger and minister. Ereš-kigal's first husband was the god Gugal-ana, whose name probably originally meant 'canal inspector of **An**' and who may therefore have been identical with **Ennugi**. In the Sumerian poem 'Inana's Descent to the Underworld', **Inana** tries to gain entry to the underworld by claiming that she has come to attend the funeral rites of Gugal-ana, the 'husband of my elder sister Ereškigal'. The son of Ereškigal and Gugal-ana was the god **Ninazu**. In another tradition, Ereškigal married the god **Nergal**, as related in the poem 'Nergal and Ereškigal'.

Ereškigal lived in a palace located at Ganzir, the doorway to the underworld, protected by seven gates, all of which could be bolted and each of which was guarded by a porter.

See **Ĝeštinana**.

Eridu

Eridu was a city on the south-western edge of Mesopotamia, sacred to the god **Enki**, and believed by the Sumerians to be the first city and to be at least 250,000 years old! Excavations have revealed that the site (now called Abu Shahrain) is very ancient indeed, but in historical times Eridu consisted of little more than the temple buildings and sacred precincts. Originally the marshes came close to Eridu, and fish offerings were regularly made to the god (see **sacrifice and offering**). The temple of Enki, known as the E-abzu ('**Abzu** House') or E-engura ('House of the *engur*' (another word for *abzu*)), was an extremely important shrine, which was ritually 'visited' (see **journeys and processions of the gods**) by other gods travelling in their boats (see **boats of the gods**). Its gates were guarded in Sumerian times by two great stone lions, one of which was excavated almost intact and now stands in the Iraq Museum, Baghdad.

Sometimes in incantation rituals (see **magic and sorcery**), the magician is told 'Now you cast the Spell of Eridu', although we never learn what the Spell of Eridu was – possibly it was a secret formula that was transmitted orally. Enki, of course, was closely involved with magic.

See **Adapa**; **altars**; **Seven Sages**; **temples and temple architecture**.

Erra: see **Nergal**.

Erua: see **Ṣarpānītu**.

Esagil

Esagil, the 'Lofty House', is the name of the temple of **Marduk** at Babylon. It stood on the Processional Way adjacent to a very large enclosure incorporating the **ziggurat** E-temen-an-ki (see **Tower of Babel**), with shrines dedicated to a number of gods. The principal shrines were those of Marduk and his wife **Ṣarpānītu**. The temple precinct measured about 500 metres square. Esagil was already in existence in Old Babylonian times but was considerably rebuilt by Nebuchadnezzar II (reigned 604–562 BC). The incredible wealth of the temple was mentioned by the Greek historian Herodotus, who described Babylon in the fifth century BC. The ziggurat was in ruins by the time of Alexander the Great, but he died at Babylon before he could rebuild it.

Sometimes in the cult of Marduk, Esagil was accorded cosmic significance as the 'mooring post of heaven and earth'. It is represented in this way in the Babylonian Epic of Creation, where the creation of Esagil itself is an important stage in Marduk's arrangement of the world.

See **temples and temple architecture**.

E-šu-me-ša: see **Ninurta**.

Etana

According to the Sumerian King List, after the **Flood**, hegemony over Sumer fell to the city of Kiš and the kings of its First Dynasty. One of these kings was named Etana, 'a shepherd who ascended to heaven'.

What could so easily have been a tantalising hint at a story is fortunately filled out for us by Babylonian poems recording the legend. The tale begins as a fable. The serpent and the eagle

61 The legendary King Etana of Kiš riding the eagle. Detail from a cylinder seal of the Akkadian Period.

lived peaceably together in a tree, until one day the eagle gobbled up the serpent's young. The serpent went crying to Šamaš (**Utu**) who suggested a course of action. Concealed in the belly of a dead ox, the serpent lay in wait for the eagle to come to eat from the carcass. He then wrought a terrible revenge, catching the bird, breaking his 'heel', plucking him and hurling him into a deep pit.

Etana meanwhile had his own problems. Being childless, he was in search of 'the plant of giving birth' (a fertility drug?) which grew only in the heavens (see **'plant of life'**). Šamaš counselled him to rescue and befriend the eagle and to make use of him in flight. Etana followed this advice and the eagle carried him on his back, soaring the skies. As the earth began to disappear from view, Etana lost his nerve. On this cliffhanger the extant text becomes fragmentary. We may assume, perhaps, that Etana was rescued and probably that he acquired the fertility plant. According to the Sumerian King List, he lived a respectable 1,560 years and had a son and successor named Balih.

Cylinder seals especially of the Akkadian Period commonly depict scenes of a man flying on the back of an eagle, which may plausibly be 61 interpreted as representations of a version of Etana's bird-borne journey.

See **Gilgameš**.

E-temen-an-ki: see **Tower of Babel**.

eṭemmu: see **gidim**.

extispicy: see **divination**.

eye and eye-idols

The image of an eye was always a powerful amulet in Mesopotamia. In the precincts of the so-called 'Eye Temple' at Tell Brak in northeastern Syria, dated to the Late Uruk Period, excavators have found thousands of little 'eye-idols', schematised humanoid figures fashioned from alabaster, limestone, soapstone 62 and black burnished clay. In their most simple form they have a flat body with an elongated

62 A selection of various 'eye-idols' from the early historic Eye Temple at Tell Brak.
Hts. *c.*60–110 mm.

neck supporting a pair of wide eyes, infilled with black or green paint. Some examples have three eyes, or two pairs of eyes one above the other. It has been suggested that the temple was dedicated to an eye god, whose image would originally have stood upon the pedestal in the shrine. Occasionally these idols are represented as 'embracing' a child, so that an alternative view would prefer to see them as offerings to an all-seeing **mother goddess**.

An emphasis on the eyes, however, seems to have been a more general sign of extreme 'holiness', for statuettes deposited in the shrine of a Sumerian temple at Ešnunna (the so-called 'Square Temple'), surely representing worshippers rather than gods, look with abnormally large eyes and wide stares as if into some other world.

The eye is a recurrent motif in art from the Early Dynastic to the Neo-Assyrian Period, although it is not easy to decide when it had a purely decorative and when a magical function. In the case of eye-shaped **amulets** and pendants, religious overtones are more certainly apparent.

See **rhomb**.

'eyes-of-Ningal'

Models of eyes cut in semi-precious stones are known from Sumerian down to Neo-Assyrian times. These include a pair of eyes carved from a lump of onyx and dedicated by an early king of Babylon to the goddess **Ningal** (see **dedication**). This item was later plundered by the Assyrians and rededicated to the same goddess, in Assyria, some ten centuries later. Because other models of eyes were dedicated to this deity, they are generally referred to by archaeologists as 'eyes-of-Ningal', but such models were also dedicated to other deities.

Ezida

Ezida (probably 'Righteous House') is the name of temples of the god **Nabû**. Originally the name referred to the temple at Borsippa, just south of Babylon, where Nabû was worshipped from the Old Babylonian Period. It was from this temple that Nabû came to 'visit'

his father **Marduk** during the annual Babylonian **New Year ceremonies**. When Nabû was adopted as a popular god in Assyria also, a temple to him was built on the acropolis of the Assyrian royal capital Kalhu (modern Nimrud). It is known that the Assyrian king Assurnasirpal II refounded this Ezida in 879 BC. An extensive library of cuneiform tablets was kept in the Ezida at Kalhu, in a room across the courtyard from the twin shrines of Nabû and his wife Tašmētu.

See **temples and temple architecture**.

fan: see **Bau**.

fertility

Although the all-embracing 'fertility cult' aspects of Mesopotamian myth and religion have certainly been exaggerated as a result of

63 A fertility god, from a monumental stone relief discovered next to a well within the temple of the god Aššur in the city of Aššur. Probably it dates to the second half of the second millennium BC. Ht.1.36 m.

the anthropological climate of the 1950s and 1960s, when there was a tendency to see fertility rites in almost every aspect of ancient (and 'primitive' modern) religions, there is no doubt that agriculture and the productivity of the land was of fundamental importance in much of Mesopotamian life, and that this was reinforced by religious belief and ritual. This is well demonstrated by the importance placed on the cult of **Dumuzi**, and pictorially by the place given to water symbolism with such recurrent motifs as the **vase with streams** and certain agricultural elements such as the fan of **Bau, barley stalk, plough** and **spade (symbol)**. The abundance of the land was thought to be dependent upon the wellbeing of the gods and upon the life and health of the ruler. Neo-Assyrian prayers and incantations for the life of the king make clear a belief in a causal connection between the ruler's personal health and the wellbeing of the state, including the condition of agriculture. The ritual for the substitute king and queen (see **human sacrifice**) was intended to save the life of the king and probably, thereby, that of the whole community. Human sexual intercourse is depicted, notably on baked clay plaques and model beds of the Isin-Larsa/Old Babylonian Period and by Middle Assyrian lead figurines from the temple of Ištar (**Inana**) at Aššur. The latter appear to show intercourse taking place on an **altar** (see **prostitution and ritual sex**).

The **Sacred Marriage** seems to have been a rite related to fertility.

See **mother goddesses and birth goddesses; nude woman; Šerida**.

'Figure with Mace': see **mace**.

figurines

Figurines or statuettes (including plaques) were made in almost every period of ancient Mesopotamia. Most of those that survive are of clay, but there are also examples of stone and metal (including gold, silver and copper or bronze), while incantations and descriptions of rituals refer to the fashioning of figurines also of perishable materials, such as wood (especi-

Margin references (left column): 17,63, 4,115, 153; 9,121; 129; fr.,8, 9,11, 12,33, 40,57, 64,70, 5,109 2,116, 8,120

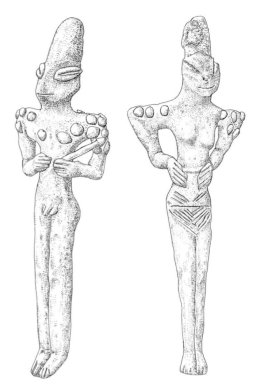

64 Ubaid Period (fifth millennium BC) male and female baked clay figurines, from Eridu and Ur respectively. Hts. 137, 152 m.

ally tamarisk), dough (see **flour**), bitumen and wax.

No single purpose can be ascribed to the use of figurines. Some of the human and animal figures may possibly have been children's toys. When found in graves they may sometimes serve as attendants upon the dead, substitutes for human and animal victims (see **animal sacrifice; human sacrifice**). Others again were dedicated to gods (see **dedication**): in all probability human figures normally represented the worshippers, while figures of gods and animals (such as the statuettes of **dogs** found in the temple of **Gula** at Isin) symbolised the deities concerned (see **beasts of the gods**). It is sometimes unclear whether anthropomorphic figures represented deities or persons, as with figures of the **nude woman**. Human figurines 118 fashioned of dough or wax were used to represent the witch in rituals to counteract sorcery. These figurines were destroyed as part of the rites (see **magic and sorcery**).

38 The Neo-Sumerian metal figures of 'basket-bearers' are thought to represent the ruler engaged in ritual labour in connection with a new building. In a different type of building ritual of the Neo-Assyrian Period, magically 9,11, protective figurines of clay and wood rep-12,40, resented various minor gods and beneficent 57,136 demons and monsters. These were buried or placed in the rooms. In many of these cases, the efficacy of the figurines depended upon the supposed localisation of the power of a supernatural being within the figurine itself (a parallel to the procedure concerning the preparation of **cult statues**).

Certain figurines and plaques had very specific functions in particular rituals. Among 151 these were those used to exorcise **Lamaštu**. Others were used to restore potency, possibly including the scenes of sexual intercourse and 124,129 the models of human sexual organs, the latter particularly associated with the cult of Ištar (Inana) (see **prostitution and ritual sex**). Models of other parts of the body, such as feet, are also known, and were possibly offerings made in connection with specific ailments.

See **creation; eye and eye-idols; fish-garbed figure; ğipar; 'hands of Ištar'; Huwawa; magic circle; mother goddesses and birth goddesses; wrestlers**.

'filling motifs'

The various smaller figures, animals, symbols and other elements found surrounding the principal scenes in Mesopotamian art, especially on seals, are generally referred to as 'fillers' or 'filling motifs'. Certain scholars, however, regard this term as inappropriate: the combinations of such elements, they believe, are almost always deliberate and have a magical, thematic and iconographic relevance to the figurations of the main scene.

See, for example, **fish; fly**.

fire: see **Gibil; Išum; magic and sorcery; Nusku**.

fish

Fish offerings were made in Mesopotamia from early times (see **sacrifice and offering**). The 36 fresh water of the Euphrates and Tigris rivers, which was believed to well up from the **abzu**, 151 teems with fish, mostly species of carp, and it was natural for the fish to become associated with the water god **Enki**. Since he was a wise 19,60 god, the fish also symbolised wisdom.

On seals, especially of Old Babylonian date, the image of the fish is often placed (as a so-called **'filling motif'**) close to figures and elements of ill omen for mankind, such as gods and demons attacking men. It may be that in such contexts the fish was intended to give a certain balance, as a sign of beneficence, to malevolent forces. Neo-Assyrian cylinder seals show fish offerings on tables, perhaps **altars**.

When the Assyrian king Sennacherib (reigned 704–681 BC) made an offering to Ea (**Enki**) of a golden boat, he also cast into the sea a pair of objects of gold, one of which was the model of a fish.

See **fish-garbed figure; goat-fish; lion-fish; merman and mermaid; vase with streams**.

fish-garbed figure

The term is used to refer to a bearded human-bodied figure with, above the human face, a fish-head drawn over the scalp, and the full body of a fish hanging down the back, complete with caudal and dorsal fins. The type first occurs in the art of the Kassite Period, after which it passed to Assyria, becoming popular in the art of the Neo-Assyrian and Neo-Babylonian Periods. From Assyrian palace sculpture the figure was copied in the early Persian Period. A similar figure, perhaps the Oannes of **Berossos**, was known in Seleucid times. In the fourteenth to tenth centuries BC, the figure was depicted with a fish-skin reaching to the ground. In the ninth century this was shortened to a cape terminating in a 65 fish-tail just below the man's waist. From the eighth century, however, there was a reversion 18, 82 to the longer form. 108

From representations on magical plaques,

65 A human-looking figure dressed in the skin of a fish and holding a bucket and (originally) a cone. Drawn from a monumental stone relief, one of a pair flanking a doorway of the temple of the god Ninurta at the Assyrian city of Kalhu (modern Nimrud), where they had been erected during the reign of King Assurnasirpal II (reigned 883–859 BC). Drawn by the archaeologist Sir Austen Henry Layard, who conducted excavations at the site in the mid-19th century.

where a pair of fish-garbed figures is shown 151 flanking the bed of a sick man, the figures of this type have been interpreted by some as exorcist **priests**, dressed in the bodies of fish or in costumes imitative of them (see **animal** 104 **skins**). The presence of the type at doorways in Assyrian palace and temple sculpture, however, demonstrates the magically protective nature of the figure. So does the discovery of **figurines** of the creature buried under the floors of buildings. Texts concerning the ritu- 12 als for making such images and placing them about the house identify the type as a form of *apkallu* 'sage'. The rituals prescribe figurines of this type to be buried in groups of seven (see **numbers**); those examples that have been found intact conform to this. Though perhaps sometimes imitated by priests, the being must in essence be a supernatural creature, an antediluvian sage whose traditions are reflected in the myths of the **Seven Sages**.

See **bucket and cone**.

fish-man and fish-woman: see **merman and mermaid**.

Flood

Both great rivers of Mesopotamia, the Tigris 4 and the Euphrates, are prone to flood when swollen by the spring rains and the snow-melt. The Tigris especially can rise during the period February to May and cause destructive floods of immense proportions over a very wide area of the flat alluvial plain. These sudden, violent floods were a frequent feature of life in southern Mesopotamia until flood-control 66 engineering in the 1950s. Archaeological excavations have revealed evidence of several extensive floods at various sites and at different periods.

So it was natural for floods to be a powerful literary image, and the destructive inundation was a favourite metaphor for the destructive power of a deity. Nor is it surprising that Mesopotamian mythology should include legends of one great Flood accompanied by torrential rainstorms that was more extensive than any

66 A view of the marshlands in the far south of Mesopotamia, in present-day Iraq.

other – that covered the whole world, in fact. The Sumerian King List gives the names of eight kings of five cities who ruled before the Flood (other sources mention nine or ten kings). The last of these was the father of **Ziusura**, the sage who with his family was chosen by the god **Enki** to survive the Flood, when the rest of mankind perished. In other Mesopotamian versions of the story he is called Atra-hasīs or Ūt-napišti.

From Mesopotamia the myth of the universal Flood spread to Ugarit, and to Palestine, where it was incorporated into the Hebrew Book of Genesis. Possibly the Greek flood myths of Deukalion, Ogyges and Dardanos are influenced by the Mesopotamian story also. Personified, 'Flood' (*abūbu*) was the name of a winged cosmic monster.

Some modern authorities have implausibly interpreted the story of the Flood as a metaphor for a 'flood' of people, relating it to the Semitic immigrations onto the Mesopotamian plain.

See **Gilgameš; lion.**

flour

Numerous different types of flour were used in a variety of rituals. Flour might be used for making a magic drawing, e.g. of a sorcerer thought to have bewitched the patient. In various divinatory and exorcistic rituals, flour is scattered on the ground, and a special ritual use of flour is to make small heaps of it (*zidub-dubbû*, literally 'piled up flour'), sometimes together with *šebirbirredû* (scattered grains). When separate heaps of flour are made in front of gods, or in front of other objects symbolising the gods, the heaps represent offerings. In other rituals, as explicitly stated, the heaps themselves symbolise certain gods whose presence is desired during the procedures.

Various doughs made from different cereal flours were used, mixed with herbs, to make pastes for medical treatments. They were also used ritually in the manufacture of **figurines** for magical rituals intended to improve sexual potency or to undo the effects of sorcery.

See **diseases and medicine; magic and sorcery; prostitution and ritual sex.**

'flowing vase': see **vase with streams.**

fly

In the Mesopotamian versions of the **Flood** story, the bodies of dead humans floating on the flood waters are compared to flies. When Ūt-napišti (**Ziusura**), the survivor of the Flood, makes the first **sacrifice** after the ark comes to land, the gods sniff the savour and buzz around like flies. To express her regret that the Flood was ever sent, the mother goddess Nintu (or Bēlet-ilī in the version of the story in the Epic of **Gilgameš**) (see **mother goddesses and birth goddesses**) touches the necklace of fly-jewels that Anu (**An**) made her, swearing that she will never forget the terrible event. Lapis lazuli beads in the shape of flies have been found in Mesopotamia, and other fly-jewellery is known from temple inventories.

In a Sumerian poem, a little fly helps **Inana** when the **galla** demons are hunting down **Dumuzi**.

The image of a fly on Old Babylonian seals has been thought possibly to be a symbol of **Nergal** as god of disease and death.

food and drink of the gods

Unlike the Greek Olympians with their ambrosia and nectar, the Mesopotamian **gods** had no special foods which were the privilege of divinity. However, in the story of the sage **Adapa**, Anu (**An**) decides that Adapa shall be offered the 'bread of life' and the 'water of life' when he visits heaven, and it is clear from the context that to have consumed these would have conferred (eternal) life. In fact, believing them to be the bread and water of death, he declines and loses his chance of immortality.

The gods lived on the sacrifice of sheep, fish, cereals and oil which mankind was obliged to offer them regularly: the same foods as were consumed by man himself. They drank beer and wine (probably date wine as well as grape wine), and in a number of myths gods are depicted as imbibing to excess. **Inana** has to feign sexual innocence to ward off the drunken advances of her brother **Utu** in one Sumerian poem, and in 'Inana and Enki' she plies **Enki** with beer and sweet wine to the point where he agrees formally to bestow on her the **me** or divine powers of the universe, an action he bitterly regrets when he wakens from his drunken stupor.

See **alcohol**; **animal sacrifice**; **Ninmah**; **sacrifice and offering**; **Siduri**.

fork

A rare symbol in Mesopotamian art is the trident or three-pronged fishing spear. It is rep- 76 resented on seals of Early Dynastic, Akkadian, Old Babylonian/Old Assyrian and Neo-Assyrian date. It may occur in a group with other, more familiar, symbols of gods, or as an attribute held by a god or **bull-man**. On one seal from the time of the Old Assyrian trading colony in Anatolia, a god on a **bull** holds the triple fork of **lightning** while another god on a **lion** holds the trident. The two symbols should certainly, therefore, be distinguished. The trident has been explained as the Old Assyrian *mazlagum*, 'fork'. Which Mesopotamian deity the object symbolised, however, is unknown.

fortune-telling: see **divination**.

foundation deposits: see **building rites and deposits**.

frog

In the Sumerian poem 'Inana and Enki', when **Enki** awakes to find that in a drunken gambling game he has allowed **Inana** to win from him all the **me**, he attempts to recover them by sending various watery creatures chasing after Inana's boat. The first is a little frog, whom he grasps 'by its right hand'. Apparently the frog fails, and other creatures are sent on the same errand.

A frog occurs as a symbol or '**filling motif**' on cylinder seals of the Kassite Period. Weights were sometimes made in the shape of frogs.

galla

The *galla* (Akkadian *gallû*) is one of the numerous types of underworld demons especially responsible for hauling unfortunate humans off to the **underworld**. Often mentioned in incantations in enumerations of seven types of evil demons (see **magic and sorcery**), the *galla*s in one magical text are said themselves to number seven (see **numbers**). **Inana** is accompanied by *galla*s on her return from the underworld, and they set off in a pack to fetch the hapless **Dumuzi** to the nether regions. Several Sumerian poems describe the deserted sheepfold of Dumuzi after the *galla*s have taken him away.

Like most demons or spirits, *galla*s could exist in a favourable form too. In Gudea's hymn the minor god Ig-alima is described as 'the great *galla* of Ĝirsu' (see **Ninĝirsu**).

see **Ĝeštinana**.

Ganzir: see **Ereškigal**; **gatekeepers**; **underworld**.

gatekeepers

152 The entrances to heaven, the **underworld** and the **abzu** were usually guarded by one or a pair of lesser divinities. In the poem 'The Descent of Ištar (**Inana**)' and in Babylonian magical incantations, a god called Neti guards the gate of the underworld (called Ganzir). In '**Nergal and Ereškigal**', the gatekeeper of the underworld is not named. In the myth of **Adapa**, the gods **Dumuzi** and Gišzida (**Ningišzida**) are found guarding the gate to the heaven of Anu (**An**), but this was a rôle not usual for them.

Particularly in Assyrian times, gateways were protected by a flanking pair of hybrid animals or animal-men (see **demons and monsters**), sometimes semi-divine (see **lama**).

See **Lugal-irra and Meslamta-ea**; **Utu**.

Ĝatumdug

Ĝatumdug was a goddess of the city-state of Lagaš and, like **Bau**, with whom she was later equated, she was regarded as a daughter of **An**. She is sometimes called 'Mother of Lagaš' or 'Mother who founded Lagaš'. Gudea, the prince of Lagaš who rebuilt the temple of **Ninĝirsu**, describes in his great hymn on that subject how he visited the temple of Ĝatumdug on his way to the temple of **Nanše** to obtain an interpretation of a **dream**. He addresses Ĝatumdug as mother and father and asks for the protection of her favourable **udug** and **lama** deities.

Ĝatumdug's temple was originally in the temple area at Lagaš but was subsequently moved to Ĝirsu.

generations of gods

Information about the generations of **gods** is contained in many myths and literary works and also in ancient Mesopotamian **lists of gods**, set out according to their 'households', with consort, offspring, other relatives, minister, household staff and so on. 'Marriages' and 'parenthood' among the gods are sometimes attributable to geographical closeness of the cult centres where they were worshipped. However, the same god was sometimes worshipped in different places, each with its own traditions, and it was a persistent feature of the history of Mesopotamian religion for local traditions to be gradually syncretised as, throughout the centuries, political units grew larger and larger. So it is sometimes impossible to present unified data since several discrepant traditions may be recorded for the same period. The table on page 87 shows the 67 family relationships of some of the principal gods according to the best-known traditions. But it cannot be regarded as exclusively correct and is far from presenting a complete picture: the reader is advised to consult the entries on individual gods and goddesses. In some cases the use of the terms 'brother' and 'sister' in Mesopotamian texts may imply no more than that the deities concerned were of the same 'generation'; similarly 'father' sometimes means 'ancestor', and so forth.

genies

A number of so-called 'genies' are found in Assyrian monumental and minor arts, often engaged in royal rituals. Sometimes animal hybrids such as the **griffin-demon** appear to take part in rituals, but more often such participants are anthropomorphic. Some types are clearly minor deities, since they wear the **horned cap** as a mark of their divinity; others may be human. A male winged god, standing or kneeling, holds a **bucket and cone** and can be 37 involved in the scenes of 'ritual' centred on the

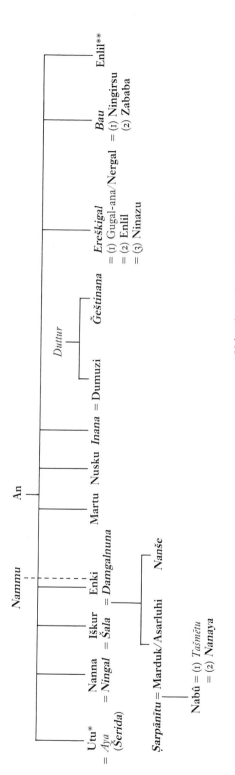

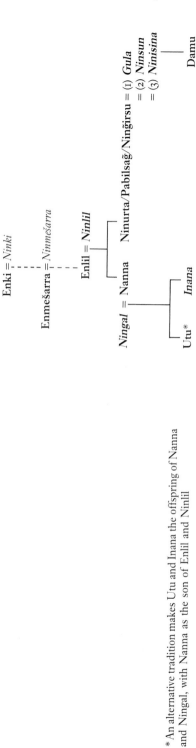

Nammu

An

Utu*   Nanna   Iškur   Enki
= *Aya*   = *Ningal*   = *Šala*   = *Damgalnuna*
(*Šerida*)

     Martu   Nusku   *Inana* = Dumuzi

     Duttur

     Geštinana

     Ereškigal
     = (1) Gugal-ana/Nergal
     = (2) Enlil
     = (3) Ninazu

     Bau   Enlil**
     = (1) Ningirsu
     = (2) Zababa

Šarpānītu = Marduk/Asarluhi

     Nanše

Nabû = (1) *Tašmētu*
      = (2) *Nanaya*

An alternative tradition about the parentage of Enlil was:

Enki = *Ninki*

Enmešarra = *Ninmešarra*

Enlil = *Ninlil*

Ninurta/Pabilsaǧ/Ninǧirsu = (1) *Gula*
                  = (2) *Ninsun*
                  = (3) *Ninisina*

Damu

Ningal = Nanna

Utu*   *Inana*

** An alternative tradition about the parentage of Enlil was:

* An alternative tradition makes Utu and Inana the offspring of Nanna and Ningal, with Nanna as the son of Enlil and Ninlil

67 Genealogical table of Mesopotamian gods and goddesses. Female deities are indicated in *italics*. Dotted lines indicate descent rather than parenthood, or else a variant tradition.

68 A winged genie with a sacrificial deer. From a monumental stone relief in the throne-room of the royal palace of the Assyrian king Assurnasirpal II (reigned 883–859 BC) at Kalhu (modern Nimrud).

49 **stylised tree**. A similar female figure holds a chaplet of beads. Such figures might be covered by the Akkadian term *aladlammû*, which seems also to have been applied to **bulls and lions with human head** (see **lama**). A third figure carries a flowering branch, some-
68 times also a sacrificial(?) goat. Sometimes he wears the horned cap, and even when he does not he often has wings. Presumably, therefore, such figures are also non-mortal; they may represent the **Seven Sages** in human guise.

See **fish-garbed figure**.

Ḡeštinana

Ḡeštinana is the goddess who was the faithful sister of **Dumuzi** and, like him, a child of the sheep goddess Duttur. Her cult was widespread over Sumer until the Old Babylonian Period. She seems to have been thought of sometimes as an 'old woman, an interpreter of dreams', as 'Mother Ḡeštinana'. When **Inana** determines that, in order to secure her own release from imprisonment in the **underworld**, her husband Dumuzi shall take her place, **galla** demons come to fetch the young shepherd god from his sheepfold in the country. Ḡeštinana, his sister, who is also a rural deity after whom fields were named (hence too her equation with the later Akkadian goddess Bēlet-ṣēri, 'Lady of the open countryside'), helps her brother to hide from the demons by sending him successively to four different hiding places. In another version of the story, she refuses to give him away even when tortured. In the event a friend of Dumuzi reveals his whereabouts to the demons. Ḡeštinana sings a death lament for him. It was believed that subsequently she and Dumuzi alternated six-month periods in the underworld, where she sometimes functioned as scribe to **Ereškigal**.

ghosts: see **gidim**.

Gibil (Girra)

Gibil or Girra (Akkadian *girru*) is deified fire. Viewed as a god, Girra was thought to be a son of Anu (**An**) and the goddess **Šala**. He represented fire in all its aspects: as a destructive force and as the burning heat of the Mesopotamian summer; and, as a creative force, the fire in the smith's furnace and the fire in the kiln where bricks are baked, and so as a 'founder of cities'.

See **Nusku**.

gidim

The *gidim* (Akkadian *eṭemmu*) is, first of all, the spirit of a dead person, living in the **underworld**, who must be propitiated and revered. The condition of such spirits is not, in general, happy, and regular funerary offerings of food and drink must be made to them. If not fed, they can become restless and liable to haunt the living. The *gidim* is also, then, the ghost who returns from the underworld to persecute the living. Especially those who had died violent deaths were likely to be unsettled in the underworld and to return and 'seize' living persons. They might enter the body through the ear. Magic could be employed against them.

Necromancy, the deliberate raising of ghosts, was known and practised in Babylonia. Questions about the future could be put to a ghost raised in this way, although it was recognised that this was a very dangerous activity, since a ritual exists to counteract the ill effects caused by practising necromancy (see **magic and sorcery**).

Ghosts were also thought to be able to cause some **diseases**. *Qāt eṭemmi* (literally 'hand of the ghost') seems to have been a more or less psychological illness. On the other hand, *ṣibit eṭemmi* ('seizure by the ghost') appears to have had definite physical symptoms.

See **afterlife**.

Gilgameš

Most scholars take the view that Gilgameš probably was a historical king of the Sumerian city Unug (in Akkadian, Uruk) some time during the early part of the Early Dynastic Period. However, we can definitely say that during the later Early Dynastic Period a *god* Gilgameš (or Bilgames, to give the early Sumerian form of his name) was already being worshipped at a number of different places in Sumer. The first certain connection of this god with Uruk was when Utu-heǧal, king of Uruk, adopted Gilgameš as his patron deity. Under Utu-heǧal's immediate successors, the Third Dynasty of Ur, Gilgameš was also worshipped at a small town near Ur. This may be why the kings of the Third Dynasty were especially attached to Gilgameš, calling him their 'divine brother' and 'friend'. Probably from this period derive the various legends according to which Gilgameš was a famous king of Uruk, contemporary with En-me-barage-si, a historically attested early

ruler of the city of Kiš, or with the latter's son Agga.

The five independent narrative poems in Sumerian survive in manuscripts from the first half of the second millennium BC and are usually called by the titles given to them by their modern editors. 'Gilgameš and Agga' is the story of the successful rebellion of Gilgameš against his overlord and benefactor, King Agga of Kiš. 'Gilgameš and Huwawa' (or 'Gilgameš and the Cedar Forest') relates how the hero and his serving man **Enkidu** defeat and kill the monster **Huwawa**, who had been appointed by **Enlil** as guardian of the Cedar Forest. 'Gilgameš and the Bull of Heaven' tells how the heroic duo defeat and kill the **Bull of Heaven**, sent against Gilgameš by the goddess **Inana** perhaps after he had rejected her sexual advances. 'The Death of Gilgameš' is poorly preserved, but apparently referred to an important state funeral and the arrival of the deceased in the **underworld**. It may perhaps have been misinterpreted, as it could refer rather to the death of Enkidu. In 'Gilgameš, Enkidu and the Nether World', Gilgameš questions the shade of Enkidu about conditions in the underworld.

By the Old Babylonian Period, stories about Gilgameš and his adventures had been elaborated into one or more poems in Akkadian. However, the most complete version, a grand epic which survives in twelve fragmentary tablets, was compiled by one Sîn-leqe-unninnī, probably in Middle Babylonian times, and first discovered in the excavation of the library of the Assyrian king Assurbanipal (reigned 668–c.627 BC) at his capital Nineveh. Some of the gaps in the narrative can be filled by fragments found at other sites in Mesopotamia, Anatolia and the Levant.

The epic opens with a prologue in praise of Gilgameš, builder and first king of Uruk, the great warrior, one-third human, two-thirds divine. There is allusion, however, to the king's 'oppression' of the city, usually interpreted either as his tyrannical compulsion of the citizens to forced labour or as his sexual oppression of the population. In order to curb

69 Gilgameš and Enkidu pin down and slaughter the monster Humbaba. From a baked clay moulded plaque of the Old Babylonian Period.

these excesses, Anu (**An**) creates Enkidu, an uncivilised brute of a man who at first runs wild among the animals. Tamed and initiated into the ways of the human world by his encounter with the prostitute Šamhat, however, Enkidu journeys to Uruk for the inevitable confrontation with the king. Gilgameš is ready for him. The second tablet describes a wrestling bout between the two men (see **wrestlers**). Gilgameš is the victor, but the strength and tenacity of his opponent win his lasting respect and friendship. Enkidu hereafter is treated as the equal partner and companion of Gilgameš (not his slave as in most Sumerian versions).

In tablets III–V the companions travel together to the distant Cedar Forest, guarded in the name of Enlil by the terrifying Humbaba (the Akkadian name for Huwawa). The rest of the engagement is lost to us, but it is likely that Humbaba is defeated and killed. When the sixth tablet begins, Gilgameš has returned to his city. The city goddess Ištar (Akkadian name of Inana) proposes marriage, but Gilgameš rejects her advances and, with Enkidu's help, slays the dreaded Bull of Heaven that the vengeful goddess sends against him.

At the beginning of tablet VII Enkidu recounts a **dream** in which Anu (**An**), Ea (**Enki**) and Šamaš (**Utu**) had decided that for killing Humbaba and the Bull of Heaven either Gilgameš or Enkidu must die. They choose Enkidu. (In the Sumerian poem 'Gilgameš and

Huwawa', Enkidu's specific crime was his lack of compassion for Huwawa.) Enkidu subsequently sickens, and dreams of the underworld that must await him. He dies. The lament of Gilgameš for his late friend and the details of the state funeral are narrated in the eighth tablet.

The next episode (in tablets IX–XI) leads up to the story of the **Flood** and its hero, which in Sumerian literature had been an independent poem. Depressed by the death of Enkidu and feelings of his own mortality, Gilgameš makes a long journey, involving many dangers, to the home of Ūt-napišti (**Ziusura**), to learn from him the secret of immortality. When he finally arrives, Ūt-napišti relates the story of his escape from the Flood and his attainment of eternal life. In response to the plea of Gilgameš for immortality, Ūt-napišti challenges him to defy sleep. This Gilgameš fails to do, immediately falling asleep and not awakening for seven days. If not eternal life, Ūt-napišti is still able to offer restored youth, directing Gilgameš to the place of a plant which has the property of rejuvenation. Gilgameš picks the plant, but he leaves it on the shore while he takes a refreshing swim, and its smell is caught by a nearby serpent, who snatches it. Hurrying away, the serpent sheds its old skin for a new one. (See **'plant of life'**.)

Despondent, Gilgameš returns to Uruk, showing off his city to Ūt-napišti's boatman Uršanabi (called Sursunabu in the Old Babylonian version).

The twelfth tablet is an appendix relating to the loss of certain objects which had been given to Gilgameš by Ištar. This is a close parallel to part of the Sumerian 'Gilgameš, Enkidu and the Nether World' that did not fit well into the new epic and so was relegated to the end. The poem thus concludes with a vision of the spirit of Enkidu, who promises to recover the lost items, but who gives a bleak report on conditions in the **afterlife**.

From some (probably three) of the Sumerian Gilgameš poems and other material, some romantic narratives and others more philosophical, the Akkadian Epic of Gilgameš creates a work of outstanding sensitivity and beauty. The focus is on the sharp contrast between the hero's disdain of danger in the first part and his haunting terror of death in the second.

There is one important event in the life of Gilgameš that neither the Sumerian nor the Akkadian version treats: the hero's birth. Since his exploits might have been considered of more interest, this might not, perhaps, be surprising in itself. Yet birth legends were a common feature of Mesopotamian and Near Eastern heroic romances, and the omission is the more striking because there is a chance mention of Gilgameš's birth preserved in the work of a classical author, Aelian's *On the Nature of Animals*. According to this account (narrated as an illustration of the kindness of animals to men), King 'Seuechoros' of 'the Babylonians' had been warned by his magicians that a son born to his daughter would usurp his throne. He therefore kept the girl at the acropolis under close guard. Nevertheless, she became pregnant, and the guards, fearing the king's wrath, cast the child from the summit. The baby was saved by an eagle in flight (recalling the story of **Etana**). The bird took him to an orchard, where the child was carefully set down. The caretaker of the place found the baby and took care of him. The child, who was later to become king, was called 'Gilgamos'. The story is in the tradition of other Near Eastern birth legends (Sargon, Cyrus, Moses). This account and the Hittite version of the epic do, however, hint at traditions about the birth and early life of Gilgameš at a time before he became king of Uruk, and it has been suggested that this could help to explain his unpopularity in his own city at the beginning of the epic. If he were a usurper of the throne, a certain resentment and a degree of repression might be expected.

Although the stories about Gilgameš had a long currency and were apparently widely known in the Near East, depictions of the legends in art are hard to come by. The 'hero' figure with long hair, typically with four or six large curls (see **Lahmu**), and his concomitant bull-man, common in Mesopotamian art of most periods, have popularly been taken to represent Gilgameš and Enkidu, but this is incorrect. Some works of art of the second and first millennia BC, however, mostly clay plaques (**figurines**) and seals, do seem to depict two of the episodes in the Gilgameš stories. In one a pair of human figures attack a demonic figure, often a version of the 'hero' with curls; the two men stab or hack at the demon with their weapons, each using one leg to pin him down. This must be the slaughter of Huwawa/Humbaba. A second scene shows a similar human pair attacking a monstrous winged human-headed bovine, almost certainly the Bull of Heaven.

g̃ipar

The *g̃ipar* (Akkadian *giparu*) was the residence of the *en* priest or priestess (Akkadian *ēnu* or *entu*) (see **priests and priestesses**) and the administrative centre of their households. The *g̃ipar* at Ur was rebuilt by the Neo-Babylonian king Nabonidus when, reviving the ancient office, he dedicated his daughter En-nigaldi-Nanna as *entu* of **Nanna** following an eclipse of the moon on 26 September 554 BC. The building was excavated by Sir Leonard Woolley. The original *g̃ipar* (built during the time of the Third Dynasty of Ur), located adjacent to the main temple enclosure of Nanna which included the **ziggurat**, was divided into two sections, one the residence proper of the *entu* and her household, including a cemetery of former *entu* priestesses, and the other incorporating the *entu*'s personal temple to the goddess **Ningal** (the wife of Nanna). As rebuilt by Nabonidus, the *g̃ipar* was relocated slightly further east. A new temple of Ningal was built inside the enclosure of the temple of Nanna.

In the time of the Assyrian governor Sîn-balassu-iqbi, during the reign of Assurbanipal (reigned 668–c.627 BC), the original site of the *g̃ipar* had been occupied by a building heavily protected by magical deposits of sun-dried clay **figurines** buried in the foundations. They were placed in boxes of 'plano-convex' bricks, unused architecturally since the Early

70 Neo-Assyrian sun-dried clay figurines of the
goat-fish and the merman, probably from the city of
Aššur. Although no details of their discovery are
known, they will have been placed within a brick box
buried in the foundations of a building to counter evil.
Lengths 140, 130 mm.

Dynastic Period and probably excavated from an ancient ruin (see **building rites and deposits**).

Girra: see **Gibil**.

Gišzida: see **Ningišzida**.

goat-fish

A creature with the head and forelegs of a goat and body of a **fish** is represented from Neo-Sumerian through to Hellenistic times, and even had a revival, as Capricornus, at the hands of the Romans (especially in Augustan art, Capricorn being the emperor's zodiac sign). The identification of the Mesopotamian creature with the *suhurmašû*, 'carp-goat', is proved by a **kudurru** caption and by the inscriptions prescribed in Assyrian rituals for **figurines** of the type, which appear on actual examples. Association with the god Ea (**Enki**), suspected from the frequent iconographic juxtaposition with the ram-headed staff (see **standards, staves and sceptres of the gods**), is confirmed by texts, but the figure could also be a generally magically protective type, often paired with the **merman** in pictorial representations.

goat-headed staff: see **standards, staves and sceptres of the gods**.

gods and goddesses

The gods of the ancient Mesopotamians, in historical times, were almost without exception anthropomorphic, male or female. It seems that they were imagined as of gigantic size and of superhuman powers, although the power of all the gods was by no means equal: some were relatively minor or of restricted influence. They shared the emotions and foibles of mankind. Generally speaking they were immortal, although there are certain gods, such as **Dumuzi**, Gugalana (see **Ereškigal**), **Ĝeštinana** and the **Slain Heroes**, about whom myths are recounted which involve their deaths, or visits to the **underworld** (see **dead gods**). Typically the gods exuded or, as the Mesopotamians said, 'wore' **melam**, which

71 Gods fight among themselves. Modern rolled impression of a lapis lazuli cylinder seal of the Akkadian Period from Kiš. Ht. 280 mm.

72 Head, broken from a baked clay statuette of a goddess, wearing the distinctive horned cap as a mark of her divinity. Probably Neo-Babylonian. Ht. 133 mm.

73 King Nabû-apla-iddina of Babylon is
introduced into the presence of the sun god
Šamaš. Before the shrine the god's solar disc
is suspended on an altar. From a stone tablet
commemorating the restoration of the Temple
of Šamaš at Sippar in *c.*870 BC.

covered them in a terrifying splendour.
Although they lived in heaven or the underworld, an extension of their personality also
inhabited the various **cult statues** erected to
them by mankind: when a statue was first
dedicated, the Babylonians performed the
'Washing the mouth' and 'Opening the mouth'
rituals for it in order to enable it to become
imbued with the divine presence.

49,87

The largest group of gods are the deities of
the various city **pantheons**. To these can be
added gods and goddesses representing
natural forces (**Gibil, Nisaba, Iškur,** etc.),
birth goddesses (see **mother goddesses and
birth goddesses**), groups of anonymous gods
(such as the **Anuna, Igigū** or gods of the
night), minister deities (minor deities who
attend more important gods and goddesses), as
well as deities of inchoate personality assigned
to the primordial period before the splitting of
heaven and earth. Next come the **personal
gods** of individuals ('a man's god') chiefly dis-

74 A man worships before two altars, each
supporting a divine symbol (in this case the
lion-headed standard of the underworld god
Nergal and the crescent of the moon god Sîn).
From a cylinder seal, Neo-Babylonian Period.

75 Two images of kingship. (*left*) Narām-Suen, god-king of Agade (2254–2218 BC), wearing the horned cap of divinity. From his stela commemorating victory over the Lullubū, found at Susa in north-west Iran, where it had been taken as booty in antiquity. (*right*) King Assurnasirpal II of Assyria (reigned 883–859 BC) in ceremonial religious dress. Assyrian kings were not deified, but were the chief priests of the god Aššur. From an ivory casket (?) panel from Kalhu (modern Nimrud).

tinguished by their not being named. **Demons**, which can be both beneficent or evil, are normally under the command of gods, and usually operate very much in the world in which mankind lives. Finally some human beings were deified: most of the Akkadian, Sumerian and Babylonian kings from Narām-Suen (reigned 2310–2274 BC) to Samsu-ditāna (reigned 1681–1651 BC) were deified in their own lifetimes and received a cult in temples throughout their kingdoms, but the practice died out thereafter.

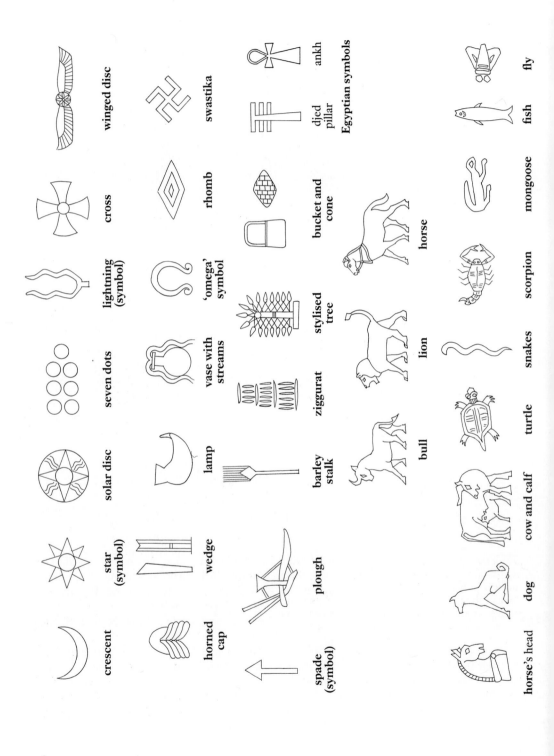

winged disc

cross

lightning (symbol)

seven dots

solar disc

star (symbol)

crescent

swastika

rhomb

'omega' symbol

vase with streams

lamp

wedge

horned cap

ankh

djed pillar

Egyptian symbols

bucket and cone

stylised tree

ziggurat

barley stalk

plough

spade (symbol)

horse

lion

bull

fly

fish

mongoose

scorpion

snakes

turtle

cow and calf

dog

horse's head

96

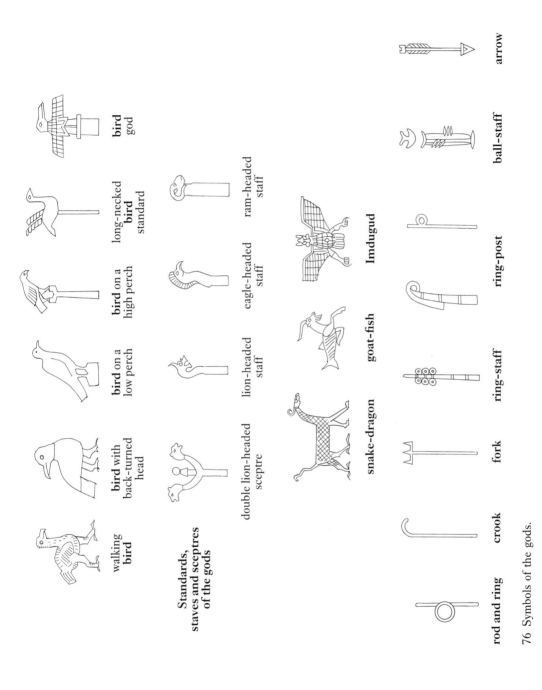

arrow

ball-staff

bird god

long-necked **bird** standard

ram-headed staff

bird on a high perch

eagle-headed staff

Imdugud

ring-post

bird on a low perch

lion-headed staff

goat-fish

ring-staff

bird with back-turned head

double lion-headed sceptre

snake-dragon

fork

walking **bird**

Standards, staves and sceptres of the gods

crook

rod and ring

76 Symbols of the gods.

97

In order to deal conceptually with the extreme proliferation of deities (more than 3,000 names have been recovered), the gods were organised by the Mesopotamians into groups for which the metaphors of 'household', 'extended family' or 'state' can be used. The divine patrons of the various cities participate, in myths, in a consultative **assembly of the gods**, which may reflect a human political phenomenon of the Third Dynasty of Ur. The gradual organisation of the **local gods** into a national pantheon, like a great tribe with several generations, also threw up anomalies: a god worshipped under the same name in two different places might have two quite different cults and would then be distinguished as, for example, Anu (**An**) of Uruk or Anu of Dēr, Ištar (**Inana**) of Arba'il or Ištar of Uruk, or Nineveh. **Aššur** was sometimes called the 'Assyrian **Enlil**'. In due course the overall number of deities was reduced by the expedient of equating or regarding as forms of each other deities whose character was similar. At its most extreme this led to the so-called monotheistic tendencies of the cult of **Marduk**, in which, at one point, *all* the other male gods' names were alleged to be no more than the 'names of Marduk'.

When depicted in art, from at least the third millennium BC, gods are generally shown 72 wearing the **horned cap** with up to seven superimposed sets of bulls' horns. This is described as a mark of their divinity. They can also be identified by their distinctive symbols 73,74, and attributes. The majority of these, some 76 first depicted in the prehistoric, others in the Akkadian Period, are found with very little change in form or meaning down to the time of the Persian conquest (and in a few cases beyond). When not represented together with a god, these motifs nevertheless symbolise their associated deities.

See **Anuna; generations of gods; 'great gods'; Igigū; lists of gods.**

'God with mace': see **mace.**

'God with staff': see **Ninšubur (god).**

good and evil

Every human society has notions of good (morally laudable) and bad (morally reprehensible) behaviour. When these notions are elevated to be independent abstract principles we speak of good and evil, and some religious systems can be interpreted in terms of these two opposing powers, sometimes seen as constantly locked in combat with each other. The complexity of ancient Mesopotamian religion, resulting from the syncretism over many years of numerous local cults, was not conducive to such a view, even if in the Standard Babylonian tradition and in Neo-Assyrian religion we occasionally come across personified concepts like Kittu (Truth, a daughter of Šamaš/**Utu**), Mīšaru (Justice, a son of Šamaš) and Dayyānu (the Judge) as deities.

While the principal deities **Enlil**, **Utu/Šamaš** and **Enki**/Ea promote justice and activities beneficial to man, protect the weak, widows and orphans, and destroy the wicked, these are secondary characteristics of their divine personalities, rather than their personalities being an extension of their rôle as a personification of good. The 'wicked' are often not distinguished from the 'enemy'. The Sumerian **gods**, amongst themselves, behave amorally, even immorally.

Many of the spirits we call '**demons**', such as the **udug, lama,** *alad* or **galla**, were originally neutral, and the evil forms of them are specifically identified as 'evil *udug*s', 'evil *gallas*' (except that in certain contexts reference to the evil form is taken for granted). Perhaps the nearest to a specifically evil personification in the Mesopotamian record is the demon often mentioned in magical incantations called *Mimma lemnu*, which means 'All that is evil'. No information survives about how the physical features of this demon were envisaged.

See **Lamaštu; sin.**

goose: see **Bau.**

graves: see **death and funerary practices.**

'great gods'

The term 'great gods' is used sometimes, apparently, for the **gods** in general, but more usually for the principal divinities of the **pantheon**. When the deities referred to are enumerated or invoked by name, the list varies slightly from time to time, but the most usual inclusions in Assyrian royal inscriptions are seven or twelve in number. The personal preferences of individual kings (see **personal gods**) would affect the inclusions and the order. For example, the devotion of Assurnasirpal II (reigned 883–859 BC) to the god **Ninurta** placed this god among, and perhaps at the head of, this group, but he is thereafter seldom acknowledged. **Aššur** was normally placed at the beginning of the list, but Assurbanipal favoured especially the goddess Ištar (**Inana**), who seems to take precedence during his reign (668–*c.*627 BC).

On the stelae erected by Assyrian kings (or, exceptionally, provincial governors) to commemorate special events or the limits of successful campaigns, the king is always shown below symbols of the principal gods. These 21 and usually additional deities are invoked in the accompanying inscriptions.

See **Igigū**.

griffin

Griffin (from Greek *gryphōn*) was the name used in medieval Europe, and today in studies of art, for a fabulous composite animal, typically having the body (winged or wingless), hind-

77 Ivory furniture inlay showing a winged griffin, from Kalhu (modern Nimrud). Neo-Assyrian Period. Ht. 190 mm.

78 A monumental stone relief from the royal palace of the Assyrian king Assurnasirpal II (reigned 883–859 BC) at Kalhu (modern Nimrud). It depicts a so-called 'griffin-demon', thought of at the time as an ancient sage in bird-guise. He carries a bucket and cone for purification. The inscription across the middle of the relief records (in a way common to all the slabs from this palace) the conquests of the king. Ht. 2.32 m.

legs and tail of a **lion** and the head and fore-parts of a **bird**, usually an eagle. Probably originating in Syria in the second millennium BC, the griffin was known throughout the Near East, including Mesopotamia, and in Greece by the fourteenth century BC. It is often paired with the sphinx (see **bulls and lions with human head**). In Assyrian art it is sometimes depicted together with the **griffin-demon**.

The beast can be shown recumbent or seated on its haunches. The Near Eastern version has a crested head, while the Greek is usually shown with a row of spiral curls forming a mane. Often, in both the Near East and Greece, the creature has large **donkey ears**, perhaps from some assimilation to the **lion-dragon**. The beak is often parted to show the curling tongue.

Apparently the creature had some religious significance, being shown in the Near East among other **beasts of the gods** and in the West in funerary art. It may have been magically protective, but its precise associations and functions are unknown.

griffin-demon

With possible antecedents from the Old Babylonian Period, and with close analogues in Mitannian art, the griffin-demon first appears in his familiar form – a human-bodied figure with bird's head and wings – on Middle Assyrian seals, and became a very popular figure in Neo-Assyrian art, especially in the ninth century BC. After the seventh century BC, the figure is rare, but occurs on Seleucid Period seals. The private quarters of the palace of Assurnasirpal II (reigned 883–859 BC) were dominated by reliefs depicting this creature.

In the Neo-Assyrian Period figures of this type were explained as representations of the Babylonian **Seven Sages**, and groups of seven **figurines** of them were used as foundation deposits to protect houses and palaces (see **building rites and deposits**) – alongside very different anthropomorphic figures and figurines of the **fish-garbed figure** (also supposed to represent the Seven Sages).

See **bucket and cone**; **Nisroch**.

'Guardians of the gate': see **gatekeepers**.

gud-alim: see **bison**; **bull-man**.

Gugal-ana: see **Ereškigal**.

Gula

The goddess Gula (whose name means 'great') was a healing goddess, who 'understands disease', and a patroness of doctors. She was also worshipped under the names Nintinuga, Ninkarrak and Meme, originally the names of other goddesses; and as **Ninisina**, 'Lady of Isin'. Her principal shrine was the E-gal-mah at Isin, but she also had temples at Nippur, Borsippa and Aššur. She was regarded as the wife of **Ninurta** or **Pabilsaǧ**, or else of the minor vegetation god Abu. Gula was the mother of the healing god **Damu**, and of the god **Ninazu** (also associated with healing).

Her sacred animal was the **dog**, and small model dogs were dedicated to her by worshippers (see **dedication**).

See **diseases and medicine**.

79 The goddess Gula and her dog. Detail from the carving on a *kudurru* of the reign of the Babylonian king Nabû-mukīn-apli (reigned 978–943 BC).

hand

Because the hand symbolises control or seizure, a number of diseases have names in Akkadian which indicate that they were thought to be directly attributable to the power of various **gods**: 'hand of Šamaš (**Utu**)', 'hand of Ištar (**Inana**)', 'hand of the ghost (**gidim**)', 'hand of the god' (see **diseases and medicine**). It is not usually possible to identify these illnesses or groups of symptoms in modern medical terms.

Small models of hands, made from stone, bone or shell, were common **amulets** in the Early Dynastic Period, and are known occasionally from later periods. The symbol of a hand, sometimes mounted on a pole, and with varying numbers of fingers, is seen on seals of the Old Babylonian Period; its significance is unknown.

'hands-of-Ištar'

Qāt Ištar, 'hand of Ištar (**Inana**)', is the name of a psychological illness of some sort (see **hand**). In modern archaeological jargon, however, the term has been used to refer to a particular type of object: baked clay images of clenched fists. They were inserted into the walls of the major buildings of the Assyrian kings Assurnasirpal II (reigned 883–859 BC) and his son and successor Shalmaneser III (reigned 858–824 BC). The inscriptions on the backs of the hands record the name of the king and of the palace or temple into which they were set. They have sometimes been regarded as magical devices for the aversion of evil from the buildings, although some commentators have not unreasonably explained them simply as consoles for supporting (perhaps in a decorative rather than structural sense) the beams of the ceiling or of an upper storey. Since they were coated in bitumen, it is very likely that they also functioned as stoups to drain off the rain water. In any event, the use of the term 'hands-of-Ištar' for these devices has no textual basis.

Haniš: see **Iškur**.

Haya: see **Nisaba**.

heaven: see **cosmology**.

Hendursag̃: see **Išum**.

'hero' with curls: see **Lahmu**.

horned cap

From the early third millennium BC onwards a cap with up to seven superimposed pairs of horns is the distinctive head-dress of divinity. It is seen as a separate symbol, often standing on a podium, from the late Kassite Period down to the Neo-Babylonian, and continued to be represented as a mark of divinity in Achaemenid art. Originally a general indication of divine status, its use as a symbol of a particular major deity was never consistent. On Kassite **kudurrus** the symbol is named as that of the supreme god Anu (**An**), but in Neo-Assyrian art it was apparently transferred to the new national god Aššur. Sometimes, however, three caps then represented Aššur, Anu (**An**) and **Enlil**, or in Babylonia two such caps symbolised the latter two, with very occasionally a third cap standing for Ea (**Enki**) in place of his ram-headed staff. The style of the divine cap changed from time to time according to fashion, being either domed or flat-topped, sometimes trimmed with feathers or surmounted by a knob or *fleur-de-lys*.

fr., 16,
71,72
92,10
132,1

80,15

21
10

90

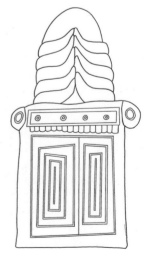

80 The symbol of the multi-horned cap placed on an altar, as it was commonly carved on the Babylonian *kudurru* stones.

The horned cap may well be derived from the horns of wild cattle (*Bos primigenius*), which, even after the domestication of cattle, 127 remained as a separate species throughout the Near East. They still roamed the plains of north-western Mesopotamia as late as Neo-Assyrian times, when they were hunted by Assyrian kings. The wild bull must have been a truly awe-inspiring beast, six feet tall at the shoulder and with an enormous pair of wide-sweeping horns. Domestic cattle were tiny by comparison. As a visual and literary image of power and strength, wild cattle preoccupied the Mesopotamian imagination, a metaphor for deity or a suitable comparison for heroes or kings.

horoscopes: see **zodiac**.

horse

The horse had been introduced into Mesopotamia by the first half of the second millennium BC. A winged horse or a **centaur** is to be 43 seen on some Middle Assyrian seals. The motif of a horse's head occurs as a divine symbol on a seal of the second millennium BC and on Neo-Assyrian seals, as well as on a **kudurru** of the

81 Symbol of a horse's head on an altar. Detail from the carving on a *kudurru* of the Babylonian king Nebuchadnezzar I (reigned 1125–1104 BC).

82 (*below*) Detail from a Neo-Assyrian cylinder seal. The sun god Šamaš, within his winged disc (supported by bull-men), stands on a horse, while a fish-garbed figure and worshipper (representing the owner of the seal) flank the scene.

Babylonian king Nebuchadnezzar I (reigned 1125–1104 BC), where it may represent a constellation (see **rainbow**). In the Neo-Assyrian Period, the horse is the animal of the sun-god Šamaš (**Utu**), if we may trust this identification of the deity on the basis of the associated **winged disc**.

81,90

31

82

Assyrian business documents sometimes specify as penalties for breach of contract, the **dedication** of two or four white horses to the god Aššur. These were probably live horses, given to the temple or (as the chief priest of the god) the king, rather than statues.

House God and House Goddess
A pair called 'House God' and 'House Goddess' were magically protective deities in Neo-Assyrian and Neo-Babylonian buildings. Clay **figurines** of them were buried in the foundations to ward off **demons**. The form of these figures is at present unknown.

See **building rites and deposits**.

Hubur: see **river of the underworld; river ordeal**.

human sacrifice
For Early Dynastic Sumer large-scale **sacrifice**, on the **death** of a lord or lady, of the retinue of the household, human as well as animal (see **animal sacrifice**), is scarcely if at all hinted at in documentary sources. Nevertheless, it is unequivocally attested by Sir Leonard Woolley's excavations of the 'Royal Tombs' at Ur. The principal occupants of these tombs were attended by numbers of victims, from six

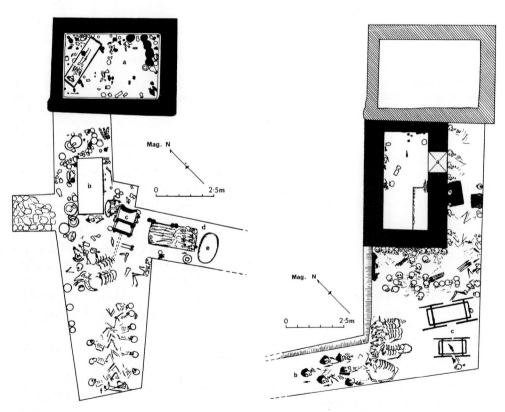

83 The plans of two important Early Dynastic burials at Ur, as excavated by Sir Leonard Woolley. (*left*) The so-called 'King's Grave' and (*right*), lying above it, the grave of Queen Pu-abi.

84 A reconstruction, in a painting by A. Forestier (1928), of the scene of sacrifice in the 'death-pit' of the 'King's Grave' at Ur, based on the archaeological excavations.

to eighty persons, equipped with the tools and weapons that had been appropriate to them in their lives of service. The principal body was laid inside a specially built stone or brick tomb-chamber. The human victims were then 83 either placed in the filling of the grave-shaft, in separate chambers, or, more usually, in a great 'death-pit' (a large dug-out rectangular open-air trench), the walls and floor lined with reeds, and with steps or a ramp cut on one side, at the bottom of which the tomb was built. Usually the lord or lady was first installed and sealed within the tomb, accompanied by three of four crouching attendants. Into the pit was then led the procession of courtiers, soldiers, 84 musicians, servants, animal-driven chariots and carts with drivers and grooms. Each person held a small vessel of clay, stone, or metal, from which we assume (by the peaceful con-

dition of the bodies which showed no sign of violence or a struggle), they drank their poison or sleeping-drug. The animals were then killed, and the great pit filled in with earth. Doubtless the entire process was accompanied by elaborate ceremonies. 35,52

This large-scale sacrifice of the Early Dynastic Period was apparently short-lived and was subsequently abandoned. However, in the seventh century BC, when an eclipse was thought to portend the death of the Assyrian king, there was a procedure for choosing a temporary substitute king and queen. The couple were for a time ceremonially treated as if royal (but given no political power) and then, at the time of the predicted fatality, were put to death.

See **death and funerary practices; figurines**.

Humbaba: see **Huwawa**.

Hurrian gods: see **Išhara; Iškur; Šala; Tišpak**.

Huwawa (Humbaba)

Huwawa (Akkadian Humbaba) appears in the **Gilgameš** stories as **Enlil**'s guardian of the Cedar Forest. Described as a giant protected by seven layers of terrifying radiance (see **melam and ni**), he was killed by Gilgameš and **Enkidu**.

85   In art, Humbaba is typically portrayed as a human-bodied figure with lion's claws for hands, a monstrous face, long hair and whiskers. Clay plaques and seals of the second and first millennia BC depict his killing by Gil-
69 gameš and Enkidu: they pin him down with

85 A baked-clay relief plaque depicting Huwawa or Humbaba, Enlil's guardian of the Cedar Forest. Probably Isin-Larsa or Old Babylonian Period. Ht. 105mm.

their feet while Enkidu cuts off his head with his sword.

Babylonian models of the face of Humbaba (ranging in date from the Old Babylonian to the Neo-Babylonian Periods) were connected 8 with **divination**: some are inscribed with omens for 'when the intestines are like Humbaba', or 'if a woman bore [a foetus] in the shape of Huwawa' – the prognostication is always revolution in the state! It has been thought that such models were used to instruct in divination, but in the Old Babylonian Period faces of Humbaba are frequently seen on clay plaques and on seal designs, set high in the background, as if they were hung on the wall – perhaps as magical charms. The face of Humbaba was carved in stone on one side of the entrance to the Old Babylonian Period temple at Tell al-Rimah.

Huwawa/Humbaba is perhaps a form of the **Elamite god** Humban. The name and rôle of Humbaba survive in that of Kombabos, a guardian figure in a legend from Hellenistic north Syria.

hybrids: see **demons and monsters**.

hydra: see **snakes**.

Ig-alima: see **Bau; local gods**.

Igigū

Igigū or Igigi is a term introduced in the Old Babylonian Period as a name for the (ten) **'great gods'**. While it sometimes kept that sense in later periods, from Middle Babylonian times on it is generally used to refer to the gods of heaven collectively, just as the term Anunnakkū (**Anuna**) was later used to refer to the gods of the **underworld**. In the Epic of Creation, it is said that there are 300 Igigū of heaven.

Ilaba

Ilaba is now thought to be the correct reading of the name of a god whose worship was briefly but importantly prominent during the Akkadian Period, as a warrior god and personal

86 The lion-headed bird Imdugud. Detail from the carving on a stone relief dedicated by the priest Dudu, found at Ḡirsu (modern Tello). Early Dynastic Period.

deity of the kings of that dynasty. His name is sometimes found inscribed on the attractive cylinder seals of the period.

After the Akkadian Period he appears to have become almost completely obscure, and is mentioned only occasionally, as for instance on a **kudurru** of the eighth century BC. There was a temple of Ilaba at Babylon. The constellation known to the Babylonians as the Harrow is described in an astronomical explanatory text as the 'weapon of Ilaba'.

The suggestion that the god is represented 103 by the so-called 'Figure with **mace**' is without foundation.

Il-abrāt: see **Ninšubur (god)**.

Imdugud (Anzû)

Imdugud is probably the correct reading of the 86 Sumerian name of the monstrous bird who is called Anzû in Akkadian. Envisaged as bird-like but having the head of a lion, and of gigantic size so that the flapping of its wings could cause whirlwinds and sandstorms, the Imdugud was probably originally a personification of an atmospheric force (its name is used to write a word meaning 'fog' or 'mist'). Other descriptions of the Anzû indicate that it had a beak 'like a saw', and so presumably a bird's

head. In Neo-Assyrian art, a monster combining bird and lion elements may be the Anzû or the Asakku (**Asag**) (see **lion-** 6,117 **dragon**).

The Imdugud or Anzû steals the **tablet of destinies** from **Enki** (Sumerian version) or from **Enlil** (Akkadian version), and the bird is killed by **Ninurta** who eventually returns the tablet to its rightful owner. This must be a very early myth (although not attested until the Old Babylonian Period) since the Imdugud is already depicted as a heraldic animal associated with **Ninḡirsu** on the 'Stela of the Vultures' (late Early Dynastic Period) and referred to in connection with this god in a **dream** recounted by Gudea of Lagaš. The association is presumed to derive from Ninḡirsu/Ninurta's defeat of the bird (see **Slain Heroes**). On seals of the Akkadian Period, a **bird-man** is commonly shown being brought before Ea (Enki) as a prisoner, and 88 some have thought to relate this to an early version of the Imdugud/Anzû story.

In the Sumerian poem of **Lugalbanda**, when he is wandering in the Zagros mountains, the hero comes upon the Imdugud fledgling in its nest. The Imdugud and its wife soon return. In 'Gilgameš, Enkidu and the Nether World', the Imdugud and its fledgling nest in a sacred *halub* tree which **Inana** has planted in Uruk.

Later the term *anzû* is used (in the plural also) to refer to heraldic representations of the Anzû bird on buildings etc.

See: **E-kur**.

Iminbi (*Sebittu*): see **Seven (gods)**.

immortality: see **Adapa**; **dead gods**; **Gilgameš**; **Ziusura**.

Inana (Ištar)

The goddess Inana or Ištar was the most important female deity of ancient Mesopotamia at all periods. Her Sumerian name Inana is probably derived from a presumed Nin-ana, 'Lady of Heaven'; it also occurs as Innin. The sign for Inana's name (the **ring-post**) is found in the earliest written texts. Ištar (earlier Eštar), her Akkadian name, is related to that of the South Arabian (male) deity 'Athtar (see **Arabian gods**) and to that of the Syrian goddess Astarte (Biblical Ashtoreth), with whom she was undoubtedly connected.

The principal tradition concerning Inana made her the daughter of **An**, and closely connected with the Sumerian city of Uruk. According to another tradition she was the daughter of the moon god **Nanna** (Sîn) and sister of the sun god **Utu** (Šamaš). She was also regarded as daughter of **Enlil** or even of **Enki** in variant traditions. Inana's sister was **Ereškigal**, queen of the **underworld**. Her minister was the goddess **Ninšubur**. The fact that in no tradition does Inana have a permanent male spouse is closely linked to her rôle as the goddess of sexual love. Even **Dumuzi**, who is often described as her 'lover', has a very ambiguous relationship with her and she is ultimately responsible for his death. Nor were any children ascribed to her (with one possible exception, **Šara**).

It seems likely that with the persona of the classical goddess Inana/Ištar a number of originally independent, local goddesses were syncretised (see **local gods**). The most important of these was certainly the Inana of Uruk,

87 Aspects of Ištar: details of cylinder seals of the Akkadian and Neo-Assyrian Periods. The goddess is shown respectively in a state of undress, dressed to kill and (as cult statue) in astral aspect receiving worship.

where her principal shrine **E-ana** ('House of Heaven') was located. But other local forms of the goddess were recognised and received independent cults: Inana of Zabala (in northern Babylonia), Inana of Agade (especially honoured by the kings of the dynasty of Agade), Inana of Kiš; and, in Assyria, Ištar of Nineveh and Ištar of Arba'il.

Inana was also intimately associated with the goddess **Nanaya,** with whom she was worshipped at Uruk and Kiš.

87   The 'personality' of Inana/Ištar can be divided into three quite separate strains. One aspect is that of a goddess of love and sexual behaviour, but especially connected with extramarital sex and – in a way which has not yet been fully researched, notwithstanding the remarks of Herodotus on the subject – with **pros-**
124 **titution.** Inana is not a goddess of marriage, nor is she a mother goddess. The so-called
129 **Sacred Marriage** in which she participates carries no overtones of moral implication for human marriages. The sixth tablet of the Babylonian Epic of Gilgameš, in which **Gilgameš** reproaches Ištar for her treatment of a whole series of lovers, and declines to become the latest in the list, is an important source for this aspect of Ištar, as are the various Sumerian poems about Inana and her love for Dumuzi.

The second aspect of the goddess's personality is that of a warlike goddess who is fond of battle, which is proverbially described as the 'playground of Ištar'. Violent and lusting after power, she stands beside her favourite kings as they fight. In a Sumerian poem, Inana campaigns against Mount Ebih. Her journey to **Eridu** to obtain **me** and her descent to the
frontis. **underworld** are both described as intended to extend her power. Especially, Ištar of Arba'il was a war goddess for the Assyrians.

The third aspect of Inana is as the planet Venus, the morning and evening star. 'I am Inana of the sunrise', she declares in 'Inana's Descent to the Underworld'. In this form she was sometimes known under the name Ninsianna. Her transformation to this aspect is celebrated in a poem composed probably in the Kassite Period.

Other myths concerning Inana are 'Inana and Bilulu' (in which Inana turns the old woman Bilulu into a waterskin, believing her to be responsible for the death of Dumuzi); 'Inana and Šu-kale-tuda' (concerning the gardener Šu-kale-tuda), and 'Gilgameš, Enkidu and the Nether World', in the first part of which Inana transplants a sacred *halub* tree to Uruk, from the wood of which her chair and her bed are later made.

In art, Inana is usually represented as a warrior-goddess, often winged, armed to the 87
hilt, or else surrounded by a nimbus of stars. 16,41,
Even in this aspect she may betray – by her pos- 49
ture and state of dress – her rôle as goddess of sex and prostitutes. In Neo-Assyrian and Neo-Babylonian art, a female, shown full frontal and nude or nude from the waist down, who has wings and wears the **horned cap** of divinity, probably depicts Ištar more specifically in her sexual aspect.

Ištar's beast was a **lion.** Her usual symbol 16,31
was the **star** or star disc. She may also have been symbolised for a time by the **rosette.**

See **Anunītu; bull and 'winged gate'; Bull of Heaven; cow and calf; E-ana; 'hands-of-Ištar'; Išhara; La-tarāk and Lulal; nude woman; 'omega' symbol; sacrifice and offering; standards, staves and sceptres of the gods; temples and temple architecture; Zababa.**

incantations: see **demons and monsters; magic and sorcery.**

incense
Incense, scattered on lighted coals in a censer which was moved through the air to disperse a fragrant smoke, was a regular element in Babylonian religious ceremonies. Incense 'offerings' were a normal part of sacrificial rituals, and the use of incense was often called for in magical rituals also. In medical practice, incense, cedar resin or shavings, and other fumigants (usually plants) or aromatics were used as a form of fumigation.

In Old Babylonian times, a form of **divination** was practised in which omens were observed in the shape of the smoke rising from the incense.

Innin: see **Inana**.

Isimud (Usmû)

Isimud, or in Akkadian Usmû, is a minor god who functions as a minister to **Enki**/Ea. He acts as a messenger for the god in the Sumerian poems 'Enki and Ninhursaĝa' and 'Inana and Enki' (in which he tries to persuade Inana to return the **me** to her father). His name seems to be identical with a word (occurring in both masculine and feminine forms) explained in a commentary as 'with two faces', and so he can 60,88 be identified with the two-faced deity associated in Mesopotamian art with Enki.

Išhara

Išhara was a goddess who seems to have been more closely connected with the Semitic tradition than the Sumerian. Her worship may have spread into southern Mesopotamia from the Middle Euphrates region. She seems to have been associated with **Dagan**, possibly as his wife in one tradition. As a goddess of love, she is equated with Ištar (**Inana**); in other guises she is associated with war and with extispicy (see **divination**), or else appears to be

a **mother goddess**. An explanation of a ritual describes her as mother of the *Sebittu* or **Seven (gods)**. Earlier her associated animal was the *bašmu* snake (see **snakes**), replaced from late 139 Kassite times by the **scorpion**. Astronomically 130 Išhara is the constellation Scorpius.

An important goddess of the same name was worshipped in south-east Anatolia and northern Syria, within the Hurrian pantheon. She was associated with the **underworld**.

Iškur (Adad)

The god who embodied the power of storms was known to the Sumerians as Iškur. The Akkadian equivalent of this deity was Adad (also called Addu or Adda). More at home in the West Semitic area was a related deity called Wer or Mer. Most ancient Near Eastern peoples worshipped a storm god, and Adad was sometimes equated with the Hurrian god Tešup or the Kassite god Buriaš (whose name may be distantly connected with the Greek god of the north wind, Boreas) (see **Kassite gods**).

Iškur/Adad was usually regarded as the son of **An**. According to an older tradition, he was the son of **Enlil**. His wife was the goddess **Šala**, possibly of Hurrian origin, also treated as the wife of **Dagan**. His ministers were the pair of minor deities Šullat and Haniš.

88 The double-faced minister god Usmû ushers a bird-man into the presence of the water god Ea. From a cylinder seal of the Akkadian Period.

89 The weather god standing on his beast. (*left*) Iškur or Adad on lion-dragon, from a cylinder seal of the Old Babylonian Period. (*right*) Adad on his bull, from a Neo-Assyrian stela found at Arslan Tash.

The worship of Iškur probably goes back as far as the Early Dynastic Period at least: the sign for his name (the same as the sign for 'wind') appears in the earliest list of gods. Karkara, a town in Babylonia whose name was also written with the sign 'wind', was a cult centre of Adad. Later Anu (**An**) and Adad shared a double temple, with twin **ziggurats**, at Aššur.

While Iškur, associated with the Sumerian south, tended to be connected with thunderstorms, hail and flood, Adad also had a beneficial aspect as a god of fruitful rain and mountain streams, possibly in areas where rain was more important for agriculture.

A representation of **lightning** symbolised such storm gods. Adad might also (rarely) be represented, it seems, by a symbol of flowing streams. The **beast** of Iškur is thought to have been the **lion-dragon**; that of Adad was the lion-dragon or the **bull**. Storm clouds were called Adad's 'bull-calves'.

See **ring-staff**; **Sacred Marriage**; **standards, staves and sceptres of the gods**; **wedge**.

Ištar: see **Inana**.

Ištaran

The cult of the god Ištaran is attested from the late (Third) Early Dynastic Period onwards. It appears to have continued vigorously until the Middle Babylonian Period, after which his name no longer occurs in personal names. His principal rôle was as **local god** of the town of Dēr, located on the border between Mesopotamia and Elam, east of the Tigris. Ištaran's wife was known simply as Šarrat-Dēri, 'Queen of Dēr', and his minister was the **snake god** Nirah.

Already in the Early Dynastic Period we hear of Ištaran invoked as a god who will adjudicate in a border dispute between the city-states of Lagaš and Umma. It is possible that he was invoked in this case because there was a shrine of his in the locality: but also possible that he was felt to be specially qualified because of the location of his own city of Dēr. Gudea, ruler of Lagaš, mentions installing a shrine for Ištaran in the great temple of **Ninĝirsu** at Ĝirsu, and speaks of the god as a deity associated with justice.

On **kudurrus**, Ištaran's **beast** and symbol is a **snake**, probably representing Nirah.

Išum

Išum was a popular, if not very important god, known from the Early Dynastic Period onwards. He may have been connected with the Sumerian god Hendursağ, with whom he shared a wife (the goddess Ninmug). According to one text, Šamaš (**Utu**) and **Ninlil** were his parents.

The generally benevolent aspects of his character include being a protective night-watchman and a herald; he is also associated with the **underworld** and the god Erra (**Nergal**), in contrast to whose violent behaviour he acts as a calming influence.

His name may be connected with words in various Semitic languages meaning 'fire'; but he is not a god of fire (see **Gibil**).

No symbol of Išum is known.

journeys and processions of the gods

The **gods** (or rather their **cult statues**) were transported about the country by chariot and by barge (see **boats of the gods; chariots of the gods**). A group of Sumerian literary compositions concerns boat journeys by the gods (e.g. 'The Journey of **Nanna-Suen** to Nippur'), and there is plenty of non-literary evidence to show that regular journeys really took place in the Early Dynastic Period and under the Third Dynasty of Ur. Usually they were to Nippur or to **Eridu**, to obtain a 'blessing' from **Enlil**, as head of the **pantheon**, or from **Enki**, as distributor of the **me**. Frequently kings repaired or replaced the processional barge, and this was commemorated in year-names of the Third Dynasty of Ur (but only once thereafter).

'The Journey of Nanna-Suen to Nippur' describes the building of the barge, the offerings that are to be taken on board for the journey, and the six stages – presumably each a day's travel – of the 150 km journey. At each stage the barge is stopped and greeted by the goddess of the town in question, who tries to restrain Nanna-Suen from continuing on his journey. The poem is set in a world populated exclusively by gods: it may represent a 'journey of the god', in which the god's statue was

36,45

physically transported to Nippur, but in the poem it is presented as a 'real' visit by the deity of his own volition and by his own agency.

It is possible that after the Third Dynasty of Ur, when Sumer was increasingly occupied with civil and inter-state war, there was no opportunity for the splendid, leisurely progresses of the gods to continue. No year-names after 2033 BC commemorate the building or repairing of barges. However, transport of divine images certainly occurred again later in the Babylonian **New Year ceremonies**, when Nabû's statue was brought by barge from Borsippa to Babylon, and the images of all the gods were transported from **Marduk**'s temple on wagons to the quay and then upstream by barge to the *bīt akīti*.

There is a text copied in the Seleucid Period which relates the route and procedures to be followed in a pageant of the cult statue of the god Anu (**An**) at Uruk, starting at the god's temple and ending at the *bīt akīti* outside the city. On the way the procession passes the quay where Anu's barge is moored.

Kassite gods

The worship of various gods was introduced by the Kassites into Babylonia and, generally speaking, did not survive the end of their rule. Most are known only from personal names:

Harbe (equated with Babylonian **Enlil** or Anu (**An**));

Buriaš or Hudha (= Adad/**Iškur**; cf. Greek Boreas);

Šuqamuna (= **Nergal**, **Nusku**; see **birds**) and Šumalia;

Šuriaš or Sah (= Šamaš (**Utu**));

Bugaš;

Maruttaš (= **Ninurta**);

Šipak;

Turgu.

Ki

Ki is the Sumerian word for earth, and was sometimes personified as a goddess and female counterpart to **An** (heaven). In some Sumerian accounts, An copulates with Ki to produce a variety of plants. An and Ki themselves were thought to be the offspring of the goddess **Nammu** (representing the subterranean waters).

Kingu: see **Qingu**.

Kišar: see **Anšar and Kišar**.

Kittu and Mīšaru: see **good and evil**.

kudurrus

*Kudurru*s are large polished stones carrying inscriptions concerning land grants, usually involving the crown, or land sales. They are often of hard stone, including black basalt; there are rare examples of rather smaller but related monuments of baked clay. Those *kudurru*s known from excavations were found mostly in temples, standing as records of the royal grants, but it is supposed that these represent replicas of such stones placed on the boundaries of the land allotments themselves (hence the term 'boundary stone' as a common translation of *kudurru*). The stones have been found only in the south of Mesopotamia. They were perhaps introduced by the Kassites and were used from that time down to the Neo-Babylonian Period (seventh century BC). Although the form was not adopted by the Assyrians in the north, after the time of the fall of Assyria no further *kudurru*s are known.

On the upper parts of *kudurru*s or on one face were symbols of deities which were apparently 90 supposed to solemnise the agreements. Dire curses upon those who broke the agreements were included in the text, made in the names of other gods (never those whose symbols are depicted).

On some of the stones the symbols are 'labelled' with the names of the deities they 7 represent, which is a valuable source for identification of the meaning of such symbols (see Introduction). *Kudurru*s with such labelling are among those looted from Babylonia in antiquity by the Elamites and discovered in excavations at the Elamite city of

90 A carved *kudurru* with symbols of different gods, found at Sippar. The inscription on the other side of the stone records a grant of land and privileges from the Babylonian king Nebuchadnezzar I (reigned 1125–1104 BC). The carved images were thought to invoke the protection of the legal arrangements by the deities symbolised. Ht. 0.56 mm.

Susa: it has been suggested that the labels were added by the Elamites as a 'key' to the symbols of the Babylonian gods. Some of the symbols may represent constellations (see **rainbow**).

It has been thought by some that the positions of the symbols on the stones were related to the relative ranking of the deities shown, and even if not a deliberate and conscious procedure, a rough correlation is likely because the more important deities would come to mind first, the less important being added lower down on the stone if space permitted. If true, the suggestion has implications for the detailed reconstruction of Babylonian theological changes and shifts of power of different interest groups attached to the various temples.

The term 'ancient *kudurrus*' is used by scholars to refer to land exchange transactions of the Early Dynastic Period which bear no relation to the later Babylonian *kudurrus* proper.

kur

The word *kur* in Sumerian has two separate meanings. One of these is 'mountain' or, more generally, the 'mountains', especially the Zagros Mountains to the east of Mesopotamia. Because of this it can also refer to a 'foreign land' (other than Sumer) or in the plural to 'foreign countries', since the foreign countries with which Sumerians had to do, whether in war or in peaceful trade contacts, were above all those in or beyond the Zagros Mountains.

The second meaning of *kur* (which may be in origin a completely different word, a cognate of **Ki**, 'earth') is 'earth, ground', and in particular *kur* is one of the names for the world under the ground we live on: the **underworld** or abode of the dead.

Although there are no grounds for positing a Sumerian belief that the underworld was located in the mountains, it was probably believed that the entrance to the *kur* (underworld) was located in the mountains to the east of Mesopotamia where the sun could be seen to emerge every morning. Certainly in some myths the mountains (*kur*) are treated as an other-worldly locale in the same way as the underworld (*kur*) in other myths is an otherworld which deities try to visit or to obtain power over.

Labbu: see **Tišpak**.

lahama

Among the creatures associated with the Sumerian god **Enki** are the 'fifty *lahama* of the *engur*' (*engur* is a synonym of **abzu**). They are among the creatures sent to try to recover the **me** from **Inana** in the myth 'Inana and Enki'. They were especially associated with the *abzu* and with **Eridu**, but it is not known in what form they were imagined.

A secondary use of the term *lahama* in Sumerian seems to refer to guardian figures (statues) which stood in the gateways of great temples such as the **E-kur** in Nippur or the E-ninnu at Ĝirsu. These are also sometimes called '*lahama* of the *abzu*'. Again it is not known in what form they were represented.

The word *lahama* is borrowed from Old Akkadian *lahmum* (probably meaning 'hairy').

See **Lahmu**.

91 The god Lahmu ('Hairy') more than holds his own with a fierce lion. Modern impression from rolling a cylinder seal of the Neo-Babylonian Period. The inscription is a dedication of the seal 'for his life' to the god Nabû by one Nabû–šarhi–ilāni, brewer for the temple of Marduk. Ht. 44 mm.

152

Lahmu

Lahmu ('Hairy') is the name of a protective and beneficent deity, originally associated with **Enki**/Ea, later associated with **Marduk**. **Figurines** of the god, who was represented with long hair and beard (often with four or six large curls), were used in the Neo-Assyrian Period as foundation deposits to ward off **demons** and sickness. In art this figure (inappropriately termed the 'Nude Hero') is often closely associated with the *kusarikku* (see **bull-man**).

In the Babylonian Epic of Creation, Lahmu and Lahamu are a male and female pair of primordial deities (see **Anšar and Kišar**). Their names are probably derived from the same root (and do not mean 'muddy' as was formerly believed).

See **lahama**; *lahamu* under **Tiāmat's creatures**; **vase with streams**.

lama (lamassu)

The Sumerian term *lama* (Akkadian *lamassu*) refers to a beneficent protective female deity, imagined as human in form. Generally such a deity was anonymous. (The corresponding male deity was called *alad*, Akkadian *šēdu*.)

In Neo-Sumerian, Old Babylonian, Kassite and Neo-Babylonian art such goddesses are depicted in a quite consistent form, usually introducing worshippers into the presence of important deities, and wearing a long, often flounced skirt, with one or both hands raised in supplication to the major god.

Later, the related term *aladlammû* (if that is the correct reading of the cuneiform) seems to have been used to designate the winged human-headed bull and lion colossi which guarded the gateways of Assyrian palaces and temples. The corresponding winged female human-headed colossi were called *apsasû*. (See **bulls and lions with human head**.)

Lamaštu

Although she is usually described in modern works as a 'demoness', the writing of the name of Lamaštu in cuneiform suggests that in Babylonia and Assyria she was regarded as a

92 A stone stela carved with the figure of a *lamassu*, one of a pair that probably flanked the entrance to a shrine. Kassite Period. Ht. 0.84 m.

kind of goddess. As a daughter of Anu (**An**), she was above the common run of 'evil' **demons**. Unlike such demons, who acted only on the commands of the gods, Lamaštu practised evil apparently for its own sake – and on her own initiative.

Lamaštu's principal victims were unborn and newly born babies: both miscarriage and cot death were attributed to her. Slipping into the house of a pregnant woman, she tries to touch the woman's stomach seven times to kill the baby, or she 'kidnaps the child from the wet nurse'. Magical measures against Lamaštu included the wearing by a pregnant woman of a bronze head of **Pazuzu** (see **amulets**). Offerings of creatures and objects (such as centipedes and brooches) were made to tempt Lamaštu away. The so-called 'Lamaštu plaques' of metal or stone which often depict her doubtless also had a magically protective purpose. Lamaštu is shown being forced back to the **underworld** by Pazuzu. On these plaques, however, we see a bed-ridden man rather than a pregnant woman, so the plaques seem to relate to another function of Lamaštu, as a bringer of **disease**.

Lamaštu is described as having the head of a **lion**, the teeth of a donkey, naked breasts, a hairy body, hands stained (with blood?), long fingers and finger nails, and the feet of Anzû (**Imdugud**), that is, **bird talons**. Thus too, in the art of the ninth to seventh centuries BC, she is depicted, also with upright ears which resemble those of a donkey (see **donkey ears**). A piglet and a whelp suckle at her breasts; she holds **snakes** in her hands. Like other deities (see **beasts of the gods; boats of the gods**) she has her distinctive animal, a donkey, and her boat, in which she floats along the **river of the underworld**.

93 A lamp, symbol of Nusku.

lamp

The lamp occurs as a divine symbol from the Kassite to the Neo-Babylonian Periods, and is identified on the **kudurrus** as a symbol of the god **Nusku**.

Laṣ: see **Nergal**.

La-tarāk and Lulal

Either Lulal is a Sumerian god and La-tarāk is an Akkadian name for the same deity, or the two gods were originally distinct but closely related. In the later second millennium BC Lulal and La-tarāk were treated as a pair, and in Neo-Assyrian times **figurines** of them were buried at doorways as magically protective deities. It has been suggested that they might be represented visually at this time as respectively an anthropomorphic god with raised fist (see **Smiting god**) and a lion-headed human-bodied figure cloaked in a lion's pelt and carrying a whip. In a magical text they are listed among deities protective against **witchcraft**.

94 A 'lion-genius', possibly the god La-tarāk, with whip. Detail from a cylinder seal of the Neo-Assyrian Period.

Lulal is connected with the city of Bad-tibira and in the Sumerian poem 'Inana's Descent to the Underworld', Lulal has a close but unclear relationship to **Inana**. He seems to have been a warrior god, but is also connected with domestic animals.

The meaning of both names is uncertain: La-tarāk is probably connected with a word meaning 'whipping'.

lecanomancy: see **divination**.

letters to gods

Just as some Sumerian literary compositions purport to be letters sent by one famous king to another, or from a hero or mythical sage to another, others are composed in the form of a letter addressed by their authors to **gods**, or to deified kings. They are composed in ornate artistic language to incorporate some special request, and although they may originally have been composed for a specific occasion, these 'letter-prayers' seem to have been absorbed into the literary tradition.

Two letters to gods are known from the Old Babylonian Period at Mari in Syria, and others are known also from Neo-Assyrian times. Of three surviving, the most famous is in the form of a letter addressed to the god **Aššur**, the gods and goddesses of the city, the city itself and its people, and its king, Sargon II, containing an account (narrated by the king in the first person) of his eighth campaign (in 714 BC). These Neo-Assyrian letters to gods are each preserved in one text only, presumably the original which was actually offered in the god's temple and preserved there as a record – as much for future human readers as for the information of the god himself – of the king's activities as priest of the god Aššur.

libanomancy: see **divination**.

libation

The practice of libation – pouring out a liquid for ritual purposes – was an essential accompaniment to all forms of **sacrifice and offering** in ancient Mesopotamia. Sometimes cool water from a well, or holy water, was libated to the gods. In Babylonian ritual offerings to the dead, it seems that only water was used. In other rituals it was much more common to pour beer and wine (see **alcohol**), and sometimes milk, honey, oil or cream were added to these. One ritual to counteract nightmares calls for the libation of vinegar.

The liquid(s) were poured onto the ground, all around the sacrificer, from a cup, bowl or flask, sometimes made of precious materials; or else onto the head of a sacrificial sheep, or into a river or spring, or into a second vessel, or at a gateway. Libations to the dead were poured down a clay tube inserted into the ground. Normally the libation would be made before the **cult statue** of the god, or else in front of the **incense** burner or the brazier, sometimes immediately after censing or, in a **sacrifice**, after the presentation to the god of the meat offerings.

Unlike the various sacrificial foods, which were actually redistributed to the temple staff afterwards, libated liquids were not recoverable. In the case of libations to the dead, the ritual act probably was thought to be a way of giving them a drink. In hot countries the first

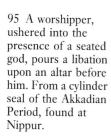

95 A worshipper, ushered into the presence of a seated god, pours a libation upon an altar before him. From a cylinder seal of the Akkadian Period, found at Nippur.

act of hospitality is to offer cool water. However, the very ancient practice of pouring drink offerings onto the ground may be connected with an idea of sacred wastefulness.

See **animal sacrifice**.

lightning (symbol)

The representation of a single lightning flash (zigzag line), found very rarely in the art of the Akkadian and Old Babylonian Periods, apparently gave way in the latter period to the double- or triple-lightning fork, which occurs thereafter until Neo-Babylonian times. It should be distinguished from the **fork** or trident. As is known from inscriptional evidence, it was at all times and in all regions a symbol of the storm god, whether Adad (**Iškur**) in Assyria or some localised deity. Sometimes it was held as an attribute by the god. On a famous monumental relief carving of the Neo-Assyrian Period, the god **Ninurta**(?) holds triple-lightning symbols, perhaps because he has taken over a mythical rôle once attributed to Adad (see **Asag**).

See **ring-staff**.

21,90,
96,151

10,89,
132

117

96 Forked lightning, symbol of the weather god.

Lil: see **Šul-pa-e**.

lilītu

The male *lilû* and the two females *lilītu* and *ardat-lilî* are a sort of family group of **demons**. They are not gods. The *lilû* haunts desert and open country and is especially dangerous to pregnant women and infants. The *lilītu* seems to be a female equivalent, while the *ardat-lilî* (whose name means 'maiden *lilû*') seems to have the character of a frustrated bride, incapable of normal sexual activity. As such, she compensates by aggressive behaviour especially towards young men. The *ardat-lilî*, who is often mentioned in magical texts, seems to have some affinities with the Jewish Lilith (e.g.

Isaiah 34:14). 'She is not a wife, a mother; she has not known happiness, has not undressed in front of her husband, has no milk in her breasts.' She was believed to cause impotence in men and sterility in women.

A plaque thought possibly to depict her shows a scorpion-tailed she-wolf about to devour a young girl.

See **nude woman**.

lion

The last lion in Mesopotamia was killed in the twentieth century AD, although the exact date is disputed. Until the end of the third millennium BC lions were common throughout the country. Thereafter they are not much mentioned in southern Mesopotamia, although on the Middle Euphrates and in Assyria they remained such a nuisance that lion-hunting, made famous by the Assyrian kings (see **animal sacrifice**), was a genuine necessity. In the Babylonian Epic of **Gilgameš**, the gods discuss whether a plague of lions would not have been a more appropriate chastisement of mankind than the **Flood**.

22

91

In literature, the lion is a favourite metaphor for warlike kings and fierce deities, especially **Ninurta** or **Inana**. A popular saying was: 'He who seizes the tail of a lion will drown in the river; he who seizes the tail of a fox will be saved.'

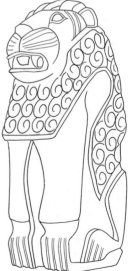

97 This colossal stone lion originally stood in the temple of Enki at Eridu. It probably dates to the Neo-Sumerian Period. Ht.1.64m.

As far as the Sumerians were concerned, the lion was grouped together with **dogs** and wolves as a 'canine', rather than as a feline.

97 Two gigantic stone lions guarded the entrance to **Enki's** temple **E-abzu** at **Eridu**: one of these is now in the Iraq Museum, Baghdad, while only fragments of the other were recovered. In the poem 'Inana and Enki', Enki entertains his daughter Inana to a beer-drinking party 'in front of the lions'. In the Neo-Assyrian Period rhyta with their bases shaped in the form of a lion's (or a ram's) head, were luxury drinking vessels.

A standing lion surmounting a standard is depicted on Sumerian stelae and on seal impressions of the time of the Third Dynasty of Ur. Since all the relevant material comes from the city of Ğirsu, the lion-standard has been regarded as an emblem of the god **Nin̄ĝirsu**.

The lion is known in the Akkadian Period as 87 the attribute of a goddess, usually a heavily *frontis.* armed deity, perhaps Ištar (**Inana**) in her guise 16 as warrior-goddess. Monumental stone lions of King Assurnasirpal II of Assyria (reigned 883–859 BC) were dedicated to an aspect of Ištar and placed at the gateway to her temple at Kalhu (modern Nimrud), and it is probably she who is represented as standing on a lion on the 31 seventh-century BC Maltai rock panels. On the same reliefs Mullissu (**Ninlil**) is enthroned on a lion. The lion also seems at least in the Neo-Assyrian Period to have been associated with the goddess Damkina (**Damgalnuna**).

On a 'Cappadocian' seal (that is, from the Old Assyrian trading colony in Anatolia), the lion is associated with a male deity who holds the **fork** emblem.

In the Neo-Assyrian Period, the natural lion is also a generally magically protective type, known as *urgulû*. An evil **demon** who lay in 98 wait in washrooms was envisaged in the form of a lion (see **lion-centaur**).

The constellation called Lion corresponds 159 to our constellation Leo (see **zodiac**).

See **bulls and lions with human head**.

lion-centaur

The so-called lion-centaur of Middle Assyrian and Neo-Assyrian art is a hybrid creature with a lion's lower body (including all four legs), and the head, upper body and arms and 98, 99 hands of a man. He often wears the **horned cap** of divinity. The creature's name was *urmahlullû*, 'lion-man'.

Representations of him were placed outside ablutions rooms, where he fended off the attacks of the leonine demon *Mukīl-rēš-lemutti*, 'Evil attendant'.

See **merman and mermaid**.

lion-demon

A human-bodied hybrid figure with the head of a lion, upright ears (see **donkey ears**) and the feet of a bird is present in Mesopotamian art from the Old Babylonian Period (and with more leonine features from the Akkadian 14

98 A 'lion-centaur' (*urmahlullû*) attacks the demon Mukīl-rēš-lemutti, shown in the form of a lion. From a cylinder seal of the Middle Assyrian Period.

99 'Lion-demons' and a 'lion-centaur' threaten and bar the way to evil forces. A monumental stone relief which stood in a niche in a room of the royal palace of the Assyrian king Assurbanipal (reigned 668–*c.*627 BC) at Nineveh. Ht. 1.47 m.

100 A so-called 'lion-dragon' or 'lion-griffin'. Detail from the carving on a *kudurru* of the late Kassite Period.

Period) until the Persian conquest, when it passed into Achaemenid, and then Seleucid, art. The demon most often (and always in the first millennium BC) raises one hand with a dagger and holds in the other, lowered, hand a mace. His torso is generally naked. Usually he wears a short kilt, but when he is fully naked he has a curly lion's tail.

At least for the Neo-Assyrian and Neo-Babylonian Periods, the type can be certainly identified as the *ugallu*, 'big weather-creature', a beneficent demon protective against evil demons and illnesses. He is depicted on Neo-Assyrian palace reliefs, and clay **figurines** of him were among those placed in houses or buried in the foundations in magically protective rituals (see **demons and monsters**). He is often associated with the figure of the **Smiting god**. On Old Babylonian seals, however, he often holds a man upside down by one leg, and is associated with the 'god with scimitar', probably the underworld god **Nergal**. It has been suggested therefore that at this early time he represents an attendant of Nergal, and is a bringer of **disease**.

lion-dragon

The lion-dragon (or lion-griffin) with lion's foreparts and bird's hind-legs, tail and wings

is represented from the Akkadian Period down to the Neo-Babylonian, including on an Assyrian wall-relief from the Temple of Ninurta at Kalhu (modern Nimrud). As the creature is often clearly male, suggested identifications as **Lamaštu** and **Tiāmat** can be discounted. It is possible that the monster is the Asakku (**Asag**) or the Anzû (**Imdugud**). A recent suggestion makes the creature sometimes the (*ūmu*) *nāʾiru*, 'roaring (weather-beast)', the animal of the god **Iškur**; this would account for the beast's wide-open mouth. A slightly variant horned lion-dragon with scorpion tail is found in Neo-Assyrian art. On the rock reliefs, probably of Sennacherib, at Maltai, three different gods stand upon such a beast, probably **Aššur**, Sîn (**Nanna-Suen**) and Adad (**Iškur**).

See **griffin**.

lion-fish

A motif on Old Babylonian seals is a figure with the head of a lion and the body of a fish. Its significance is unknown.

lion-garbed figure: see **La-tarāk and Lulal**.

lion-headed bird: see **Imdugud**.

Margin references: 99; 4,32, 151; 55; 100; 6,117; 45,89, 132; 31; 53

lion-headed staves: see **standards, staves and sceptres of the gods.**

lion-humanoid

101 In Kassite, Neo-Assyrian and Seleucid art we find, if rarely, a minor deity (in **horned cap**), human above the waist but with two lion's legs and lion's hind-quarters, including a curled-over lion's tail. **Figurines** of the type are some-times paired with those of a **bull-man** and the creature may similarly be associated with Šamaš (**Utu**). In any event he seems to be a late invention based upon the bull-man and the **scorpion-man**. He is a protective figure. His Akkadian name seems to have been *uridimmu*, which could be translated as 'mad lion' (literally, 'mad canine').

lion with human head: see **bulls and lions with human head**.

Lisin

The goddess Lisin, together with her brother Ašgi, was worshipped in the Sumerian cities of Adab and Keš. Her husband was Ninsikila, but later his name was misinterpreted as that of a goddess, and Lisin was accordingly treated as a god. In Sumerian times she was sometimes called 'Mother Lisin' and, as a **mother god-dess**, was either equated with **Ninhursaǧa** or regarded as a daughter of Ninhursaǧa. As the name of a star, Lisin is α Scorpionis.

lists of gods

Detailed lists of **gods** were prepared by the peoples of ancient Mesopotamia for pedagogic use in the training of scribes; clearly they are also extremely useful to us for collecting information about Mesopotamian religion. Already in the early third millennium BC tra-ditional lists were being recorded in writing: sometimes arranged by graphic principles, but more often arranged according to the theological importance of the gods listed, and so of great interest. Some lists have an explana-tory subcolumn giving extra details about the divinities, and the largest list gives the names of nearly 2,000 gods. Typically they are

101 A leonine human figure as protective demon. Drawing of a (now lost) monumental stone relief found at Nineveh in the royal palace of Assurbanipal, king of Assyria (668–*c*.627 BC). Drawn by W. Boutcher, artist to the archae-ological excavations, in *c*.1854.

arranged with the deity followed by his or her spouse, then their eldest son, his wife and family and attendants, then the rest of their offspring, and finally the 'courtiers' (minister, administrator, throne-bearer, gatekeeper – all gods) of the principal pair. It is fascinating to study the reordering of these lists as the theological ranking of the gods changes with the passage of time, as minor gods become amalgamated into one personality, or as epi-thets of major divinities are separated off and invested with divine status of their own. Some deities even change sex.

See **pantheon**.

local gods

One of the most ancient features of Mesopotamian religion was the survival of local gods and goddesses – deities special to individual towns or villages. The sense of place was highly developed among the peoples of ancient Mesopotamia and it is entirely in keeping with the original development of urban settlement in this part of the world that local deities – urban religion – should be a feature of the **pantheon**. Generally speaking a deity is identified as special to a particular town if the town is associated with his or her name in epithets, if there is a temple to them in the town, if administrative or other documents reveal the existence of a localised cult to them, or if personal names incorporating the name of the deity are specially common in a particular area. There are very few Mesopotamian deities who are not specially associated with some town or other where their cult was pre-eminent, but whereas some remained minor gods whose cult was later eclipsed, others rose in stature from local to national deities. The process of political development played its part in this: a city which became the capital of an empire would export the cult of its local gods.

In some cities a group of local deities – sometimes linked together in family relationships – was worshipped. The Early Dynastic Sumerian city-state of Lagaš provides a good example of this, where a complex localised pantheon consisting of two family groups developed, probably derived from the fusing of cults local to the town and villages which made up the city-state:

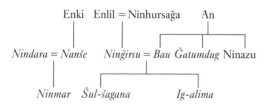

(Specifically local deities are in italics, although some of these were also worshipped elsewhere.)

At other cities, the local deity had no more

individuality than a name based on that of the geographical locality, such as Šarrat-Dēri, 'Queen of Dēr', or Bēl-Mê-Turān, 'Lord of Mê-Turān'. Some deities appear to have had several local cults, for example **Inana** of Uruk, Inana of Zabala, Ištar (Inana) of Arba'il, Ištar of Nineveh and Ištar of Agade, a situation which may have developed from an identification of originally local deities with more prestigious national gods.

See **temples and temple architecture**.

love charms: see **magic and sorcery**.

lozenge: see **rhomb**.

Lugalbanda

The hero Lugalbanda was a deified king of the Sumerian city of Uruk. His wife was the goddess **Ninsun**. In most literary traditions they were regarded as the parents of **Gilgameš**. Lugalbanda is mentioned together with Ninsun in a **list of gods** as early as the Early Dynastic Period, and a short fragment of a literary composition about him dates from the same period. All the kings of the Third Dynasty of Ur sacrificed to the divine Lugalbanda at Nippur, and in the praise poetry addressed to these kings it is common to find Lugalbanda and Ninsun described as the king's divine 'parents' (which made Gilgameš the king's brother). Lugalbanda was also worshipped at Kuara near Uruk and at Umma.

In two heroic narrative poems, Lugalbanda succeeds in crossing dangerous mountains on his own, despite a near-fatal illness, and he clearly has a special connection with **Inana**. The Sumerian King List describes him as a shepherd who ruled Uruk for 1,200 years.

Lugal-irra and Meslamta-ea

Lugal-irra was a minor god whose name probably means 'mighty lord' and who was identified with **Nergal** in late tradition. Together with his twin, the god Meslamta-ea, Lugal-irra was worshipped at Kisiga, a town in northern Babylonia. Perhaps originally they

102 (*right*) The gods Lugal-irra and Meslamta-ea, the 'Great Twins'. From a chalcedony amuletic pendant of the Neo-Assyrian Period.

103 (*far right*) The 'Figure with mace' on a cylinder seal of the Old Babylonian Period.

were thought to stand at the entrance to the **underworld** ready to dismember the dead as they entered: certainly they were considered to be efficacious in guarding doorways, and in Neo-Assyrian times small images of them were buried at entrances, Lugal-irra on the left and Meslamta-ea on the right, identical figures in 102 **horned caps** each carrying an axe and a mace.

Astronomically, Lugal-irra and Meslamta-ea were named the Great Twins (Gemini). (The name Lugal-irra was formerly read Lugalgirra.)

Lulal: see **La-tarāk and Lulal**.

mace
103 A common representation on seals of the Old Babylonian and Kassite Periods is a male figure with prominent splayed beard, wearing a rounded cap and short wrap-around robe knotted on one hip. He strikes a distinctive posture: head and lower body in profile, farther leg forward, upper body twisted to a three-quarter view, one arm held loose by the side, the other bent at the elbow with the hand held majestically to the lower chest (in the style of

the Roman toga-wearer). In this hand the figure often, but not always, carries a mace, probably a mark of his authority. It has been thought that the figure represents a god (**Ilaba**, **Ninšubur (god)**, **Martu** or any **local god**), or, since he often stands upon a podium, the **cult statue** of a god. More recently he has usually been designated as the 'Figure (rather than god) with mace' and interpreted as a generalised representation of the king or of a deified former king.

See **lion-demon**; **Lugal-irra and Meslamta-ea**.

magic and sorcery
Magic was a normal aspect of life in ancient 104 Mesopotamia, and did not belong to a disapproved area. In a world in which one was interminably threatened by supernatural **demons** and by human sorcerers, and hemmed about by **taboos** and **oaths**, and where past, present and future were inextricably interrelated by the observation of (sometimes avertible) portents, it was normal to use white magical means, among others, to bring comfort and, possibly, healing. However, sorcery (deliberately harmful

black magic) was regarded as evil because of its social effects, but very probably its methods were the same as those used in standard magical practice.

Magic was used to insure against, to drive away or to overcome demons; to undo the bad effects of certain 'sinful' actions (usually social misdemeanours); to counteract the potential effects of certain portended events; to increase sexual potency (see **prostitution and ritual sex**); to secure the favours of a loved one; to quieten squalling infants; and, among many other functions, to frustrate the activity of hostile sorcerers.

These practices presuppose certain views of the world, namely that there is a host of demons who cause ills of all sorts, especially sickness; that human beings can bring 'sin' (Akkadian *arnu* and other words, envisaged as a sort of illness) upon themselves by unwittingly infringing taboos or committing 'sinful' acts, or disturbing the world order; that they can be bewitched by other humans; and that when ill portents are divined, their ill effect can be dissipated in advance by magic, that is, that the predetermined future can to some extent be redetermined.

Clearly the practice of magic is very close to both medicine and **divination**, and sometimes difficult to separate from them (see **diseases and medicine**). Medicine – 'scientific', surgical, herbal – certainly existed, but (since the cause of sickness was often thought to be demons) magic was often used in addition to decoctions, poultices, ointments, enemas, etc. They were carried out by the same person, the *āšipu*. Another specialist, the *asû*, was more specifically a physician. Divination was carried out by the diviner, but an *āšipu* was needed to avert the effects of ill portents. *Āšipū* might be

104 A reconstruction, in a painting by H. M. Herget, of a ritual scene that might have taken place in Assryia or Babylonia in about the 7th century BC. A priest attends a sick man, while fish-garbed figures (real or imagined) protect and purify. A diviner consults a model of a sheep's liver. See ill.151.

attached to temples as part of their clergy. (See **priests and priestesses**.)

The forms in which Babylonian magic survives to us are incantations or spells in Sumerian, Akkadian and sometimes other languages such as Elamite or Hurrian, sometimes garbled but rarely complete mumbo jumbo; 'rituals', that is, systematic descriptions (addressed to the magician) of the actions to be followed, including a list of the incantations to be used at certain points, said either by the magician or by the 'patient'; **amulets**, usually inscribed with excerpts from well-known incantations and worn around the neck, or occasionally hung on the wall of a house; and apotropaic **figurines**.

The very earliest incantations which survive date from the Early Dynastic Period, about 2400 BC, but are very difficult to read unless a clearer duplicate text of later date gives assistance. Some are intended to protect against snake-bite, against scorpions, to assist in childbirth or to consecrate objects used in magical rituals, and they are important mainly as they presuppose the existence of such rituals already at this date. By the Old Babylonian Period it is clear that the process had begun by which individual incantations in Sumerian were grouped together according to their function or the demons they were intended to give protection against. The first Akkadian interlinear translations also date from this period. This is not to imply that magical practices were already becoming matters merely of curiosity – far from it – but it does show that the magical literature had by then entered the stream of written tradition, as well as being handed on by word of mouth.

Broadly speaking, four types of incantation can be distinguished. First, those in which the magician, often addressing the demons directly, legitimates himself as the representative of those gods especially associated with white magic (**Enki**/Ea, his wife **Damkina**, and **Asarluhi** – a god of Kuara near **Eridu**, later considered as Enki's son and hence identified with **Marduk**) in order to protect himself against the demons during the course of the

ritual. These generally end 'Be conjured by heaven! Be conjured by the underworld!' Second, incantations designed to protect lay persons from the attacks of demons: the demons are first described, then banished. The third type of incantation also begins with a detailed description of the demons and what they have done. In a short narrative section, Marduk 'notices' and goes to his father Ea for advice. Ea replies in a formulaic phrase, 'My son, what is there that you don't know? What can I add? All that I know, you also know', but goes on to give appropriate ritual advice. The ritual procedure is thus encapsulated in the text of the incantation itself. In medical incantations, the narrative section is regularly absent because the ritual procedure to be followed is abstracted and recorded separately; but it was obviously a convenient way of preserving the correct ritual when the magical tradition was transmitted entirely by memorisation. Finally, there is a type of incantation addressed not to demons or to gods of white magic but to the cultic objects that are to be used in the ritual. By being 'enchanted' the objects become more effective in their magical function. These are generally a variety of perfectly ordinary objects: the stove or brazier with the fire in, onions, branches of dates, reed matting, a flock of wool, goat's hair, red-dyed wool, **flour**, tamarisk branches, reeds, salt, cedar or juniper, aromatic resins, **incense**, sea water and so on.

One of the best-preserved Babylonian magical collections is that called *Šurpu* ('burning'), also one of the most interesting in content. *Šurpu* is performed when the magician's client does not know by what act or omission he has offended the gods and disturbed the world order. The client, or patient, has come to the magician 'in a critical state, worried, sleepless, ill', sometimes convulsing, foaming at the mouth, struck dumb, or suffering from headaches – symptoms some of which we might refer to a psychiatrist. In the ritual all possible 'sins' are exhaustively enumerated, including the effects of the 'oath' – either a broken oath returning in the form of a curse, or an oath sworn in good faith but arousing thereby magical powers which could be sources of evil. The 'burning' is a part of the ritual in which the patient peels an onion into the fire, strips dates from a branch into the fire or unravels matting into the fire, all the while reciting incantations in which the 'undoing' of his sins is compared to the activity he is performing. Finally the magician extinguishes the fire, and the sins. Clearly, to the extent that the patient's troubles are psychological in origin, the ritual might have a calming effect on him.

Quite different in nature are the incantation rituals called in Akkadian *namburbû*, which are intended to undo or avert the effect of future evil detected in advance by portents (see **divination**). Typically a *namburbû* ritual involves a sequence of five rites. First, enclosure rites are performed, designed to separate off the ritual site from the world outside, perhaps by performing them inside a reed hut, or by delimiting the area with a **magic circle**. Then, in **purification** rites, the patient is washed, bathed, shaved; tamarisk is used to asperge and incense to fumigate; the area is swept clean, possibly a goat is sacrificed (see **animal sacrifice**); a copper **bell** is rung and a drum beaten. Next, food and aromatics are offered to the gods and to the deified River (because it will carry away waste matter). The principal rites are apotropaic and might consist of the destruction, for instance, of an ominous, monstrous animal birth; the sealing up of a doorway (with bat's blood, crushed spider and fly, and scorpion); substitution or simulation, e.g. making an image where the object concerned is itself inaccessible, or touching parts of a building as a symbolic destroying of the whole of an accursed house. The final rites involve further purification, unravelling plants, or actions restoring the patient to the outside world again (he is told not to look round as he leaves, or is told to go and enter a tavern), and magical prescriptions to be followed for a particular period (to avoid garlic, to wear a special necklace for seven days).

Some aspects of these rites recur in the long nocturnal ritual known as *Maqlû* (also meaning

'burning'), performed when the patient is convinced he has been bewitched. The text is always careful to specify 'sorcerer *or* sorceress' but the verb forms are usually feminine, suggesting that fear of witches was more prevalent than fear of wizards. 'She goes about in the street, enters houses . . . stands in the street. By her look she has taken the pleasure of a young woman . . . When the sorceress saw me, she walked behind me; she crossed my path with her magic; she has taken away my (personal) god and goddess', and so on. Figurines of wax, wood, dough, bitumen or clay are melted or burnt in the fire – representing, of course, the sorcerer. The incantations are addressed to the gods of the **night**, the fire god **Gibil** or other gods, or else to the sorcerers themselves.

The above are merely examples from the copious magical literature. One question prompted by study of the literature is who exactly used these rituals, who resorted to the services of the magician? Certainly there is no doubt that some of the very long and complicated rituals were performed only for socially very highly placed, perhaps wealthy, people. One cannot imagine that the magicians gave so much of their time and skill free of charge. Certain of the rituals were specifically envisaged for the king – for instance those designed to ward off the evil portended by lunar eclipses (see **human sacrifice**), since celestial omens typically concerned the king or the state directly. At the other end of the scale, we can probably say that all classes regarded the use of magic as more or less normal, and shared the view of the world which made its practice possible. But for most of these people we have no surviving evidence. We know nothing, either, of the practices of sorcerers and how sorcery was carried out. It may have been very similar to the magic used to counteract it, or it may have been less refined and more simple.

A development can be recognised in the history of Babylonian and Assyrian magical practices. The gradual grouping of related incantations, already referred to, into collections (so-called 'series') presupposes more than mere editorial activity on the part of magician scholars, since the series are organised into, and accompanied by directions for, complex rituals in which the sequence of actions and incantations is crucially important. The incantations have been gathered from various sources and woven into a ritual sequence in the belief that proliferation of the magic would make it more effective. A single example may be given: two copies of the 'same' ritual exist, separated by a thousand years, in which the number of paraphernalia required, in this case cylinder seals hung around the neck of the patient, has been increased from one to nine, evidently in the belief that the magic would thereby become the more powerful.

magic circle

In magical rituals it is common to demarcate a circle by sprinkling a trickle of **flour** on the ground (Akkadian *zisurrû*, literally 'flour which makes a boundary'). The patient or, if the patient is too ill to move, the patient's bed, may be surrounded by such a magic circle. Ritual actions are carried out inside the circle, and magical **figurines** may be surrounded with a circle of flour. It is said that the power of the circle is such that certain **demons** cannot enter it, and in commentaries the circle is 'explained' as symbolising certain protective deities.

In other rituals a magic circle might be painted in whitewash or dark wash to the left and right of a doorway, for apotropaic purposes.

magical figurines: see **building rites and deposits; demons and monsters; figurines**.

Magillum-boat: see **boat with human head; Slain Heroes**.

Maltese cross: see **cross**.

Mami (Mama): see **mother goddesses and birth goddesses**.

Mamītu: see **Nergal**.

Mamu

An originally Sumerian deity, one of several associated with **dreams** (*mamud* being the Sumerian word for 'dream'), Mamu was sometimes regarded as female (and a daughter of the god **Utu**) and sometimes as male (and referred to as 'god of dreams'). When Assurnasirpal II of Assyria (reigned 883–859 BC) refounded the town of Imgur-Enlil (modern Balawat), he built a temple there to a god whose name is written in the same way, possibly in origin a local deity with a similar name.

Marduk

The god Marduk was the patronal god of the city of Babylon from at least as early as the Third Dynasty of Ur. His worship is attested as early as the Early Dynastic Period, although nothing further is known of his origin. The conventional writing of his name with the signs meaning literally 'bull-calf (of) the sun' is probably a popular etymology. Later on Marduk was often known simply as Bēl (Lord).

Quite early on, Marduk seems to have absorbed the personality of a local deity of the **Eridu** region, **Asarluhi**, who was regarded as a son of **Enki**; consequently Marduk became the son of Enki/Ea. Marduk's great shrine was the temple called **Esagil** at Babylon, where he was worshipped together with his wife Ṣarpānītu. Occasionally the goddess **Nanaya** was treated as his wife. **Nabû**, worshipped at nearby Borsippa, became in due course the son of Marduk.

The rise of the cult of Marduk is closely connected with the political rise of Babylon from city-state to the capital of an empire. From the Kassite Period Marduk became more and more important until it was possible for the author of the Babylonian Epic of Creation to maintain that not only was Marduk king of all the gods but that many of the latter were no more than aspects of his persona – hence the hymn of the Fifty Names of Marduk incorporated into the Epic, to which a contemporary **list of gods** adds sixty-six more.

Marduk was also a popular god in Assyria, from about the fourteenth century BC. Because of his supreme position, it is difficult to identify specific traits in his character, but **magic** and wisdom (derived from his connection with Asarluhi), water and vegetation (connected with his father Ea) and judgement (suggesting a connection with the sun god Šamaš (**Utu**)) can be adduced. In the reign of Sennacherib (704–681 BC), however, some aspects of Marduk's cult, mythology and rituals were attributed to the Assyrian state god **Aššur**.

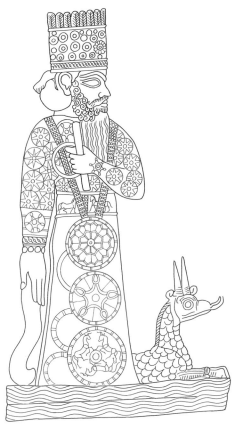

105 The god Marduk and his snake-dragon (*mušhuššu*). Detail from a large lapis lazuli cylinder dedicated to Marduk by the Babylonian king Marduk-zākir–šumi I (reigned *c.*854–819 BC). According to the accompanying inscription, the cylinder was to be set in gold and hung around the neck of the god, i.e. to be attached to the cult statue in Esagil, Marduk's temple in Babylon. It was found at Babylon in the house of a bead-maker of the Parthian Period.

The worship of Marduk in its most extreme form has been compared with monotheism, but it never led to a denial of the existence of other gods, or to the exclusion of female deities.

In the Epic of Erra (see **Nergal**), when the god Erra wants to unseat Marduk so that temporarily he, Erra, can rule the world, Marduk is presented, possibly with humorous intent, in a very uncharacteristic form as a bumbling old incompetent whose insignia need repairing and cleaning.

Marduk's symbol of a triangular-headed 141 **spade** or hoe, the *marru*, may possibly reflect an origin of the god as a local agricultural deity. The **snake-dragon** (*mušhuššu*) as animal of 158 Marduk and Nabû was taken over from **Tišpak**, local god of Ešnunna, possibly soon after the conquest of that city by Hammurabi of Babylon.

See **New Year ceremonies**; **Sacred Marriage**.

marru: see **Marduk**; **spade (symbol)**.

Martu (Amurru)

The god Martu (Akkadian Amurru) is a god who destroys cities and rages over the land like a storm. He was regarded as a son of **An**, and was sometimes said to be a son of **Ninhursaǧa**. According to some traditions his wife was Bēlet-ṣēri ('Lady of the Desert') or else Ašratu. There seems little doubt that he represents a personification of the nomadic peoples of the desert who began to appear on the horizon of settled Mesopotamia at least as early as the later third millennium BC, originally from the west, but gradually infiltrating the Mesopotamian area so that they also occupied lands to the east in the foothills of the Zagros. The first waves of these people were called Martu in Sumerian, and we tend to use the Biblical term 'Amorites'. The name of the god Martu, or Amurru, is used in personal names from the end of the third millennium BC.

In a Sumerian poem called 'The Marriage of Martu', the daughter of the god **Numušda**, patron god of the city Kazallu in southern

Babylonia, insists on marrying Martu even though he 'digs up truffles in the foothills, eats raw flesh, and has no permanent home' – a partially accurate description of a desert nomad even today. The poem clearly indicates an attempt to absorb this god of the nomads into the general **pantheon** of Mesopotamia. The metaphor of a storm was frequently employed to describe the incursions of these people who 'knew nothing of agriculture'.

In Old Babylonian and early Kassite art, Amurru is represented as a god in long robes who carries a **crook** or a scimitar, and is sometimes associated with a gazelle. Chronologically the occurrence of this figure in art corresponds roughly with the flourishing of the god's cult in Babylonia, and the figure of a man with a crooked stick might be thought an appropriate form for a god of travelling nomads.

In Akkadian *amurru* continued to be used as the normal word for 'west'. It was also a name of the star group Perseus.

See **mace**.

106 The god Amurru. Detail from a cylinder seal of the Old Babylonian Period.

maškim: see **demons and monsters**.

me

The Sumerian term *me* (pronounced 'may'; rendered by Akkadian *parṣū*) is a plural, inanimate noun, and expresses a very basic concept in Sumerian religion. The *me* are properties or powers of the **gods** which enable a whole host of activities central to civilised human life, especially religion, to take place. A related term, *ǧiš-hur* ('plan, design'), denotes how these activities ought, ideally, to be: the *me* are the powers which make possible the implementation of the *ǧiš-hur* and which ensure the continuation of civilised life. They are ancient, enduring, holy, valuable. Mostly they are held by **An** or **Enlil**, but they can be assigned or given to other gods of, by implication, lesser rank. Some *me* are conceived in very concrete terms – the throne of kingship (symbolising the activity of kingship) or a temple drum (symbolising the performance of ritual music) – and consequently are sometimes said to be 'carried', 'worn', 'sat on'. In times of social upheaval the *me* may be 'dispersed', 'forgotten' or 'gathered together and stood in a corner'. In the poem 'Inana and Enki', the two gods gamble drunkenly over the *me*, and **Inana** wins them all from her father **Enki**.

medicine: see **diseases and medicine**.

melam and ni

Melam and *ni* are two Sumerian words which are often linked. Strictly speaking *ni* seems to denote the effect on human beings of the divine power *melam* (Akkadian *melammu*). The Babylonians used various words to capture the idea of *ni*, including *puluhtu*, 'fear'. The exact connotation of *melam* is difficult to grasp. It is a brilliant, visible glamour which is exuded by **gods**, heroes, sometimes by kings, and also by temples of great holiness and by gods' symbols and emblems. While it is in some ways a phenomenon of light, *melam* is at the same time terrifying, awe-inspiring. *Ni* can be experienced as a physical creeping of the flesh. Both Sumerian and Akkadian are rich in words to describe this phenomenon and its effects. Gods are sometimes said to 'wear' their *melam* like a garment or a crown, and like a garment or a crown, *melam* can be 'taken off'. If the god is killed (see **dead gods**), his *melam* disappears. While it is always a mark of the supernatural, *melam* carries no connotation of moral value: **demons** and terrifying giants can 'wear' it too.

Meme: see **Gula**.

merman and mermaid

A figure with the head, arms and torso of a man but with the lower body and tail of a fish exists in most periods of Mesopotamian art from Old Babylonian times onwards. In the Middle Assyrian Period he may have been displaced by the analogously composed **lion-centaur**, 98 but if so he was revived as a popular figure in Neo-Assyrian times. Continuing into the Achaemenid and Seleucid Periods, the figure is perhaps the prototype for the merman figure in Greek and medieval European art and literary tradition. To the Assyrians, the creature was known simply as *kulullû*, 'fish-man', and with the *girtablullû* (**scorpion-man**) and

107 A swimming merman. Detail from a monumental stone relief from the royal palace of the Assyrian king Sargon II (reigned 721–705 BC) at Dūr-Šarkēn (modern Khorsabad). Ht. of figure 255 mm.

108 A stylised tree flanked by a 'fish-garbed figure' and a merman and mermaid. Detail from a cylinder seal of the Neo-Assyrian Period.

urmahlullû ('lion-man', the lion-centaur) he forms a group of analogous human-animal hybrids. Together with other **demons and monsters**, representations of these figures were used in Neo-Assyrian art for the purpose of

107 protective **magic**, both as monumental palace and temple sculpture and as small protective

70 **figurines**. Although of a general protective nature, and not the symbol of a specific deity, the merman sometimes appears to have a special and understandable relationship to the water-god Ea (**Enki**), and is known as one of the creatures of the *apsû* (**abzu**).

108 In Old Babylonian, Neo-Assyrian and Neo-Babylonian art, a female version of the figure (half fish and half woman) occasionally appears, and may be the *kuliltu*, possibly meaning 'fish-woman'.

See **goat-fish**.

Meslamta-ea: see **Lugal-irra and Meslamta-ea**; **Nergal**.

minister deities: see **gods and goddesses**.

mongoose
The mongoose or palm-rat is often found in southern Mesopotamia. Ningilin (Ninkilim) is the name of a goddess (or possibly a god) who was connected with the mongoose, the Akkadian word for which was later written with the deity's name. Ningilin may at an early date have been confused with a god of **magic** called Ningirima, who was invoked in spells to drive away **snakes**. In a Babylonian popular saying, a mouse who has fled from a mongoose into a snake's hole greets the snake with: 'I bring you greetings from the snake-charmer!' Since snakes are the natural prey of mongooses it is easy to see how the deity and the mongoose came to be associated.

In Old Babylonian glyptic art, a creature with something of the appearance of the mongoose is a common motif, but is of unknown significance.

monsters: see **demons and monsters**.

morality: see **divine intervention**; **good and evil**; **sin**.

mother goddesses and birth goddesses
The term 'mother goddess' is widely used 109 in popular writing about polytheistic, pre-modern or so-called primitive religions, with great variety of meaning, and considerable overlap with other terms like 'earth mother', 'earth goddess' or '**fertility** goddess'. It is common to assume the existence of such female deities for prehistoric periods on archaeological or artistic evidence alone, although it is often impossible to distinguish what might be representations of such a goddess from, for example, **figurines** of a pregnant woman made in connection with magical attempts to secure conception or an easy delivery.

For the historical periods of the ancient Mesopotamian past we have fairly definite information about mother goddesses and birth goddesses. Since one image for the **creation** of natural forces or **gods** was the sexual act performed between two deities, there is a sense in which any goddess could become a 'mother goddess' – a goddess who is a mother – and

109 A goddess with newly born babies, probably Nintu as 'lady of birth'. Baked clay relief plaque probably of the Isin-Larsa or Old Babylonian Period. Ht. 115 mm.

many examples could be given. However, usually motherhood of most of the early gods was ascribed to one particular goddess who by the second millennium BC appears under a variety of interchangeable names, some of which are really titles, but who may in origin have been several different deities. These are:

Aruru;

Mami or Mama (clearly 'mother');

Dingirmah ('exalted deity');

Ninmah ('exalted lady');

Nintu ('lady of birth');

Ninmena ('lady of the crown');

Bēlet-ilī ('lady of the gods' in Akkadian);

Nammu.

Damgalnuna seems earlier to be a mother goddess but later to have a more specialised rôle as the wife of **Enki** (and hence mother of **Marduk**). Ninmah's name was changed by her son **Ninurta** to **Ninhursağa** ('lady of the mountains') to commemorate his creation of the mountains. Nammu is usually creatrix of **An** and **Ki**, and of the early gods, including Enki, but she also creates mankind in one poem (see **creation**).

The making of a figurine of clay which is then brought to life is another image for creation. Usually it is a goddess (under one of the above names) who pinches off and moulds the clay, especially in connection with the creation of mankind (although occasionally Enki is responsible), and she becomes thereby a mother goddess in a second sense. An additional goddess sometimes acts as 'midwife' in both these types of creation, and these divine midwives can conveniently be termed birth goddesses.

The term *šassūru*, meaning in Akkadian literally 'womb', is sometimes used to refer to the mother goddess herself. But in the complex account of the creation of the first seven men and seven women in the Epic of Atra-hasīs (**Ziusura**), the mother goddess is assisted by fourteen *šassūrātu*, each of whom oversees the

'shaping' or 'preparing' of one of the clay figurines during a period of ten (lunar) months.

Finally, to complete the clay figurine imagery, we may note that in the Atra-hasīs story, Enki assists Mami as she mixes the clay and blood – clay for moulding or potting must be prepared by levigating beforehand – and, likewise, in the poem 'Enki and Ninmah', the creatures called *sig-en-sig-du* nip off the clay into lumps for Nammu to mould after she has first kneaded it, while Ninmah acts as midwife. This fourth function is not necessarily performed by a female deity. In addition, in this case, seven minor goddesses 'stand by' to assist Nammu, presumably as servants might be in attendance at a birth.

See **Anunītu**; **Išhara**; **Lisin**; **Ninlil**; **nude woman**; **'omega' symbol**. For the birth goddess Erua, see **Ṣarpānītu**.

Mullissu: see **Ninlil**.

mušhuššu: see **snake-dragon**.

Nabû

Nabû (earlier Nabium; Biblical Nebo) is the Mesopotamian scribe god, the divine scribe of the destinies. As such he is also a scribes' god and patron of writing, although no myths are related about him. Because so much learning was transmitted in writing, he later joined Ea (**Enki**) and **Marduk** as a god of wisdom, and in some traditions he absorbed attributes of **Ninurta** and was therefore associated with irrigation and agriculture. His spouse was the goddess Tašmētu. He may have been identified with the planet Mercury.

The worship of Nabû may have reached Babylonia from Syria with the nomadic Amorites in the early second millennium BC. His cult centre came to be at Borsippa near Babylon, and he was absorbed into the circle of the god Marduk, first as Marduk's minister and later (from the Kassite Period) as his son. Later **Nisaba** was regarded as his wife. At the **New Year ceremonies**, Nabû was brought from Borsippa to 'visit' his father Marduk at Babylon (see **purification**). In time Nabû

110 The scribal god Nabû holding his wedge-shaped writing stylus and standing on his snake-dragon. (The god's eye is obliterated on the original and is restored in this drawing.) Detail from a cast copper or bronze amuletic plaque of the Neo-Assyrian Period.

became supreme god of Babylonia alongside Marduk. In Neo-Assyrian times his worship was accepted in Assyria too and he almost became an 'Assyrian' god in the reigns of Esarhaddon (680–669 BC) and Assurbanipal (668–*c.* 627 BC).

154   A symbol of Nabû is a single **wedge**, vertical or horizontal, possibly a writing stylus, sometimes resting on a clay tablet. Occasionally this, or the god himself, is shown riding on the back 31,110 of a **snake-dragon**.

The worship of Nabû was long-lived and spread outside Mesopotamia among expatriate communities of Aramaic-speakers in Egypt and Anatolia during the fourth century BC. By the time of Augustus a Mesopotamian pan-

theon of gods including Nabû was being worshipped in central and northern Syria at Palmyra and Dura Europos, and survived until at least the second century AD. In post-Babylonian Mesopotamia, Nabû's cult continued and he was identified by the Greeks with Apollo.

See **Arabian gods**; **Dilmunite gods**; **Enzag**; **Ezida**; **Sacred Marriage**.

Nammu

Nammu was a goddess who was considered, in some traditions, to have given birth to **An** (heaven) and **Ki** (earth) and to many more of the more ancient **gods**. Especially she was regarded as the mother of **Enki**. She came to be thought of as one of the **mother goddesses**.

Her name is written with the same sign as *engur*, a synonym of **abzu**, and it is probable that she was originally a personification of the subterranean ocean.

Namrasīt: see **Nanna-Suen**.

Namtar

Namtar or Namtaru was a minor deity who acted as minister of **Ereškigal**, queen of the **underworld**. In one tradition he was the offspring of **Enlil** and **Ninlil**. The same name was also given to one of the **demons** of the nether regions, a harbinger of death. Originally Sumerian *namtar* meant 'destiny' or 'fate'.

Nanaya

The goddess Nanaya, who seems to have shared some of the sexual aspects of **Inana**, was worshipped together with her daughter Kanisura (Akkadian Uṣur-amassa) and Inana of Uruk in a sort of trinity of goddesses at Uruk, and later at Kiš, during the Old Babylonian Period. Later Nanaya's name was used in cultic texts to denote little more than another aspect of Inana/Ištar.

See **Sacred Marriage**.

Nanibgal: see **Ennugi**; **Nisaba**.

Nanna-Suen (Sîn)

In ancient Mesopotamia both the sun and the
111 moon were male deities. In Sumerian, the
moon god was called Suen or Nanna (Nannar),
and sometimes he was called by both names
together, Nanna-Suen. In Akkadian, Suen was
later pronounced Sîn. Other names included
Ašimbabbar, Namraṣīt ('Who shines forth') and
Inbu ('the Fruit', perhaps referring to the
natural waxing and waning of the moon). His
name is also written simply with the number 30,
the number of days in a lunar month.

Nanna was the son of **Enlil** and **Ninlil**. The
story of Enlil's rape of the young goddess is
told in a Sumerian poem: Enlil was banished
by the other gods, but Ninlil followed him,
already pregnant with Nanna. Nanna's wife
was the goddess **Ningal**, and their children
were **Utu**, the sun god, and the goddess **Inana**.

The most important shrine of Nanna was the
temple E-kiš-nu-ğal at Ur, but another cult
centre which became of great importance in the
Neo-Babylonian Period was the temple at Harran in northern Syria, where under the name
Sîn the god was worshipped together with
Nusku as his son. The temple at Harran was
especially popular with the Babylonian king
Nabû-na'id (known in Latin as Nabonidus;

reigned 556–539 BC), whose mother was a
priestess there. Nabû-na'id made his daughter
high priestess of Sîn at Ur.

Although a very popular deity in Old Babylonian times, Nanna always remained subordinate to the chief gods of the **pantheon**,
and in 'Nanna-Suen's Journey to Nippur', he
travels by barge to Nippur to obtain the blessing
of the god Enlil (see **journeys and processions of the gods**).

A symbol of Nanna was a recumbent **cres-** 47
cent moon. His beast was a **bull** or a **lion-** 31
dragon.

See **Arabian gods**; **'omega' symbol**.

Nanše

The Sumerian goddess Nanše belongs to the
local pantheon of the city-state of Lagaš in
south-east Sumer (see **local gods**). Her temple
was located at a small town near Lagaš. She was
regarded as a daughter of **Enki**, but also as the
sister of **Ninğirsu** (the local form of **Ninurta**)
and **Nisaba** in a parallel tradition. Her husband was Nindara and her minister **Hendursağ**. Nanše was especially associated with **divination** and the interpretation of **dreams**, and
with **birds** and **fishes**. In an extended Sumerian hymn addressed to her, she is also praised
as a benefactor of the socially disadvantaged
and as responsible for checking the accuracy of
weights and measures.

See **Damu**.

Narūdu: see **Seven (gods)**.

necromancy: see **divination**.

Nergal (Erra)

The gods Nergal and Erra were originally
separate deities, but later became so closely
identified as to lose their independent characters. Since Nergal was worshipped at the
temple called E-meslam (or 'Meslam House')
at Kutû in Babylonia, he was also sometimes
known under the name Meslamta-ea, 'he who
comes forth from the Meslam'; later he was
also identified with **Lugal-irra**. Another cult
centre was Maškan-šāpir (Tell Abu Dhawari).

111 The moon god
Sîn. Detail from a
cylinder seal of the
Neo-Babylonian
Period.

Nergal was associated with the **underworld** and was usually regarded as the husband of **Ereškigal**, queen of the underworld. Their love story is related in the myth 'Nergal and Ereškigal'. Other goddesses sometimes regarded as the wife of Nergal were Laş and Mamītu. Nergal was considered to be a son of **Enlil** and **Ninlil**, or else of Bēlet-ilī.

In addition to his underworld connections, Nergal was also associated with forest fires, fevers and plagues, and sometimes had a war-like aspect.

Erra was, especially, a violent warlike god, particularly responsible for plagues. He too was worshipped at the E-meslam at Kutû, with his wife Mami (probably the same as Nergal's wife Mamītu, and not the Mami who is counted among **mother goddesses and birth goddesses**). Erra's father was said to be **An**.

In the Babylonian poem 'Išum and Erra', the god acquires temporary control of the world and (apparently because destruction is simply in his nature, rather than to punish any **sin**) ravages and lays waste Babylonia: the mythical narrative may mirror invasions of the country between the twelfth and ninth centuries BC by tribal, nomadic peoples such as the Aramaeans or 'Suteans'.

In Babylonian art, Nergal is represented as a god dressed in a long, open-fronted robe, often with one leg bared and advanced, his foot often placed upon a raised support or trampling a man. He usually carries a scimitar and a single- or double-headed lion-sceptre, which, as independent motifs, also served to symbolise the god (see **standards, staves and sceptres of the gods**). A god shown at rest in a coffin may also be Nergal (see **dead gods**).

In the Parthian Period, Nergal was identified with the Greek Herakles.

See **Arabian gods**; **fly**; **lion-demon**.

New Year ceremonies

The New Year ceremonies were celebrated at Babylon from the first to the twelfth of Nisannu, the first month of the year, which fell approximately at the time of the spring equinox. The ceremonies at Babylon were

112 A god apparently lying in his sarcophagus, thought by some scholars to be Nergal, god of the underworld. Baked clay figurine, possibly of Isin-Larsa or Old Babylonian date. Ht. 133 mm.

centred on the cult of **Marduk**, but related ceremonies were performed at other cities for other deities, and had been performed for a very long time. The *akiti* festival performed at Ur under the Third Dynasty, for the god **Nanna**, took its name from the Akkadian *akītu*, one of the New Year ceremonies.

The Babylonian ceremonies consisted of a sequence of rites which were concerned (1) with celebrating or marking the spring barley harvest; (2) with a patronal festival of the city-god, Marduk, including his enthronement (known as 'taking Bēl by the hand'), incorporating (3) symbolic representation of certain episodes in the Babylonian Epic of Creation (see **creation**); (4) with marking the calendrical aspect of the New Year; (5) with the affirmation of the king as bearer of the sacred duties of kingship; and (6) with the reception and enthronement of the god **Nabû**. A very late copy of a set of ritual instructions for the **priests** gives precise details of the ceremonies of the second to fifth days, but the sequence of events on the other days is far less clear. It certainly included a procession and journey out to the *bīt akīti* or *akītu* building, a ritual humiliation of the king, and an 'offering' (most probably a reading), on the fourth day, of the Epic of Creation, in addition to a whole series of magical and cultic rites of various significance.

The last known occasion when the *akītu* of Marduk was celebrated at Babylon was when Cambyses, king of Persia, 'took Bēl by the hand' in 538 BC. However, *akītu* ceremonies were still celebrated for the deities Anu (**An**) and Ištar (**Inana**) at Uruk during the second century BC.

See **Aššur**; **purification**; **Sacred Marriage**.

Nidaba: see **Nisaba**.

night
The Babylonians appear to have believed that at dusk the sun god Šamaš (**Utu**) entered through a gateway at the western horizon into the 'interior of heaven', where a chamber was located where he spent the night. In the morn-ing he emerged from a corresponding gate at the eastern horizon. It is clear that his radiance was believed to diminish during the night-time hours, but it is not yet quite clear how this view can be harmonised with another tradition that he illuminated the **underworld** during the night.

Certain rituals had to be performed during the night. These included extispicy rituals and, especially, magical rituals intended to destroy the power of sorcerers, and some *namburbû* rituals (see **magic and sorcery**). Because of this, such rituals often included special prayers addressed to the (unnamed) gods of the night, or to the stars.

Nikkal: see **Ningal**.

Nimrod
In Genesis 10, we read that Nimrod was 'a mighty hunter before the Lord', and that 'the beginning of his kingdom was Babel [Babylon] and Erech [Uruk], and Accad and Calneh in the land of Shinar'. The context suggests that Nimrod here stands for the Babylonian nation. Nimrod survived as a figure in Islamic tradition and is perpetuated in the modern names of the ruins of Kalhu (Nimrud) and Borsippa (Birs Nimrud). However, no Mesopotamian source for the legend can be identified.

Ninazu
The god Ninazu was regarded as a son of **Ereškigal**, queen of the underworld; he was also the father of **Ningišzida**. His connection appears to be with the **underworld**. It seems that during the third millennium BC he was worshipped at the city of Ešnunna, but that his cult was later replaced there by that of the god **Tišpak** (in origin the Hurrian storm god Tešup). Ninazu's divine beast seems to have been the **snake-dragon** (*mušhuššu*), apparently taken over by Tišpak and so later by **Marduk**.

It is possible that the Ninazu who was worshipped at Enegi in southern Sumer, whose father was **Enlil**, is in origin a different god.

Nindara: see **local gods**; **Nanše**.

113 A diorite statue of the goddess Ningal of the Isin-Larsa Period, found in the *ĝipar* at Ur, and heavily restored. (When found the statue was headless and very broken.) The inscription is a dedication of the statue to Ningal by En-ana-tuma, daughter of King Išme-Dagan of Isin.

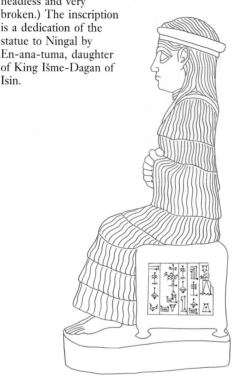

Ningal

The goddess Ningal was the wife of the god **Nanna**/Sîn and the mother of the sun god **Utu**/Šamaš. She was worshipped with Sîn at Ur, and also at Sîn's sanctuary at Harran in northern Syria. Her cult developed independently in Syria as early as the second millennium BC, where her name was altered to Nikkal, a form which is also used in Babylonia sometimes. The cult of Nikkal seems to have lasted in Syria well into the first millennium AD.

See **'eyes-of-Ningal'**.

Ningilin: see **mongoose**.

Ninĝirsu

The god Ninĝirsu (whose name means 'Lord of Ĝirsu') was important from the Early Dyn-

astic Period until the Old Babylonian Period as a local form of the god **Ninurta** (see **local gods**). He was the most prominent of the local **pantheon** of the city-state of Lagaš, within whose borders the town of Ĝirsu (modern Tello) lay, where he was regarded as a son of **Enlil**, the husband of **Bau** and brother of the goddesses **Nanše** and **Nisaba**.

Ninĝirsu was the god for whom Gudea, ruler of Lagaš, rebuilt the great temple E-ninnu, 'House of the Fifty [**me**]' (see **numbers**), celebrated in a lengthy Sumerian hymn. 114 In the hymn, Gudea dreams that Ninĝirsu appears before him commanding the rebuilding: instead of appearing in human form, the god appears as the lion-headed **Imdugud** (Anzû) bird (see **dreams and visions**). Since in the older versions of the Akkadian 'Anzû' poem, it is Ninĝirsu who defeats the Anzû when the bird has stolen from Enlil the **tablet of destinies** (while the later versions have Ninurta as the divine avenger), it is possible to see how what must originally have been a victim – a 'trophy' – of the god later became so closely identified with him as to be able to stand as a symbol for the divine presence.

Also alluded to in Gudea's hymn is the myth of the **Slain Heroes**, a group of bizarre minor deities – some anthropomorphic, some monstrous and some inanimate – conquered by Ninĝirsu (or in other versions, Ninurta). 135

In general Ninĝirsu was, on the one hand, a warrior god, as the above exploits suggest; on the other hand, he was associated with the fruitfulness of cultivation and vegetation, with the regulation of canals essential for irrigation and with fecundity. On **kudurrus** of the Kassite Period, the **plough** is named as his symbol. 121 As Ĝirsu became less important (being absorbed into the empire of the Third Dynasty of Ur), less is heard of Ninĝirsu, and his myths were attributed to Ninurta.

See **lion**; **Zababa**.

Ningišzida

The god Ningišzida was an **underworld** deity, son of the god **Ninazu**. His name may etymologically mean 'Lord of the Good Tree'.

114 An Early Dynastic Period *abzu* basin from the Temple of Ninĝirsu at Ĝirsu (modern Tello), photographed where it now stands in the Museum of the Ancient Orient at Istanbul.

115 Gudea, prince of Lagaš, is introduced to the god Enki by his personal deity Ningišzida, shown with horned serpents (*bašmū*) rising above his shoulders. Detail from Gudea's own cylinder seal, Neo-Sumerian Period.

In the Sumerian poem 'The Death of Gilgameš', **Gilgameš** meets Ningišzida and **Dumuzi** together in the underworld. Babylonian incantations name Ningišzida as a guardian over **demons** who live in the underworld. The god's name is also mentioned in laments over the death of Dumuzi.

Gudea, the Sumerian ruler of Lagaš who built the temple of **Ninĝirsu**, regarded Ningišzida as a personal protective deity (see **personal gods**), and recorded his appearance to him in a **dream**.

Unexpectedly, in the myth of **Adapa**, the sage who travelled to heaven, we encounter Dumuzi and a god called Gišzida, certainly an abbreviated form of Ningišzida, guarding the gate to the Heaven of Anu (**An**), the highest heaven (see **cosmology**). Adapa is told that he must say, in reply to the gods' questions, that he is in mourning for two gods who have disappeared from earth, namely Dumuzi and Gišzida. This, together with the complicated interplay of the themes of death and immortality in the poem, makes it clear that it is exceptional that Dumuzi and Gišzida are found in heaven on this occasion.

The symbol and beast of Ningišzida was the horned snake or dragon *bašmu* (see **snakes**) and astrologically Ningišzida was associated with the constellation we know as Hydra.

The god's name may have been pronounced 'Ningizzida'.

See **Damu; snake-dragon; snake gods.**

Ninhursaĝa

Ninhursaĝa was the Sumerian name of one of the **mother goddesses,** who was known as 'mother of the gods' and was certainly thought to have been responsible for the birth of many of the **gods and goddesses.** Many human rulers liked to name her as their 'mother' also.

In the Sumerian myth 'Enki and Ninhursaĝa, Ninhursaĝa (who is also called Nintur, **Damgalnuna** and Ninsikila in the poem) is inseminated by **Enki,** who then rapes the daughter of their union in the first of a series of incestuous rapes. Eventually they have intercourse again and Ninhursaĝa gives birth to eight divinities favourable to man. In another poem, *Lugale*, a myth explains the origin of Ninhursaĝa's name: the god **Ninurta,** having defeated the demon **Asag** and his army of stone allies, builds the mountains out of stones, and decides to rename his mother **Ninmah** with the new name Ninhursaĝa ('Lady of the Mountain').

Being virtually identical with the goddess Ninmah, Ninhursaĝa was worshipped at the temple E-mah in the city of Adab. However, it appears that she was also connected with the city of Keš, since she is sometimes known as the 'Bēlet-ilī of Keš' or as 'she of Keš'.

See **Dilmunite gods; Lisin; 'omega' symbol; Šul-pa-e.**

Ninisina

Ninisina, whose name means 'Lady of Isin', was the patronal goddess of the Sumerian city of that name (see **local gods**). She was a daughter of the goddess Uraš. Her husband was **Pabilsaĝ** and her son **Damu.** Already in the third millennium BC she was worshipped in Sumer outside Isin, for instance at Lagaš, but with the rise of the kingdom of Isin shortly after 2000 BC her importance as a special deity of Isin increased. From this period, too, she was known by the epithet 'great doctor of the black-headed (that is, human beings)', and, like her son, Damu, she was specially associated with healing (see **diseases and medicine**). She was compared with **Inana** and was sometimes known as 'great daughter of **An**' and other epithets proper to Inana. Since Ninisina is really a title rather than a name, it seems that Ninisina was in fact identical with **Gula,** 79 who was known under a variety of names.

Ninkarrak: see **Gula.**

Ninkilim: see **mongoose.**

Ninlil (Mullissu)

The goddess Ninlil was the wife of the god **Enlil.** While it is likely that she was an 'artificially invented' deity (since the prefix Nin-usually means 'lady', just as En- means 'lord'), named so as to provide a wife for her important husband, she is often also called 'mother', 'merciful mother' and so on and may perhaps have been a form of **mother goddess.** As a merciful and benevolent deity, she often interceded with her husband on behalf of mortals. The Sumerian poem 'Enlil and Ninlil' recounts a story of Enlil's rape of the young Ninlil, for which he was banished by the other gods, and of how subsequently she became his wife. In the different tradition of the poem 'Enlil and Sud', Enlil marries the goddess Sud, who is then renamed Ninlil (see **Nisaba**).

Since in Assyria **Aššur,** the national god, was in some respects equated with Babylonian Enlil, Ninlil was regarded as the wife of Aššur. In Assyria she was worshipped under the name

31 Mullissu (an Assyrian dialectal form of Mulliltu, derived from a Sumerian dialectal form of Ninlil).

In Assyria, Mullissu's animal was the **lion**. See **E-kur**.

Ninmah

The goddess Ninmah acted as midwife when **Nammu** created mankind, according to the Sumerian poem 'Enki and Ninmah' (see **creation; mother goddesses and birth goddesses**). Later, when celebrating, **Enki** and Ninmah drank too much beer and became merry. Having played a subsidiary rôle in the creation, Ninmah now challenged Enki to the effect that, however favourable or unfavourable mankind's bodily form might be, she could make his destiny good or bad as she chose. Enki, accepting the challenge, claimed 'If the fate you choose is bad, I will improve it.' A drunken game followed, in which Ninmah became furious with Enki's success. They reversed rôles, and Enki soon created a creature so sick or weak in every part of its body that Ninmah could not improve it at all. The victory was granted to Enki.

Ninmah was also the name of a constellation. See **Ninhursağa**.

Ninmar: see **local gods**.

Ninmena: see **mother goddesses and birth goddesses**.

Ninmešarra: see **Enmešarra**.

Ninsianna: see **Inana**.

Ninsikila: see **Ninhursağa**; **Lisin**; **Dilmunite gods**.

Ninsun

The name of this goddess means 'lady wild-cow' and it is possible that originally her cult was associated with wild cattle (see **horned cap**). Already in the Early Dynastic Period she was regarded as the wife of the deified king of the city of Uruk, **Lugalbanda**. Lugalbanda

and Ninsun were the parents of the hero **Gilgameš**, and in the Babylonian Epic of Gilgameš, the wise Ninsun acts as an interpreter of Gilgameš's ominous **dreams**.

Ninšiku: see **Enki**.

Ninšubur (god)

A minor male deity who functioned as minister (see **gods and goddesses**) to **An**. An Akkadian form of his name was Il-abrāt. He was also assimilated to the god Papsukkal, who functioned as minister to the gods in general. Papsukkal was associated with the constellation known in modern terminology as Orion.

In Neo-Assyrian and Neo-Babylonian art, Ninšubur/Papsukkal is depicted as an anthropomorphic god, wearing a **horned cap** and a long robe; he stands, as if to attention, and holds before him a long staff, reaching from

116 A figurine of the minister of the gods, Ninšubur, in sun-dried clay with metal staff. Neo-Babylonian, from a brick box buried in the foundations of the temple of the goddess Ninhursağa at Kiš.

above the level of his head to the ground. Often he stands upon a podium. Commonly in temples (of various deities) of this period, a **figurine** of sun-dried clay of the god in this form would be buried in a brick box beneath the dais of the **cult statue**. The Old Babylonian 'Figure with mace' (see **mace**) has been regarded as an earlier iconography of the god, but it seems doubtful.

The animal symbol of Ninšubur/Papsukkal, at least from the Kassite Period, was a walking **bird**.

Ninšubur (goddess)
A minor female deity who functioned as minister (see **gods and goddesses**) to **Inana**.
See **Namtar**.

Nintinuga: see **Gula**.

Nintu: see **mother goddesses and birth goddesses**.

Nintur: see **Ninhursaǧa**.

Ninurta
There is no evidence for the meaning of the name of the god Ninurta, whose worship was very ancient in Sumer. As a son of **Enlil**, his principal cult centre was the temple E-šu-me-ša at Nippur. His wife was regarded as either **Gula** or, because of his close association with the god **Ninǧirsu**, **Bau**. Indeed, the personalities of the two gods Ninurta and Ninǧirsu are closely intertwined and, although his origin may have been independent, in historical times Ninǧirsu was a local form of Ninurta.

The most pronounced aspect of Ninurta's personality was his warlike nature. Several myths relate his martial exploits, mainly directed against the enemies of Sumer and in particular against the so-called 'rebel lands' or 'hostile lands' (the regions in the mountains to the east of Mesopotamia). Ninurta (or Ninǧirsu) is the gods' champion against the Anzû bird (**Imdugud**) when it steals the **tablet of destinies** from Enlil, thereby endangering the stability of civilisation. Ninurta (or Ninǧirsu) kills the **Slain Heroes** in a myth several times alluded to but nowhere preserved in full.

A contrasting aspect, also to be found with Ninǧirsu, is Ninurta's rôle as a farmer god. In the so-called Sumerian 'Georgica', Ninurta gives detailed advice on the cultivation of crops and preparation of the fields, in fact on the farmer's activities throughout the year. The **plough** is captioned as a symbol of Ninǧirsu on Kassite **kudurrus**, and so perhaps represented Ninurta in Neo-Assyrian art. Another symbol

117 A mythological scene on a monumental stone relief from the temple of the god Ninurta at Kalhu (modern Nimrud), belonging to the reign of the Assyrian king Assurnasirpal II (reigned 883–859 BC). Ninurta or Adad pursues a leonine bird-monster, perhaps the Anzû or Asakku.

of Ninurta in the Neo-Assyrian Period was a
76 perched **bird**.

The two aspects, warrior and farmer, are combined in the Sumerian poem *Lugale*, in which Ninurta succeeds in defeating the terrible demon **Asag** and his army of stone allies, and then proceeds to organise the world, using the stones to build the mountains in such a way that streams and lakes flow into the Tigris and Euphrates to make them useful for irrigation and to facilitate agriculture.

The Assyrian kings were devoted to the cult of Ninurta, as a warlike god who would help them against their enemies. At his new capital Kalhu (modern Nimrud), Assurnasirpal II (reigned 883–859 BC) built a temple to Ninurta adjacent to the **ziggurat** (which may also have been dedicated to Ninurta). The scene carved on stone relief slabs at either side of the main doorway of the temple may represent, uniquely
6 in Neo-Assyrian monumental art, a mythological scene: Ninurta's defeat of the Asakku
117 (**Asag**) or else of the Anzû bird (**Imdugud**).
155 According to one theory, the **winged disc** symbolised Ninurta in the official art of the ninth century BC, before it was transferred either to **Aššur** or Šamaš (**Utu**). This idea, based upon representations of a god set above the disc who seems to have a bird's tail, seen below the disc, has found little support among scholars.

See **bird gods**; **lightning (symbol)**; **Ninhursağa**; **Nisroch**; **rainbow**; **Slain Heroes**; **Uraš (god)**; **Uraš (goddess)**; **Zababa**.

Nirah: see **snake gods**.

Nisaba

As one of the group of signs used in writing her name (a pictograph of an ear of grain) shows, it is most likely that the goddess Nisaba was in origin a grain goddess. The form of the name Nisaba (or Nissaba) seems more correct than Nidaba.

The cult of this daughter of **An** and **Uraš** is attested from Early Dynastic times. Nisaba was, or became, a goddess of writing, accounting and scribal knowledge. At Lagaš

she was a member of the local **pantheon** of that area (see **local gods**), where she was regarded as a daughter of **Enlil** and hence a sister of **Ninğirsu**. The god Haya was her husband, but later, probably because of her association with the scribal art, **Nabû** (also a scribal deity) was said to be her spouse. She was also sometimes identified with the goddess Nanibgal (see **Ennugi**).

In the Early Dynastic Period, Nisaba was a **personal goddess** of the rulers of the Sumerian city of Umma. Later, however, during the Isin-Larsa Period, she was regarded as patron goddess of the city of Ereš. The goddess of nearby Šuruppag, Sud (see **Ninlil**), was regarded as her daughter. In the myth 'Enlil and Sud', when Enlil, god of Nippur, wishes to marry Sud, he has to seek the approval of Nisaba.

Nisroch

The Assyrian king Sennacherib was murdered in 681 BC, apparently by Arad-Mullissu and another of his sons (they had been passed over for succession in favour of Esarhaddon). According to the Biblical account (2 Kings: 19; also 2 Chronicles: 32, Isaiah: 37 and Tobit: 1), Sennacherib was killed while worshipping in the temple of his god, 'Nisroch'. It is not clear to which Assyrian god this refers: it has been suggested that it is a corruption of **Ninurta**, but this is unsubstantiated.

When in the nineteenth century AD Sir Austen Henry Layard excavated the palace of the Assyrian king Assurnasirpal II (ruled 883–859 BC) at the city of Kalhu (modern Nimrud), he discovered large numbers of bas-reliefs which depicted images of a winged eagle-headed figure. Referring these to the 78 Biblical story, Layard labelled the figures 'Nisroch' (in view of Ninurta's supposed character as a **bird god**). As a monumental figure-type in the palaces the eagle-headed man is now known not to be present as late as the reign of Sennacherib, the term 'Nisroch' is still occasionally found in modern art historical literature for this figure, otherwise known as the **griffin-demon**.

'Nude Hero': see **Lahmu**.

nude woman

Hand-made clay **figurines** of nude females appear in Mesopotamia in prehistoric times; they have applied and painted features. Figur- 64 ines of nude women impressed from a pottery or stone mould first appear at the beginning of the second millennium BC. Though the pos- tures vary slightly, the figurines are in most respects similar and probably were mass-pro- duced. It is very unlikely that they represent a universal **mother goddess**, although they may have been intended to promote **fertility**. Pos- sibly the same idea was responsible for a related group of female figures breast-feeding infants.

118 Early second-millennium BC seals and clay figurines commonly depict a full-frontal nude female. Often she stands on a plinth as if rep- resenting a **cult statue**. The figure never wears the **horned cap** of divinity, but she sometimes appears to be the object of worship. It has been suggested that she represents Ištar (**Inana**) in her aspect as goddess of sexual love (see **pros- titution and ritual sex**) or, according to another theory, the goddess **Šala**.

In Neo-Assyrian and Neo-Babylonian art, a frontally standing naked female who does wear 87 a horned cap and is often winged is un- doubtedly Ištar as goddess of sex (although the more menacing renderings of the type have been interpreted by some as representations of the demoness **Lilītu**). 1

Nudimmud: see **Enki**.

numbers

Some numbers acquire special religious or magical significance for essentially mathe- matical reasons. Three, for instance, has always been regarded as important because of its magical usefulness and its perfection: three points can be arranged graphically such that each point is equidistant from the others. Alternatively, if one point is taken as the centre, the other two can be placed equidistantly on either side of it. Thus the world was divided by the Babylonians into three superimposed regions, heaven, earth and **underworld**, with the earth in the middle. The heaven was divided horizontally into three regions one above the other (see **cosmology**), or the eastern horizon was divided vertically into three bands, the ways of Anu (**An**), **Enlil** and Ea (**Enki**) (see **astrology and astronomy**).

The earlier, Sumerian, cosmology of the rectangular field-shaped earth with four 'corners' was probably the origin of the four directions and four winds (usually enumerated in the order south, north, east and west).

As for Neo-Assyrian foundation **figurines**, two sets of five model **dogs** (two of each colour) 57 were deposited.

By far the most significant number for the ancient Mesopotamians was seven. It is difficult to see what the origin of this significance can have been. The group of gods called the **Seven (gods)** were equated with the Pleiades (con- ventionally seven in number). In **magic**, in- cantations must often be repeated seven times, seven demons expelled, seven gods invoked, ritual actions are carried out seven (or seven times seven) times, seven cylinder seals are hung round the neck of a patient, and so on. There are seven (or fourteen) gates to the

118 A woman in the nude standing on a plinth, (*left*) a detail from a cylinder seal, and (*right*) in relief on a baked clay plaque from Larsa. Old Babylonian Period.

underworld. Seven in some of these contexts may be replaced by eight. Sometimes 'seven' or 'eight' is used to indicate an indefinite number.

There were eleven **Slain Heroes**, and **Tiāmat's creatures** were also eleven in number.

Fifty is frequently used simply to indicate a large number. The Babylonian Epic of Creation concludes with a hymn to the Fifty Names of **Marduk**.

Since the Babylonians used a sexagesimal system of counting, multiples of sixty, and in particular the number 3,600 (60²), for which they had a special word (*šar*), and on occasion 36,000, were also used to express particularly high numbers – much as we use 'hundreds', 'thousands' or 'millions'.

Numbers were sometimes used to write the names of the most important deities: 20 (Šamaš), 30 (Sîn), 40 (Ea) and 50 (Enlil).

Numušda

The god Numušda was especially associated with the town of Kazallu in northern Babylonia. Evidence of his worship exists already in the Early Dynastic Period, but does not continue after the Old Babylonian Period. He was regarded as a son of **Nanna**, and may perhaps have been a storm god. In the myth 'The Marriage of Martu', the daughter of Numušda insists on marrying the god **Martu** despite the latter's unattractive habits and lack of a settled home.

Nungal

The goddess Nungal (or Manungal) was a daughter of **Ereškigal**, and a deity of the **underworld**. The minor god Birtum, a son of **Enlil**, was considered to be her husband. She was especially associated with the temple **E-kur** at Nippur, although she was worshipped during the late third and early second millennia BC at a number of cities, and was a member of the local **pantheon** of Lagaš (see **local gods**). Later she was identified with Nintinuga (see **Gula**).

Nusku

The god Nusku (perhaps to be read Nuska) was regarded both as a son of, and as the minister of **Enlil**. In a variant tradition he is described in a Sumerian hymn as a son of Enul and Ninul, who are also included as ancestors of Enlil in one version of his descent. Generally speaking, apart from his functions as minister, Nusku has an independent character as a god associated with fire and light. Sometimes **Gibil**, the fire god, is described as the son of Nusku. In magical incantations, Nusku is among the gods called upon to assist in the burning of sorcerers and witches (see **magic and sorcery**).

In the Neo-Assyrian Period, Nusku was among the gods who were worshipped together at Harran in north-west Syria (see **Ningal**), and at this time he seems to have acquired an importance out of all proportion to his relatively humble beginnings. At Harran he was regarded as the son of the principal deity there, Sîn (**Nanna-Suen**). This group of deities was probably worshipped by a largely Aramaic population, and Nusku is probably the same as the name 'Nasuh' found in Neo-Assyrian personal names and as the god written 'Nsk' in Old Aramaic inscriptions. These cults appear to have lasted into the early centuries AD and perhaps even longer.

The symbol of a **lamp** sometimes occurring 93 in Mesopotamian art from the Kassite to Neo-Babylonian Periods is labelled on **kudurrus** as an emblem of Nusku.   7

Oannes: see **Berossos; fish-garbed figure; Seven Sages**.

oaths and curses

In any society it is normal to solemnise statements, evidence or agreement by oaths, and to penalise those who break or go back on their oath. In the highly developed litigious world of ancient Mesopotamia, oaths were used especially in the legal sphere, as well as in treaties and political agreements, to confirm declarations of all kinds. It was normal to swear by the 'life' of one or more gods, and, especially in the period when kings were deified (see **deification of** kings), also (or instead) by the king; in early Assyria also by the city (of Aššur). In some legal cases, especially concerning boundary disputes or other matters which could not literally be brought to court, it was common to bring to the disputed site from the temple an emblem of the god, such as the saw of Šamaš (**Utu**), and for the parties to swear on the spot in its presence. Swearing by gods was also common in magical conjurations, where long lists of gods were invoked in the exorcism of demons (see **magic and sorcery**).

Dire physical and psychological penalties were foretold for those who broke oaths. It was believed that the very swearing of an oath, and even more so the breaking of an oath, generated supernatural powers which might turn against the swearer and from which he needed to be protected by magic. For this reason the oath (*māmītu*) is included in the list of potentially dangerous acts which a psychologically disturbed person might have inadvertently committed, causing his disturbance. Plaques depicting the goddess **Lamaštu** refer in their inscriptions to the affliction of a demon called Māmītu, clearly a personification of the oath, and suggest that the cause of sickness or demonic possession was thought to have been, in this case, a broken oath; it has been suggested that the symbols of the gods shown in the uppermost register of such plaques are a visual metaphor for the original oath. (See **demons and monsters; diseases and medicine**.)

151

Equally dire and explicit curses were invoked upon those who committed social crimes; in particular ample evidence survives of the curses invoked on those who damaged inscribed monuments erected by rulers, or stone monuments recording grants of land tenure (**kudurrus**). The curses are written out on the monuments for any later reader to peruse and to think twice about: 'May the god Aššur overthrow his sovereignty, smash his weapons, defeat his army, diminish his borders, decree the end of his reign, darken his days, vitiate his years, and destroy his name and his seed from the land.'

90

See **Ṣalmu**.

offering: see **boats of the gods; fish; sacrifice and offering**.

oil: see **anointing; divination; libation**.

'omega' symbol

A symbol approximating in form to an upright or inverted capital Greek letter omega, but with a number of minor variations, is first attested on an impression from an Early Dynastic seal, and is represented commonly from the Old Babylonian to the Neo-Babylonian Periods. It has variously been interpreted by modern commentators as a representation of weighing-scales, the yoke of a chariot-pole, a comet, a large-horned quadruped, a head-band, a wig, the bands used to swaddle a baby or as the uterus. Supporters of the last two suggestions usually connect the symbol with the mother goddess **Ninhursaǧa**, or with Nintu (see **mother goddesses and birth goddesses**). Some probably Isin-Larsa or Old Babylonian Period plaques of clay with moulded relief show a goddess (probably Nintu) flanked by inverted 'omega' motifs beneath which sit human forms resembling newborn babies, as if newly emerged from the womb. It has been suggested that these rather emaciated human forms might represent *kūbu*-demons (deified stillborn foetuses); such **demons** are known to have been a focus of religious feeling. Perhaps the 'omega' symbol was sometimes associated with Ištar (**Inana**) as goddess of sex and **prostitution**, for on Neo-Assyrian seals it is shown within her shrine. On a cylinder seal of Middle Assyrian date from Samsat on the upper Euphrates (in present-day Turkey) a god receives worship while standing in his boat (see **boats of the gods**). Since the deity holds in

90, 119

109

49

119 A divine emblem in a form resembling an omega. A common depiction among the symbols carved on Babylonian *kudurru* stones and seals.

one hand a **crescent**, he should be Sîn (**Nanna-Suen**) or a local moon god. In the other hand he holds the 'omega' symbol.

oneiromancy: see **divination**; **dreams and visions**.

Pabilsaǧ

The worship of the god Pabilsaǧ is attested from Early Dynastic times onwards. He was regarded as a son of **Enlil**, and was the spouse of **Ninisina**, the patron goddess of Isin (see **local gods**). As such he had cult centres in both Isin and Nippur. His personality is rather unclear, but from the Old Babylonian Period he was sometimes identified with **Ninurta/Ninǧirsu**. A Sumerian poem describes the journey of Pabilsaǧ to Nippur (see **journeys and processions of the gods**).

Pabilsaǧ was also associated with the city of Larag, one of the cities where kingship flourished in antediluvian times, according to Sumerian tradition.

Astronomically Pabilsaǧ was the constellation we know as Sagittarius (see **centaur**; **zodiac**).

Palm-tree King

The Palm-tree King is the name of one of the monsters conquered by the warrior god **Ninurta/Ninǧirsu** (see **Slain Heroes**). Very little is known about him. Probably the Palm-tree King was the name of a minor local deity of the Lagaš region whose cult was superseded by that of Ninǧirsu (leading to the myth of his conquest by Ninǧirsu). There is evidence that he was worshipped at Ǧirsu in the Early Dynastic Period.

Evidence for tree cults in Mesopotamia is very limited. The common later motif of the stylised tree is as yet unexplained.

pantheon

There is a sense in which it is impossible, in connection with ancient Mesopotamia, to speak of a pantheon ('the deities of a people collectively'). This is because under the (geographically ill-determined) heading Mesopotamia at least 3,000 years of history are included, incorporating three main peoples (Sumerians, Babylonians and Assyrians) but also various other ethnic groups who either entered as conquerors (such as Kassites) or who lived peripherally to the central area (such as Amorites, Elamites, Hurrians). Each of these groups had their own gods. Inevitably during the enormous time span, developments occurred, especially through syncretism. Second, there exists for Mesopotamia no statement, collectively and authoritatively, of all myths or all deities such as can be recognised from time to time for Classical Greek or Roman mythology (e.g. Hesiod's *Theogony* or Ovid's *Metamorphoses*). Although 'the **gods**' are often referred to generally, this certainly meant different things at different times.

On the other hand, because of the high degree of syncretism between the deities of different peoples, the pantheon can, in a sense, be viewed, together with the cuneiform script and the (in some ways) very conservative religious art, as one of the few unifying elements of 'Mesopotamian' culture.

Altogether the names of over 3,000 divinities are preserved in the cuneiform records. The largest single presentation of these is the **list of gods** called (from its first line) 'An = Anum', a Babylonian scholarly work intended to give Akkadian equivalents for the Sumerian deities; in its complete form it listed about 2,000 gods and goddesses, but the entire list has not yet been recovered.

Papsukkal: see **Ninšubur (god)**.

Pazuzu

Pazuzu was an Assyrian and Babylonian demonic god of the first millennium BC. He is represented with a rather canine face with abnormally bulging eyes, a scaly body, a snake-headed penis, the talons of a bird and usually wings. He is often regarded as an evil **underworld demon**, but he seems also to have played a beneficent rôle as a protector against pestilential winds (especially the west wind). His close association with **Lamaštu** led to his

120 A cast-copper or bronze figurine of the demon god Pazuzu. The reverse is inscribed 'I am the god Pazuzu, son of the god Hanbi, king of the evil wind demons'. Assyrian or Babylonian, 7th century BC. Ht.146 mm.

being used as a counter to her evil: he forced her back to the **underworld.** Amulets of Pazuzu were therefore positioned in dwellings or, often in the form of his head only, were hung around the necks of pregnant women.

Pazuzu, incidentally, made his latest appearance to date as the demon who possessed the girl in the Hollywood *Exorcist* films.

personal gods
Evidence from the third millennium BC indicates that rulers, at least, would sometimes regard a particular deity or deities as being in some intimate way their special protector(s).

Thus Sargon of Agade and the kings of his dynasty seem to have felt a special allegiance to **Ilaba,** and Gudea, the ruler of Lagaš, addresses the goddess Ĝatumdug as his 'mother and father'. Similarly, Utu-heĝal, who expelled the barbarian Gutians from Sumer, asks **Dumuzi** and **Gilgameš** to be his 'protectors'. The kings of the Third Dynasty of Ur regarded Gilgameš as their 'brother' and made a special cult to that god's father, **Lugalbanda**.

However, it seems to be after this period that the idea of an individual, more personal deity developed. This deity is usually not named and is referred to by the worshipper as 'my god' or 'my goddess': apparently it could be a deity of either sex, and (to judge from personal names) everyone could have such a personal god. This unidentified deity acted as a protective influence who watched over the life of the individual. Reference is often made to a person's 'god (*ilu*) and goddess (*ištaru*)'. Sometimes it is said of the personal deity that he 'created' the individual who is under his protection. Possibly the name of the deity was known to the individual but was omitted in normal speech, since occasionally a deity is named, e.g. 'Adad, your god' or 'Ištar, my goddess'.

The idea of a benevolent personal god is close to that of the benevolent *šēdu* (male) or *lamassu* (female), anthropomorphic beings who accompanied people (see **lama**). In one text the personal god is responsible for sending such beings as agents of his protection.

Clearly it was important to placate the personal god or goddess, who might be offended in all sorts of ways, deliberately or unintentionally. It was often said of an unlucky person that 'his god had left him', or of a psychologically disturbed person that he must have 'offended' his god in some way or committed an act that was **taboo** for his god.

See **'great gods'**.

'plant of life'
In the Epic of Gilgameš, when it seems clear that **Gilgameš** cannot achieve the immortality he seeks, he is given the chance of youth by the sage Ūt-napišti (**Ziusura**). Ūt-napišti reveals

to Gilgameš the whereabouts of a plant which will rejuvenate him. To fetch it, Gilgameš ties stones to his feet and enters the sea: the weights help him to sink to the bottom, where he finds a plant which is thorny like a rose. Gilgameš explains to the boatman Uršanabi that by eating the plant one can be rejuvenated: the plant is called 'The Old Man Has Become A Young Man'. While Gilgameš is bathing later, a snake smells the plant (which Gilgameš has left on the land), takes it and as a result is able to slough its skin.

A related theme is found in the poem of **Etana**, the king who travelled to heaven on the back of an eagle. What motivated Etana to begin with was the childlessness of his marriage. In a **dream**, Etana's wife saw the *šammu ša alādi*, 'plant of giving birth', and it was his prayer to Šamaš (**Utu**) for this plant which led to his journey with the eagle.

Although the phrase 'plant of life' is not used in the Epic of Gilgameš itself, it was occasionally used to refer to a mythical rejuvenating plant. It seems also to have been the name of a specific medicinal plant.

plough

The plough, which is known as a religious symbol from the Early Dynastic Period down to Neo-Assyrian times, is used on the Kassite **kudurrus** to represent the god **Ninĝirsu** (and so is in Neo-Assyrian and Neo-Babylonian art probably an emblem of **Ninurta**), although in earlier periods it is shown as the attribute of

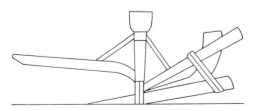

121 A seed plough. Detail from a basalt memorial stone of King Esarhaddon of Assyria and Babylonia (reigned 680–669 BC), containing an account of the restoration of the walls and temples of the city of Babylon.

various gods and goddesses. According to Sumerian tradition, the plough was an invention of the god **Dagan**.

priests and priestesses

In almost the earliest written documents are found lists of the titles of officials, including various classes of priest. Some of these are administrative functionaries of the temple bureaucracy and others are religious specialists dealing with particular areas of the cult. Later records make it clear that a complex hierarchy of clergy was attached to **temples**, ranging from 'high priests' or 'high priestesses' down to courtyard sweepers. It is not clear whether there were fixed distinctions between sacerdotal clergy and administrative clergy: one particular type of priests is called 'anointed'; others are 'enterers of the temple', suggesting that certain areas of the shrines were restricted of access. Generally speaking female clergy were more common in the service of female deities, but a notable exception was the *en* (Akkadian *entu*), the chaste high priestess in the temples of some gods in the Sumerian and Old Babylonian Periods, notably that of the moon god **Nanna-Suen** at Ur – where the office was revived by Nabonidus in neo-Babylonian times (see **ĝipar**) – and in temples at Larsa, Isin, Sippar, Nippur and Kiš. Sometimes the office was held by a daughter of the king. Other priestesses were:

nadītu, ugbabtu: these lived secluded lives in a residence within the temple, although they could own property and engage in business;

qadištu, kulmašītu: these, in contrast, may have been involved in ritual **prostitution**.

Among the classes of priests were:

en (Akkadian *ēnu*): a priest corresponding to the *entu*, but serving in the cult of female deities such as **Inana** of Uruk;

mašmaš (*āšipu* or *mašmaššu*): magicians specialising in medical and magical rites to ensure protection from **demons, disease** and sorcery (see **magic and sorcery**);

122 A female, perhaps the goddess Inana, stands in front of ring-post symbols and receives offerings from a procession of naked men, thought to be priests of her temple. Detail from a stone vase of the Late Uruk Period found at Uruk (modern Warka).

maš-šu-gid-gid (*bārû*): diviners specialising in extispicy (see **divination**);

123 *gala* (*kalû*): musicians specialising in performance of *balaĝ* and other cult songs (probably in choirs, accompanied by drums);

nar (*nāru*): musicians specialising in solo performance of praise songs, accompanying themselves on stringed instruments; in general, singers;

muhaldim (*nuhatimmu*): temple cooks (there were also slaughterers, brewers, etc.);

išib (*pašīšu* and *ramku*): priests specialising in **purification** rituals (see **anointing**);

sanga (*šangû*): generally 'priests', but also administrators;

šatam (*šatammu*): temple administrators;

ensi (female) (male *šā'ilu*, female *šā'iltu*): **dream** interpreters.

Priests and priestesses may have entered the clergy through **dedication**. They were probably distinguished by their priestly dress, especially by their hats or (in some cases) by being shaven-headed, or by their nudity. The 22 titles and functions of the priests varied, of course, from time to time and place to place.

See **animal skins**; **fish-garbed figure**; **Sacred Marriage**.

processions of the gods: see **journeys and processions of the gods**.

prostitution and ritual sex
Herodotus, writing about Babylon in the fifth century BC, states that every woman once in her life had to go to the temple of 'Aphrodite', i.e. Ištar (**Inana**), and sit there waiting until a stranger cast a coin in her lap as the price of her favours. Then she was obliged to go with him outside the temple and have intercourse, to render her duty to the goddess. The story is probably highly imaginative. However, the

123 An Assyrian *kalû* playing a musical instrument. Detail from a fragmentary stone relief from the royal palace at Nineveh of King Sennacherib (reigned 704–681 BC). Ht.1.00 m.

second-century AD writer Lucian describes, apparently from personal knowledge, a very similar custom in the temple of 'Aphrodite' (probably Astarte) at Byblos in Lebanon.

Of course prostitution existed in ancient Mesopotamia (where marriage was an important legal contract), and is often referred to. A famous prostitute in Babylonian literature is Šamhat, who first seduces **Enkidu** in the Epic of **Gilgameš**. Later, on his deathbed, Enkidu curses her in a passage which implies that the normal places for prostitutes would be in the tavern, by the city walls, at the crossroads and in the desert.

Prostitutes are mentioned together with various groups of women engaged in more or less religious activities. **Inana**/Ištar seems to have been presented as a protective goddess of 87 prostitutes. In cult songs the goddess sometimes refers to herself as a prostitute, and her temple is metaphorically called a tavern. It seems possible that prostitution was to some extent organised in the same way as other female activities (such as midwifery or wet-nursing) and in some way manipulated through the temple organisation. But this is a subject which is still not clearly understood and where further research would shed light upon the exploitation of women in Mesopotamia.

Numerous objects from Mesopotamia 129 ranging in date from prehistoric to Middle Assyrian times depict scenes of sexual intercourse, which, rightly or wrongly, have been interpreted as representations of ritual sex, in particular the **Sacred Marriage**. The practice of other sexual rituals involving lesser mortals and with less nationally important aims seems to be implicit in the many obscure allusions in the literature to sexual activities of a public nature, and the pictorial evidence should probably be related to these. Analysis is made difficult both because the few remarks in written sources are vague and obscure, and because much of the iconographic material is unpublished (a reflection of modern academic etiquette).

Depiction of frontal sexual intercourse with the man on top seems to be restricted to the glyptic art of the Early Dynastic Period (with one possible attestation in Akkadian Period art). A distinctive type of bed with animal legs, the presence of other figures besides the lovers and, occasionally, banquets suggest that a definite ritual – perhaps the Sacred Marriage – and not private intercourse, is involved.

In the early second millennium BC, numerous baked clay plaques show a scene of sexual intercourse with the man entering the woman from behind while she is bending over, drinking from a vessel through a long straw.

On Middle Assyrian lead **figurines** depic- 124 ting intercourse, the man stands and the

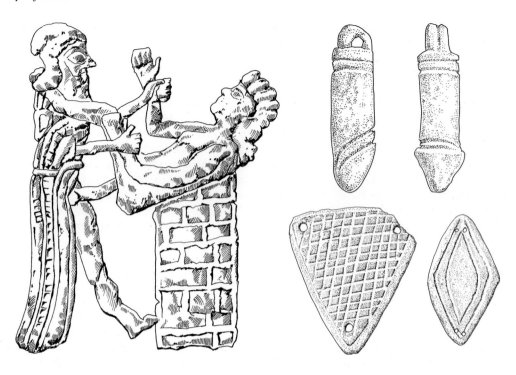

124 Some items of a sexual nature from the Middle Assyrian temple of Ištar at Aššur. A lead figurine in the form of a scene of sexual intercourse, apparently taking place on an altar. Models of human sexual organs, with holes for attachment and suspension: phalli of stone, and a pubic triangle and vulva of baked clay.

woman always rests upon a high structure, usually interpreted as an **altar**. These figurines may very likely represent ritual intercourse, although definitely not the earlier Sacred Marriage, which involved a bed and not an altar. Instead they are probably in some way associated with the cult of Ištar (**Inana**) as goddess of physical love and prostitution, and were, in fact, found in her temple at Aššur (see **temples and temple architecture**). From the same building come models of male and female human sexual organs: phalli of stone and clay, realistically pierced longitudinally down the middle (and possibly worn on the person or by wooden statues) and clay models of the female pubes and vulva.

All these objects doubtless had some amuletic property, and since sexual scenes involving only the copulating couple and no other persons are very rare, it may be that most of the representations are of some kind of cultic rather than private sex. Babylonian incantations to help overcome sexual impotence prescribe, as part of the accompanying procedures: 'You make a figurine', to be placed at the head of the bed during intercourse. Old Babylonian Period clay plaques with scenes of a sexual nature may have served such a function.

See **flour; priests and priestesses**.

purification

In order to perform the service of the gods with **sacrifice and offering**, to take part in religious rituals or to carry out effectively rites involving **magic** (especially those directed against sorcery), it was necessary for the participants to be 'pure'.

Most purification rites involve the performance of actions which are metaphors. Sweeping and water-sprinkling clear the shrine and settle the dust, (metaphorically) purifying the locality. The burning of **incense** and other aromatics cleanses the air and (metaphorically) purifies the atmosphere. Bathing and hand-washing by the participants clean the body and (metaphorically) purify the person.

On occasion **animal sacrifices** can have a purificatory effect, as in the **New Year ceremonies**: on the fifth day of the ceremonies, a magician entered and cleaned the vacant shrine of the god **Nabû** within the **Esagil** complex. (The **cult statue** of Nabû had not yet arrived from Borsippa, the neighbouring town where Nabû normally resided.) The magician summoned a slaughterer to decapitate a sheep, with the corpse of which he would purify the shrine of Nabû. (The word used, literally 'wipe clean', is often used in a transferred sense.) In due course the corpse was thrown into the river which passed by the temple; likewise the slaughterer disposed of the sheep's head. The details of this ritual are very similar to *namburbû* rituals, intended to avert the effect of future evils (see **magic and sorcery**). Clearly it concerns the shrine of Nabû, and not that of **Marduk**, usually thought of as central to the New Year ceremonies.

See **bucket and cone; stylised tree and its 'rituals'; priests and priestesses**.

Qingu

In the Babylonian Epic of Creation, after the death of Apsû (see **abzu**) at the hands of Ea (**Enki**), Tiāmat created as her champion and chief of her military forces the god Qingu (pronounced 'Kingu'). Authority was conferred upon him when Tiāmat presented to him the **tablet of destinies**. He is described as Tiāmat's lover. When Qingu's army was confronted by **Marduk**, however, it soon lost heart and evaporated. Only Tiāmat herself and her guard of monsters (**Tiāmat's creatures**) stood their ground, but in the ensuing battle they too were defeated and killed. Qingu and the gods of his host were then taken prisoner, and paraded in Marduk's triumphal procession. Marduk wrested the tablet of destinies from him and presented it to Anu (**An**).

After his victory, Marduk set about the task of reconstruction and reorganisation. With the exception of Qingu he pardoned the captured gods, pressing them into his team for the building of Babylon. Then, however, he conceived the idea of further delegating the labours to a new race: mankind. At the suggestion of his father Ea, in order to create mankind, he charged Qingu with high treason and sentenced him to death. After the execution, mankind was made from the god's blood.

See **creation; dead gods**.

rābiṣu: see **demons and monsters**.

rainbow

The crown of the god **Ninurta** was described as a rainbow. Manzât, the Akkadian word for rainbow, was also the name of a goddess and of a star in the constellation Andromeda. The star may be illustrated on a **kudurru** as a rainbow arching over a **horse**'s head. (A star called the 81,90 Horse was located near the star Rainbow.)

'Rainbow' was also a literary name of the city of Uruk.

ram-headed staff: see **standards, staves and sceptres of the gods**.

rhomb

The 'rhomb' or 'lozenge' is a pointed oval 76 within four enclosing perimeter lines. It is a very common motif in Mesopotamian art from early historic times until the Neo-Assyrian Period. Its significance is uncertain. The symbol has been variously explained as a grain of corn, a date-stone, a symbol of earth, an **eye**, or a woman's vulva. That it is closely associated in art with the goddess Ištar (**Inana**) and is similar to the clay models of 124 vulvae found in her temple at Aššur supports the last suggestion. The rhomb seems to have had a magically protective function.

right and left

The ancient Mesopotamians invariably spoke of 'right and left' in that order. The right hand was the hand of greeting or benediction, and of purity, used for eating. Presumably because of the right-handedness of the majority of people the right side (of the liver, of the moon, of constellations) was associated, generally speaking, with good fortune in **divination** while the left was associated with bad, but because of the complexity of the divination calculus and the necessity to take all ominous aspects of the entrails or other ominous material into account to produce a complete answer, this cannot be taken as an overall generalisation: in extispicy, for instance, it was not only the position of the organ, but the position of the ominous feature in the organ, that needed to be considered.

12   Divine and semi-divine protective **figurines** of the Neo-Assyrian and Neo-Babylonian Periods can have the left leg uncovered and advanced. This may be related to their function in warding off and driving out the spirits of evil (see **demons and monsters**).

In terms of divine protection, it was considered desirable to have benevolent deities standing at one's right side *and* at one's left.

ring-post

125 The ring-headed post, usually with streamers, is common in early historic art, mainly from
122 Uruk, often depicted as a doorpost for a structure built of reeds and probably made of a bundle of reeds bound together, with the upper ends bent over to make a loop for the crosspole. As this shape is the earliest form of the written sign for the name of the goddess **Inana**, it ought to be her symbol. After the Uruk Period, the symbol is to be found, though rarely, until the Early Dynastic Period, after which it disappears from art. Its disappearance may have been due to the obsolescence of pictographic writing.

A rather different ring-headed post without
139 streamer is known as a symbol in Early Dynastic art. That it is often carried as a gatepost by gods with curls (see **Lahmu**) suggests a possible association with the god **Enki**.

125 (*above*) A baked-clay model of a so-called ring-post, symbol of the goddess Inana, from Uruk (modern Warka). Uruk Period.

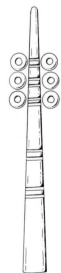

126 (*right*) A ring-staff. Detail from the carving on a stone bowl of the Uruk Period from Uruk.

127 Cattle gather around a byre, distinguished by its poles with rings. From a cylinder seal of the Late Uruk Period.

ring-staff

126 This symbol is common in early historic art and, like the **ring-post**, was used as a sign in pictographic script, but its meaning is unknown. In the earliest representations it is often seen in an architectural context and in
127 association with scenes of animal husbandry. It was most popular as a symbol and attribute in the Neo-Sumerian Period, and is last found in Old Babylonian art. When held as an object, in these later representations, it is always held by a god, never a goddess. Suggestions for the identity of this god are Adad (**Iškur**) and the sun god Šamaš (**Utu**). Advocates of the former sometimes regard the symbol as a stylisation of the **lightning (symbol)**, while supporters of the identification of the god as Šamaš have seen the ring-staff as a version of the **rod and ring**, thought by some to be a symbol of Šamaš. Whatever may be the merits of this last argument, an identification of the god who holds the ring-staff as Šamaš may be the more plausible suggestion, for the symbol is also occasionally associated with the **bull-man**.

river god: see **river ordeal**.

river of the underworld

According to some traditions about the **underworld**, it was reached, as in the later Greek tradition, by crossing a river. However, this was an untypical view rather than the usual one (according to which the underworld was located beneath the earth, beneath the **abzu**: see **cosmology**). In the Neo-Assyrian poem 'A Vision of the Underworld', the ferryman was the demon Humuṭ-tabal (whose name means 'Hurry and Take Away'). With this may be compared the ferryman Sursunabu or Uršanabi in the Epic of **Gilgameš**, who ferries Gilgameš across the waters of death. However, Uršanabi is more properly the ferryman of Ūtnapišti (**Ziusura**), and when he visited Ūtnapišti Gilgameš was not visiting the underworld.

Scenes in Neo-Babylonian art showing **Lamaštu** being driven back to the underworld typically depict her riding her donkey, set within her boat which sails upon a river, pre- 151 sumably that of the underworld.

The precise location of the river of the underworld is not clear. Sometimes it is called by the name Hubur (Sumerian *id lu rugu*, which may mean 'The river which blocks a man's way').

river ordeal

It was standard practice in Mesopotamia from the Old Babylonian Period on, when a legal dispute was not soluble by rational means (as, for example, because of conflicting sworn testimony by the parties involved), to refer the case to the River god: in other words to decide by means of a river ordeal. The judgement would then be declared in the name of Id (the 'Divine River'), or Šazi (son of the River god), or Ea (**Enki**). The person subjected to the ordeal was required to plunge into the river (at a special location in the presence of the authorities) and possibly to swim a certain distance. If they came out safe, they were cleared. If they were overcome and sank, they were guilty and had to return to the court for sentencing (fine or execution), except in the unintended eventuality of their drowning. It seems likely that only one of the litigants, selected by lot, underwent the ordeal: in which case it would be the lot, as much as the contestants' ability to swim, which determined the outcome. The river ordeal was regarded as a solemn expedient, and was in effect a form of **divination**.

The usual name for the river ordeal was *huršān* (Sumerian *id lu rugu*). Sometimes the river of the ordeal was identified with a specific
4 (deified) river, such as the Daban or Diyala (both lying north-east of Babylonia) or Hubur (possibly identical with the Habur, an affluent of the upper Euphrates). All these rivers lie outside Babylonia and it is possible that the river of the ordeal in these cases is connected with the **river of the underworld**, perhaps thought to lie at a distant extremity of the known world. Otherwise the river is simply called the (deified) River.

See **witchcraft**.

rod and ring

75 With the exception of doubtful Early Dynastic renderings, the divine attribute 'rod and ring' (apparently so called also in Akkadian) occurs in art from the Sumerian Renaissance to the Neo-Assyrian Period. It is thought to depict a pair of measuring instruments, a rule and a tape, taken as symbolic of divine justice. A par-
73 ticular association with the god Šamaš (**Utu**)
27 has therefore been suspected. Sometimes, however, the rod and ring appear to be a staff and **chaplet** of beads. It is evident that they
frontis., represent a general indication of high-ranking
105,132 divinity, for they could be held by all the major gods and goddesses. On the Neo-Assyrian re-
31 liefs at Maltai, male deities carry a 'rod and ring', female deities a ring without rod, perhaps a chaplet of beads.

See **ring-staff**.

rosette

Rosettes appear on the short ends of an Uruk Period trough from Uruk, in association with animals and a barn adorned with posts of **Inana** (see **ring-post**).

On seals of Mitannian style, the symbol of **seven dots** is normally arranged in the form of a rosette. This is not connected, however, with 21 the rosettes known from Middle Assyrian art, most commonly of faïence and found together in large numbers. Since many were found in the temple of Ištar (**Inana**) at the city of Aššur, 128 some scholars have connected the motif with Ištar, and it is possible that in the Neo-Assyrian Period the rosette occasionally replaced the

128 Middle Assyrian Period rosettes from the temple of the goddess Ištar in the city of Aššur, (*left*) in faïence and (*right*) in lead.

129 A baked-clay model of a bed, with loving couple, probably of Isin–Larsa or Old Babylonian date. Such items have been thought to have some cultic relationship with the rites of the 'marriage' of Dumuzi and Inana. L. 117 mm.

star as her symbol. The evidence, however, is unclear. Single rosettes are often seen as a decoration on wrist-straps worn by both human and supernatural figures in Neo-Assyrian monumental art.

Sacred Marriage

129 Sacred Marriage is a term borrowed from the history of Greek religion (*hieros gamos*) to describe at least two different sorts of ritual in ancient Mesopotamia. The idea of marriage between deities is used in a number of Mesopotamian myths as one way of explaining **creation**. In a ritual of which records date mostly from the Neo-Assyrian and Neo-Babylonian Periods or later, a marriage between two deities was enacted in a symbolic ceremony (called *hasādu*) in which their **cult statues** were brought together. A ceremonial bed was required so that the statues could 'marry'. Such symbolic ceremonies are known for **Marduk** and **Ṣarpānītu** (forming a part of the **New Year ceremonies**); **Nabû** and Tašmētu (or **Nanaya**), Šamaš (**Utu**) and Aya (**Šerida**); and Anu (**An**) and Antu. These 'marriages' do not appear to have been directly related to particular myths.

Quite different from this, and known from much earlier periods, is a ritual love-making apparently between a deified human king (see **deification of kings**) and the goddess **Inana**, seen as a symbolic counterpart to the mythical union of the god **Dumuzi** with Inana. The exclusively literary evidence for this 'marriage'

157

dates from the period of the Third Dynasty of Ur and the Isin Period, and it is still uncertain whether a real (temporary) 'marriage' between the king and a human priestess representing Inana actually took place, or if the whole ritual was purely symbolic. The beautiful songs and poems in Sumerian belonging to the Inana-Dumuzi cult suggest that the **fertility** of vegetation, animals and humans was believed in some way to depend upon the union of Inana and Ama-ušumgal-ana (an aspect of Dumuzi); but as no exact description of a ritual survives (in the way that details are preserved of the New Year ceremonies), it is difficult to know whether some form of dramatic re-enactment took place or not. A 'marriage' between an *entu* priestess (see **priests and priestesses**) and a local storm god, probably Adad or Wer (see **Iškur**), is known from the Syrian town of Emar in the fourteenth century BC. Possibly here too a ruler impersonated the god.

It is not known what the immediate source of information was for the story recounted by Herodotus (who may have visited Babylon in the fifth century BC) according to which a woman spent the night in a shrine on top of the **ziggurat** of Babylon, waiting to be visited by Bēl (**Marduk**) himself, although it is clearly reminiscent of what is known from earlier periods in Mesopotamia.

See **prostitution and ritual sex**.

sacred tree: see **stylised tree and its 'rituals'**.

sacrifice and offering

The widespread Mesopotamian idea of man having been created to act as the servant of the **gods** meant that it was considered necessary to feed and clothe the gods constantly and to make them presents. Among these various sorts of offering, the term sacrifice refers especially to the killing of an animal. Exactly the same foods and drinks were offered to the gods as were consumed by humans, with perhaps more emphasis on the luxury items: frequent fresh meat, fish, cream, honey, cakes and the best sorts of beer. **Incense** and aromatic woods were burned before them, as they might be at a human banquet. These sacrifices and offerings took two forms: the 'regular' offerings, offered at meal times daily throughout the year (just as daily services are performed in a Christian church); and the special, occasional offerings made at festivals which might be monthly or annual occurrences. Clothing was also offered. The actual comestibles and garments were redistributed to the temple staff (according to strict hierarchical regulations, from high **priests** down to courtyard sweepers) after being presented to the gods. In addition to the organised offerings, individuals might make personal offerings as they chose.

Offerings made as presents fall into three categories. First, those which were 'useful' to the gods – beds, chairs, boats, cups and vessels, weapons dedicated from war booty, and jewellery – were all absorbed into the temple treasury as part of the 'property' of the god. Second, statues of the offerers might be placed before the god to represent them in constant prayer before the deity. These and other thank offerings often carry inscriptions stating that they were offered 'for the life of' the offerer, or on behalf of some other person. Finally, offerings might be made as a form of request. Models of human limbs, of beds, of pregnant women and **figurines** of animals may have been of this type.

It was not only on **altars** and offering tables within temples that **animal sacrifice** was offered, for in the earliest periods certain places outside the temple proper were specifically demarcated for this purpose. In one of the series of prehistoric (Ubaid Period) temples at **Eridu** and in a room close by the entrance of another, archaeologists found heaps of ash containing great quantities of fish bones. They were apparently not part of a store of food or leftovers from the kitchens, but the remains of continual and repeated sacrifice. In a later (Uruk Period) building an enclosure was filled up with ash and fish bones. Unlike the earlier temple rooms, this enclosure was three-sided, with an open front, and represented a delineated area away from the temple itself. Fish offerings of the prehistoric and early historic periods are also known from G̃irsu (Tello) and Uruk, where large quantities of fish bones, including complete skeletons and skins, were found crammed into enclosures.

This type of large-scale fish offering is unknown from the Third Early Dynastic Period and later. Instead, from these early historic periods, enclosed deposits are found which contained mixed offerings of various animals, including fish, birds and other small animals, as well as goats and cattle. Some of these deposits also contained grain and vegetable matter. They are of two main kinds: a room containing shallow rectangular trenches, each with a slanting floor (confined to the Early Dynastic Period), and circular brick structures (found commonly up to and including the period of the Third Dynasty of Ur, with a last known occurrence in the Old Babylonian Period).

In the first of these arrangements, the areas of sacrifice were laid out almost identically to the earlier fish offering places, with a narrow trench (some four metres long by two-thirds of a metre wide) dug at an angle into the floor of an enclosure. The inside walls of the trench were plastered with clay, and replastered after each incineration. Occasionally the sides of the trench were lined with bricks. Reeds or reed mats were laid on the floor. The trench was cut straight at the entrance, but was rounded at the deeper end, where the fire was kindled. After everything was burnt, the trench was swept clean and prepared for the next incineration. At Uruk the entrance to the trench was always oriented to the north-east. In some instances large pottery vessels were placed alongside the trenches; they also contained the bones of fish, birds and other small animals. Sometimes the enclosures became so congested with sacrificial debris that the surrounding walls had to be increased in height. Some of the sacrificial trenches at Uruk (among the earliest) are located in the precinct of **E-ana**, the temple of **Inana**. At a slightly later date they were filled in with regularly laid brickwork and were no longer used.

The rounded structures seem to have served more or less the same function. They were sited either within enclosures or (apparently) on open-air plots.

We known nothing about the background to this method of sacrifice, only that they were constantly repeated in the same places, often close by the temple, but never within the sanctuaries themselves.

See **afterlife**; **dedication**; **food and drink of the gods**; **human sacrifice**; **libation**.

Ṣalmu

The Akkadian word *ṣalmu* (Sumerian *nu* or *alam*) is used to refer to any piece of representative art – figurative or not. 'Image', 'representation' or 'representative' (in the sense of an object standing for a person or creature without necessarily being a portrayal of them) are all possible translations. The word is used to refer to statues, stelae and **figurines**. It can also mean 'constellation'.

From at least the Middle Assyrian Period, Ṣalmu sometimes is used as the proper name of a deity, a sun god who can be identified with Šamaš and, in one Middle Babylonian text, is regarded as the father of the god Bunene (see **Utu**). In Neo-Assyrian sources, the name occasionally occurs in the plural, as if denoting a group of deities. The form Ṣalmu-šarri ('Ṣalmu of the king') is probably a modified name of the same god(s) (singular or plural).

It has been suggested that Ṣalmu is a name for the **winged disc**.

Samana

Incantations from the Old Babylonian Period are intended to protect infants, young men and women and prostitutes from attack by the **demon** Samana, who is described as having a lion's mouth, dragon's teeth, eagle's claws and the tail of a scorpion. The name seems also to be associated with a grain disease, possibly spread by a noxious insect.

It is not certain if this demon is originally the same as the minor deity whose worship is attested at Lagaš and one or two other Sumerian towns during the Early Dynastic Period. The writing of his name is irregular, but appears to have been pronounced Saman. He was also (under the name Saman-ana) included among the **Slain Heroes** enumerated in the poem *Lugale*.

Ṣarpānītu

Ṣarpānītu was the name of the goddess who was regarded as the wife of **Marduk**, and who was consequently the principal goddess of the city of Babylon. She was worshipped under the name Erua as a goddess of childbirth, from Akkadian *erû*, 'to be pregnant'. Her name Ṣarpānītu probably means 'she of Ṣarpān' (the name of an (as yet) unlocated town or village, perhaps near to Babylon), not, as was formerly thought, 'she who shines like refined silver (*ṣarpu*)'.

See **Dilmunite gods; Sacred Marriage**.

Sataran: see **Ištaran**.

saw: see **Utu**.

scimitar: see **Nergal; standards, staves and sceptres of the gods**.

scorpion

Representations of scorpions are known from prehistoric times onwards, but not unequivocally as a religious symbol until late in the Kassite Period on **kudurrus**, on which the creature is labelled as a symbol of the goddess **Išhara**.

Although not fatal, the sting of the scorpion found in Mesopotamia is sufficiently painful to

7, 90, 130

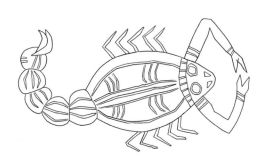

130 (*above*) A scorpion, symbol of the goddess Išhara. One of the symbols carved on a *kudurru* of the Kassite Period.

131 (*left*) Neo-Assyrian cylinder seals, with rolled impressions, depicting different kinds of scorpion-men. Hts. 29 mm.

suggest the creature as a suitable image of power and protection. Magical spells were used to counteract the effect of the sting. On representations of scorpions and **scorpion-people**, the tail is always emphasised, rising up threateningly along the back or over the head.

The Scorpion was also the Babylonian name of the constellation Scorpius (see **zodiac**).

scorpion-people

131 *Girtablullû*, 'scorpion-man', is the Akkadian term for a supernatural being with a **horned cap** of divinity, human head with beard, human body, the hindquarters and talons of a bird, a snake-headed penis, and a scorpion's tail. He may or may not have wings. The creature is first seen in the art of the Third Dynasty of Ur and of the Akkadian Period, but was common only in Neo-Assyrian and Neo-Babylonian times. The type survived in art until the Hellenistic Period. As attendants of Šamaš (**Utu**) (in art

82 often supporting the solar **winged disc** or with their heads possibly shown above its wing tips), the scorpion-men were also, by the Neo-Assyrian Period, powerful protectors against demons. Wooden **figurines** of them are prescribed, along with figurines of other beneficent **demons and monsters**, in Neo-Assyrian instructions for rituals of protective **magic**, and an actual example has been found in a storeroom at the seventh-century BC Urarṭian city of Teišebaini (modern Karmir Blur). These rituals mention figurines of 'male

and female' scorpion-people, showing that the 'scorpion-woman' was a figure in art, although no representation of her has yet been identified: pairs of scorpion-tailed figures are common but seem usually to represent two bearded males (compare **merman and mermaid**).

In the Babylonian Epic of Creation, the scorpion-man is counted as one of **Tiāmat's creatures**, while in the Epic of **Gilgameš**, a terrifying scorpion-man and scorpion-woman guard the gate of Mount Mašu, where the sun rises.

An iconographically rather different human and scorpion combination with human head, 90,131 the full body and legs of a bird, and a scorpion's tail is seen in Kassite, Neo-Assyrian, Neo-Babylonian and Seleucid Period art. It is unclear whether this is also a *girtablullû*.

seals of the gods

Like humans, the **gods** had their own seals for marking their property or for giving their agreement to legal documents. In practice they were used to signify the property or the agreement of the administration. Among the most famous are the cylinder seals of the god **Aššur** 132 rolled on the tablets of the so-called 'vassal treaties' of the Assyrian king Esarhaddon (reigned 680–669 BC), which were intended to ensure the royal succession.

Sebittu: see **Seven (demons)**; **Seven (gods)**.

132 A worshipper kneels before the god Aššur. (Behind stands the weather god Adad.) The design of a Middle Assyrian seal of the god Aššur, from its impression on one of the clay tablets of the 'vassal treaties' of King Esarhaddon. Found at Kalhu (modern Nimrud). The background was covered with a long text, now very faint and largely illegible.

serpents: see **dragons**; **snakes**.

seven: see **numbers**.

Seven (demons)

The Akkadian word *sebittu* is a singular noun meaning a 'group of seven'; Sumerian *iminbi* corresponds to it. 'The Seven' is a name given to a group of **demons**, the offspring of **An** and **Ki**, who act as assistants to the god **Nergal** (Erra). One collection of magical incantations seems to identify the Seven with seven named evil **udug**s, sometimes also called 'Seven and seven' or 'Seven times seven'.

See **Seven (gods)**.

seven dots

With possible antecedents dating back to prehistoric times, the symbol of the seven dots (or globes) is first known in unequivocal form in Mitannian glyptic art, and became common in the Neo-Assyrian and Neo-Babylonian Periods. On Mitannian seals the dots are usually arranged as six dots around a central dot, forming a kind of **rosette**. Thereafter, however, the dots are normally shown simply in 133 two rows of three, with the seventh dot placed 49,55 between the rows at the far end. From early on (at least from Middle Assyrian times), the seven dots appears as a symbol in close association with other clearly astral symbols such as 151 the **solar disc** and the **crescent**. In Assyrian, Babylonian and later art, they were regarded as a representation of the Pleiades: a new, though less popular, version of the symbol showed 87,159 seven stars rather than dots. Inscriptions also

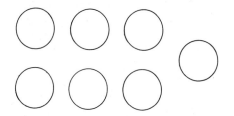

133 Seven dots, symbol of the Seven (gods), as commonly depicted in Neo–Assyrian and Neo-Babylonian art.

identify the symbol as that of the *Sebittu* or **Seven (gods)**, with whom the Pleiades were 10 evidently associated.

See **zodiac**.

Seven (gods)

As well as for a group of demons (see **Seven (demons)**), *Sebittu* (Sumerian *Iminbi*), 'the Seven', is a name given to a group of beneficent gods whose power can be harnessed against evil **demons** by means of magical incantations. 'The Seven' operate together with their sister **Narūdu**, probably in origin the Elamite goddess Narunte (see **Elamite gods**), and so may themselves be of Elamite origin. They should be distinguished from the Babylonian **Seven Sages** (*apkallū*). They may be identical with the seven children of **Ishara**. They are sometimes named (as 'Seven and seven') together with another group, who may be the seven sons of **Enmešarra**. There were temples to these Seven at the Assyrian capital cities of Kalhu (Nimrud), Dūr-Šarkēn (Khorsabad) and Nineveh. Astrologically they were identified with the star-group Pleiades.

The standard iconography of the Seven in 134 the Neo-Assyrian Period is known. They wear tall cylindrical hats with feathered upper borders, and long open robes. Each carries an axe and a knife, as well as a bow and quiver. These are the attributes prescribed for the Seven in rituals concerning the placement of protective **figurines** at set locations about a house. In practice, when in forms other than plastic art, this iconography could, it seems, pose problems, for on a stone relief slab from the palace of Assurbanipal (reigned 668–*c*. 627 BC) at Nineveh, the long bows have been carved first then erased in favour of the axes and knives.

At least in Neo-Assyrian and Neo-Babylonian art, the Seven were symbolised by the **seven dots**, sometimes substituted by seven stars (probably an allusion to the identification with the Pleiades).

See **zodiac**.

seven-headed snake: see **snakes**.

134 Three of the divine Seven, carrying axes and knives, and with their original bows erased. Monumental stone relief from the royal palace of the Assyrian king Assurbanipal (reigned 668–*c*.627 BC) at Nineveh. Ht. 0.89 m.

Seven Sages

According to Babylonian tradition, seven *ap-kallū* ('wise men' or 'sages') lived before the **Flood**. Neo-Babylonian and Neo-Assyrian ritual texts give their names and the seven cities from which they were believed to have come, although there are variant traditions which cannot be fully reconciled one with another.

Other antediluvian figures are also said to have been *apkallū*, notably **Adapa of Eridu**.

The Seven Sages should be distinguished from the **Seven (gods)** (*Sebittu*) because Neo-Assyrian instructions for rituals including protective **figurines** prescribe sets of figures of the Seven followed by those of the Seven Sages. Figures of different forms of the Seven Sages are to be made, some apparently in human form, some wearing fishes' skins (see **fish-garbed figure**), and winged figures with birds' faces (see **griffin-demon**).

The tradition of the Seven Sages seems to be preserved in **Berossos'** account of eight creatures who appeared from the sea in the 'first days', beginning with Oannes and ending with Odakon. In the Babylonian Epic of **Gilgameš**, the Seven Sages are credited with building the walls of Uruk.

See **dead gods**.

sex: see **creation; Inana; prostitution and ritual sex; Sacred Marriage**.

Sibittu (*Sebittu*): see **Seven (demons); Seven (gods)**.

Siduri

The goddess Siduri (Šiduri in the Hurrian version) is the proprietress of the ale-house at the world's edge in the Epic of Gilgameš. On his journey to Ūt-napišti (**Ziusura**), **Gilgameš** meets Siduri, who tries to persuade the hero to abandon his quest for immortality and to enjoy what fruits the present life has to offer:

Gilgameš, where are you going?
You will not find the life for which you are
  searching.
When the gods created man,
They allotted death for mankind,
Keeping life for themselves.
Gilgameš, let your belly be full,
Make merry by day and by night.
Make a feast of rejoicing every day.
By day and by night, dance and play.
Let your clothing be clean and fresh,
Your head be washed, your body bathed in
  water.
Look to the child who clutches your hand,
Let your wife enjoy herself in your lap.
This is the fulfilment of man!

sin

The various words in Sumerian and Akkadian which are translated as 'sin' (offences against moral or divine law) are equally used to refer to 'crime' (infringement of civil or criminal law) or to social ills, such as the prevalence of crime in a country. Assyrian kings were fond of talking about 'punishing' the 'crimes' of their enemies (crimes which consisted in resisting the Assyrian Empire or failing to adhere to a

treaty imposed upon them), but this is largely propaganda. Nonetheless, a distinction was recognised between offences that had to be dealt with by the courts and offences of a more social nature. Such 'sins' might be deliberate, but one whole magical rite is devoted to relieving the patient of the numerous sins which might be committed by negligence unwittingly. The patient might not even know which god or goddess he or she had offended. Such sin could be 'undone', 'expelled' or 'annulled' by a god, and it is stressed that 'prayer can undo sin'. The use of the word 'patient' in this context emphasises the Babylonian view of sin as comparable with **disease**. Sin could be transmitted by relatives or inherited from parents; it could be 'caught' by, for example, sitting on the same chair as had been sat on by a tabooed person. Like disease, it too could be cured by magic rituals involving potions and herbal ointments accompanied by incantations. In this we can recognise as 'sin' a conscious feeling of sin and guilt, a conscience, which can be salved by magical practices or by prayer. Looking at it another way, we can say that manifestations of psychological disturbance were interpreted as evidence of 'sin' and may well have been cured by rituals in which the patient had faith. The Babylonians did not have a doctrine of *original* sin, but they believed that we are all very *prone* to sin.

See **good and evil; magic and sorcery; taboos**.

Sîn: see **Nanna-Suen**.

Slain Heroes

The Slain Heroes were a bizarre group of dead 135 monsters considered to have been slain by the warrior god **Ninĝirsu** (or in another version by **Ninurta**). These include the Six-headed Wild Ram, the Seven-headed Snake (see **snakes**), the Dragon, the **Palm-tree King**, the Gypsum, the Strong Copper, the Kuli-ana, the *Magillum*-boat, Lord Saman-ana, the Bison-bull and the **Imdugud** Bird. The myth con- 35,86 cerning the 'killing' of these monsters – some animalian, some apparently inanimate – can be

135 The god Ninĝirsu or Ninurta slays the seven-headed snake monster *mušmaḫḫu*. Detail from an engraved shell inlay plaque of the Early Dynastic Period.

traced back to the period of Gudea, ruler of the Sumerian city-state of Lagaš, who rebuilt the temple of Ninĝirsu at Ĝirsu and did a lot to promote the cult of that god. Gudea arranged for the 'Slain Heroes' to receive offerings in the new temple of Ninĝirsu.

In fact there is evidence that at least the Palm-tree, the Wild Ram, the Copper and Saman were being worshipped as minor deities up to two hundred years earlier, and there is reason to believe that the myth of their 'slaying' by Ninĝirsu was an attempt to absorb them into his mythology.

Later, other trophies were added to the list, and the myth was transferred to other deities such as **Zababa, Lugalbanda, Erra (Nergal), Marduk** or even **Nabû**. Some of the once-terrifying monsters were ultimately transformed into minor **demons** and benign beings whose presence could be harnessed to ward off hostile demons. In the Neo-Assyrian Period, small clay **figurines** of beings some of whom can be traced back to the Slain Heroes of Ninĝirsu were buried in the foundations of buildings to protect their inhabitants from demonic disturbance. Traditions such as that of the Slain Heroes may ultimately have contributed to Greek myths of Near Eastern origin, such as that of the Labours of Herakles.

See **bell; bison; bull-man; dead gods; demons and monsters; dragons; merman and mermaid; Samana; Tiāmat's creatures**.

Smiting god

Since the so-called 'smiting' posture is the inevitable position for wielding certain weapons, 'smiting gods' appear in the art of all periods. The term is applied in particular, however, to a figure in Neo-Assyrian and Neo-Babylonian art who wears the **horned cap** of divinity and often a short kilt; he may be naked above the waist. He holds one fist in the air and the other hand towards the ground. He is often paired

136 A figurine of a god with raised fist 'smiting' the air, possibly the god Lulal, made of sun-baked clay. Neo-Babylonian, from a brick box buried in the foundations of a public building at Kiš.

with the **lion-demon**. He has not yet been certainly identified with any named god, although he may represent the god Lulal (see **La-tarāk and Lulal**).

snake-dragon

The snake-dragon (with horns, snake's body and neck, lion's forelegs and bird's hindlegs) is represented from the Akkadian Period down to the Hellenistic Period as a symbol of various gods or as a generally magically protective hybrid not associated specifically with any deity. By comparing the figure depicted on the gates and processional way at Babylon with the description of the building operations given by King Nebuchadnezzar II (reigned 604–562 BC), it has been possible to identify with certainty the creature's Akkadian name as *mušhuššu*, 'furious snake'. The complex mythologies and divine associations surrounding the creature have only recently been collected and explained. The *mušhuššu* was originally an attendant of **Ninazu**, the city god of Ešnunna. It was 'inherited' by the god **Tišpak** when he replaced Ninazu as city god in the Akkadian or early Old Babylonian Period, and in Lagaš became associated with Ninazu's son **Ningiš-zida**. Possibly after Hammurabi's conquest of Ešnunna, the creature was transferred to the new Babylonian national god, **Marduk**, and later to **Nabû**. The conquest of Babylon by the

Assyrian king Sennacherib (reigned 704–681 BC) brought the motif to Assyria, normally as the beast of the state god **Aššur**. On Sennacherib's rock-reliefs at Maltai, however, the creature accompanies three different gods, Aššur, Ellil (**Enlil**) and another god, most likely Nabû.

snake gods

The snake gods of ancient Mesopotamia, especially Nirah, seem to be the only fully animalian, non-anthropomorphic, deities (although **La-tarāk** may have had a leonine face and worn a lion's skin). The snake god Nirah was worshipped at the city of Dēr, located on the northern border between Mesopotamia and Elam, as the minister of **Ištaran**,

137 (*above*) Snake gods. Detail from a cylinder seal of the Akkadian Period.

138 (*left*) The snake-dragon (*mušhuššu*) as depicted repeatedly on moulded bricks of the Ištar Gate and of the Processional Way at Babylon, built for King Nebuchadnezzar II (reigned 604–562 BC).

the city god of Dēr (see **local gods**). His cult there is attested from the earliest times and was long-lived. He was also worshipped until Middle Babylonian times in the **E-kur**, the temple of Ellil (**Enlil**) in Nippur, where he was regarded as a protective deity of the temple and a protective presence. The cult of Irhan, a deity of the city of Ur and probably in origin a god representing the river Euphrates, remained independent until the period of the Third Dynasty of Ur, but was later syncretised with the cult of Nirah. It is possible that the snake symbol found on **kudurrus** represents the god Nirah (see **snakes**).

An anthropomorphic god with the lower body of a snake, shown on cylinder seals of the Old Akkadian Period, may also represent Nirah.

For the seven-headed snake, see **snakes**.

On the cylinder seal of Gudea, prince of Lagaš, the ruler is introduced into the presence of a superior deity by a god from each of whose shoulders a horned snake rises. This is probably intended to represent **Ningišzida**, regarded by Gudea as his personal protective deity (see **personal gods**).

snakes

Representations of snakes are naturally frequent in iconography from the prehistoric periods onwards, but it is not always easy to decide whether or not they carried any religious value. When depicted as attributes of deities they are seen associated with both gods and goddesses. As an independent symbol the snake appears on **kudurrus** and is identified

139 A steatite vase carved with a dragon (*bašmu*) and entwined snakes and inscribed with a dedication by Gudea, prince of Lagaš, to his 'personal god' Ningišzida. From Ĝirsu (modern Tello). Ht. 230 mm.

by the inscription on one as symbolising the minister of the god **Ištaran** (and so is possibly Nirah: see **snake gods**). Snakes continued to be portrayed in religious and secular art in later periods. As a divine symbol in Neo-Assyrian and Neo-Babylonian art, the snake can be identified from ritual texts directly as the god Nirah.

139 The motif of the two serpents entwined together as if they were a length of rope was a very common one in early historic, Sumerian and Neo-Sumerian art and thereafter occurs sporadically on seals and **amulets** down to the thirteenth century BC. One of the finest examples is carved on a steatite vase dedicated by Gudea of Lagaš to his patron god **Ningišzida**.

The horned viper (*Cerastes cerastes*), a mildly venomous snake native to the Middle East, has a pair of spike-like folds of skin on its head. In art, the form of a snake with a pair of horns rising from the forehead occurs as a symbol on Kassite **kudurru**s and in Neo-Assyrian art as an element of seal designs and in the form of magically protective **figurines**. It has been identified as the creature called in Akkadian *bašmu* (Sumerian *muš-ša-tur*). The mythological traditions are obscure, but by Assyrian times the figure was often a magically protective type. A variant horned snake with forelegs was apparently regarded as a different creature, although carrying in Akkadian the same name
139 *bašmu* (Sumerian *ušum*). This being was also known as *ušumgallu* (Sumerian *ušumgal*). Originally one of the trophies of **Ninurta** (see **Slain Heroes**), it was later – when the **snake-dragon** became **Marduk**'s animal – the symbol of various gods formerly associated with the snake-dragon, including Ningišzida.

A seven-headed *mušmahhu* monster is referred to in mythological texts and depicted in Early Dynastic art as a kind of **dragon** with
135 seven long snake necks and heads. This creature may be the seven-headed hydra killed by the god **Ninğirsu** or Ninurta (see **Slain Heroes**), also referred to in spells.

See **mongoose**; **'plant of life'**.

140 The solar disc of the sun god Šamaš.

solar disc
The disc with four-pointed star and three radiating wavy lines between each of the points occurs
from the Akkadian down to the Neo- 21,90 Babylonian Period. It almost invariably stands as a symbol of the sun god Šamaš (**Utu**). The 7,76 Akkadian names of the symbol were *šamšatu* and *niphu*. It was often represented upon a pole as a standard.

sorcery: see **magic and sorcery**; **witchcraft**.

spade (symbol)
The shaft with triangular head, as an independent symbol, sometimes on a base, and as an 141 attribute held by a figure, is known from the 49 Neo-Sumerian down to the Neo-Babylonian Period. It is inscriptionally attested on Kassite, Neo-Assyrian and Neo-Babylonian monu- 90 ments as the spade or hoe (*marru*) of the god 7,10 **Marduk**, perhaps originally an agricultural deity, who had become the national god of Babylonia. In the Assyrian Period the original agricultural purpose of the object was known, but perhaps considered to be of diminished relevance. In some Assyrian representations, especially on the palace reliefs when held by figures of **Lahmu**, it seems to have been transformed into a spear, to which the original form approximated. It is still referred to, however, as a *marru*, 'spade'.

In later Babylonian times, some slaves were branded with the device of a spade (see **dedication**).

sphinx: see **bulls and lions with human head**.

141 The *marru* 'spade', a symbol of the Babylonian god Marduk.

standards, staves and sceptres of the gods

76 A number of different standards, staves and sceptres occur as divine symbols. A ram-headed staff is known from the Old Babylonian down to the Achaemenid Period, and is identified by inscriptional evidence from
7 Kassite and Assyrian sculpture as a symbol of
10 the god Ea (**Enki**). It usually rests upon a base, but occasionally stands alone or upon the back of a **goat-fish**. Sometimes, on Neo-Assyrian seals, Ea carries a **crook**, perhaps an abbreviated form of the ram-head staff.

An eagle-headed (or griffin-headed) staff is
90 represented only on Kassite **kudurrus**, to be
7 identified from the inscription on one as a symbol of the god **Zababa**. It was later adopted as one of the Assyrian military standards.

4,142 A staff or scimitar with the head of a lion (or rather **lion-demon**, with **donkey ears**) is found as a motif from the Akkadian down to the Neo-Babylonian Period. From the inscriptions
7 on a **kudurru** and a Neo-Babylonian stela, it is shown to be a symbol of the underworld god **Nergal**.

The double lion-headed sceptre or **mace** is a common attribute and symbol in Neo-Sumerian art, and is there associated with a
13,90 variety of deities, male and female. It was apparently a symbol of a particular deity on Kassite and Neo-Assyrian monuments. Exactly which god it there represents depends upon the restoration of slight lacunae in the inscriptions
10 of two of the Bavian rock stelae of the Assyrian king Sennacherib (reigned 704–681 BC): **Nergal**, **Ninurta** and **Nusku** have each been suggested. Nergal is the most likely on epigraphic grounds. He has been discounted because his symbol on *kudurru*s is well established as the single lion-headed staff or scimitar, but perhaps the double lion-headed sceptre was regarded merely as a variant of this (and the lion-heads often have upright ears). In any event, the other two gods also each have another identified symbol on the *kudurru*s (the perched **bird** of Ninurta and the **lamp** of Nusku) and Ea is known to have two separate symbols, the **goat-fish** with ram-head staff and the **turtle**.

Neo-Assyrian military standards are occasionally shown in campaign scenes on Assyrian sculptured reliefs, especially those of Assurnasirpal II (reigned 883–859 BC). They represent various deities and it has been suggested that the army was divided into units supported by the different temples. The troops of Ištar (**Inana**) carried a banner showing the goddess herself, armed and set within a nimbus of stars. Another standard depicting a god drawing a bow and standing between streams of water and a pair of outward-facing bulls may have signified the legions of the temple of Adad (**Iškur**) – mountain streams were believed to be the responsibility of the storm god, probably because he was the god of the rains and because the reverberant sound of the waters running over the rocks was reminiscent of thunder. A military standard of the reign of Sargon II (reigned 721–705 BC) depicts an unusual god with the head of a falcon: his identity is unknown.

See **birds**; **bird-gods**; **Ninšubur (god)**; **ring-post**; **ring-staff**; **solar disc**.

star (symbol)

The eight-pointed star is known from prehis- 82,143, toric times through to the Neo-Babylonian 158

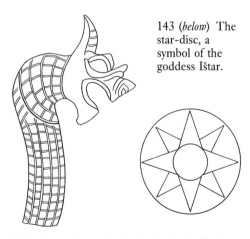

143 (*below*) The star-disc, a symbol of the goddess Ištar.

142 (*above*) A standard with the head of a lion–demon (lion with upright ears), an emblem of the underworld god Nergal. One of the symbols carved on a *kudurru* of the Kassite Period.

144 The Assyrian king, shown twice, stands on either side of a stylised tree and image of the sun god Šamaš in his winged disc. Winged protective griffin-demons with purificatory buckets and cones flank the scene. From a cylinder seal of the early Neo-Assyrian Period.

Period. In early representations it may have had a general astral significance, but at least from the Old Babylonian Period (and in all probability from the Early Dynastic) it was normally, though not always, a symbol of **In-ana**/Ištar, goddess of love and war, the planet Venus. Most commonly from the Old Babylon-ian Period onwards, the star is enclosed within a disc. On Middle and Neo-Assyrian seals, the upper body of a goddess, presumably Ištar, is sometimes set above a **crescent** surrounded by stars, a variation on the more usual armed goddess within a nimbus of stars.

7,21
73,90,
143,151

The motif of a six-pointed star occurs throughout the same period, but is of unknown significance.

In later Babylonian times some persons dedicated as temple slaves were branded with the device of a star (see **dedication**).

See **seven dots**; **solar disc**.

statues: see **cult statues**.

storm gods and storm demons: see **Iškur**; **lion-demon**; **Numušda**; **ūmu dabrūtu**.

stylised tree and its 'rituals'

The motif referred to by modern commentators as the 'stylised' or 'sacred' tree, or, more presumptuously, as the 'tree of life', has provoked more discussion and controversy than almost any other element in Mesopotamian art. The literature is almost as extensive as the representations of the motif itself, and includes a number of books devoted entirely to the subject. As with the equally ubiquitous and often iconographically associated **winged disc**, opinions vary greatly as to the meaning and significance of the symbol, and lack of explicit textual reference to the tree or its function allows speculation a free rein.

Stylised trees of one type or another are commonly portrayed in Mesopotamian art from prehistoric times through to the Neo-Babylonian Period. At one time the tree will be very formalised, often elaborate, at another tending towards naturalism, but in either case it will usually be set upon an elevation of some kind or placed in a position of prominence with respect to the other elements of a design. The tree is often flanked by animals, or by supernatural figures.

144   In scenes mostly restricted to the second and first millennia BC, and particularly popular in Assyria, a stylised tree, usually with winged disc above, is flanked by semi-human genies, 7,108 one or more possibly holding a **bucket and** 131 **cone**. The various interpretations of this so-called 'cone-smearing' ritual include a magically protective rite, a benediction, an **anointing** of a symbol of the king, or of the king himself (the cones sometimes also being held behind the king's head), a literal rendering of fruit-picking or of fertilisation of the date palm, a myth of the god **Dumuzi**, a symbolic reference to fire and water as the elements of life, or a piece of astronomical symbolism. There may be more than a single aspect involved. For example, the nature of the **genies**, almost invariably 'supernatural' rather than human, suggests some apotropaic element, while a relationship to, or even derivation from, actual date palm fertilisation (but only in the Mesopotamian south, not in Assyria) is plausible. Nevertheless, it is highly likely that the principal purpose of the rite was as a ritual of **purification** (see **bucket and cone**).

Interest in the stylised tree has been provoked, and interpretations of it often influenced, by the 'tree of life' (and the 'tree of the knowledge of good and evil') in the Garden of Eden, in Genesis 2–3. There is no reason, however, to connect the two traditions.

See **Palm-tree King**.

stylus: see **wedge**.

Sud: see **Ninlil**; **Nisaba**.

Sumuqan: see **Šakkan**.

sun disc: see **solar disc**.

sun god: see **Utu**.

145 Painted decoration on the inside of a prehistoric pottery bowl found at Samarra. The design shows birds and fish revolving around a central swastika.

swastika

The swastika or fylfot is encountered only very rarely in Mesopotamian art, but the rôle of this symbol of modern notoriety is not without interest. It is unequivocally represented on prehistoric painted pottery and early historic seal 145 impressions, but is thereafter seen again only in a single instance, on a limestone slab fronting a Neo-Assyrian temple building at Aššur, painted in bitumen. To fill the gap between these widely separated occurrences, some scholars (especially those writing just before and during the Second World War, when interest in the motif was at a peak) have attempted to see the outline of the symbol in various arrangements of men, crossed animals and geometric motifs throughout the periods of ancient Mesopotamian art, but these interpretations can stretch the imagination.

The device has been variously explained as a solar symbol derived from the wheels of the chariot of the sun god, as the sign for a fortress or fortified site, or as symbolic of a whirlwind or of the four winds. There is no convincing evidence for the motif as a solar device, at least in Mesopotamia (but see **cross**).

146 Wild animals were under the protection of the god Šakkan. Copy of a life-size wall painting of a seated cheetah from the main altar in the Late Uruk Period Temple at Tell ʿUqair. Ht. *c.*0.9 m.

Šakkan

146 In the flat, open countryside of Mesopotamia a wide range of animals lived in ancient times. Among these were the lion, cheetah, wolf, jackal, hyena, wild cattle, oryx, gazelle, wild pig, wild cat and lynx as well as the beaver and **mongoose**. In the more mountainous areas the fallow and roe deer, wild goat, ibex, wild sheep and, more rarely, the leopard and bear could be seen. The god who protected all these was Šakkan (in Akkadian, Sumuqan). In one of the Sumerian poems called 'The Death of **Gil-gameš**', offerings are made to Šakkan in the **underworld**. In the seventh tablet of the Babylonian Epic of Gilgameš, **Enkidu**'s vision of the underworld includes Sumuqan as well as **Etana** and **Ereškigal**. Possibly the connection of Šakkan/Sumuqan with the underworld is due in some way to the association of the underworld with the desert in Babylonian thought.

147 (*right*) The goddess Šala, holding a barley stalk, drawn on a clay tablet with an astronomical text, found at Uruk (modern Warka) and dating to the Seleucid Period.

Šakkan was thought of as a son of the sun god Šamaš (**Utu**). In his rôle as a protector of wild animals he was sometimes envisaged as a shepherd. He was also responsible for the **fertility** of wild creatures.

Šala

The goddess Šala (or Šalaš, which is probably a Hittite form of her name) was not a goddess of native Mesopotamian origin. She is likely to have been a goddess of the Hurrians originally, and she entered the Mesopotamian world either as the wife of Adad (**Iškur**) or, in a con-

trasting tradition, as the wife of **Dagan**. In incantations to the fire god Girra (**Gibil**), for use in magical rituals intended to undo sorcery (see **magic and sorcery**), Girra is said to be the son of Šala.

29   A symbol of Šala was a **barley stalk**, suggesting that she was perhaps an agricultural deity. One text links Šala and an ear of grain
147   with the constellation called the Furrow (Virgo), whose brightest star, in modern terminology, is Spica (Latin *virgo*, 'maiden'; and *spica*, 'ear of grain').

See **nude woman**; **zodiac**.

Šamaš: see **Utu**.

Šara

The god Šara was the **local god** of the Sumerian city of Umma, where he was worshipped in the temple E-mah. A fragment of a stone bowl dedicated to Šara was found in a rubbish dump in the Early Dynastic temple at the site in north-eastern Babylonia called today Tell Agrab, and may indicate that this city (whose ancient name is unknown) was also a cult centre of Šara.

The epithet 'hero of **An**' suggests that Šara was a warrior god, as does the fact that in the Babylonian myth of Anzû (**Imdugud**), Šara is one of the gods asked to undertake the fight against Anzû (eventually taken on by **Ninurta**). In the Sumerian poem of **Inana**'s descent to the **underworld**, Šara is one of three deities who come to pay homage to Inana after her return: this may be connected with a tradition preserved in the myth of **Lugalbanda** and a building inscription of the Third Dynasty of Ur that Šara was the son of Inana.

šēdu: see **lama**.

Šerida (Aya)

Šerida (Akkadian Aya) is a goddess of light, regarded as the consort of **Utu/Šamaš**, the sun god. She is associated with sexual love and fruitfulness. The name Aya is found in personal names from the Third Dynasty of Ur. She was particularly popular during the Old Babylonian Period, and again during the Neo-Babylonian Period. Aya was worshipped together with Šamaš at Sippar and Larsa.

See **Sacred Marriage**.

Šullat: see **Iškur**.

Šul-pa-e

The cult of the Sumerian god Šul-pa-e (*šul pa-e*, 'brilliant youth') is attested from the Early Dynastic Period on. Despite his name, he was not a youthful god but was, according to one tradition, the husband of the 'mother goddess' **Ninhursaĝa** (see **mother goddesses and birth goddesses**), who bore him three children (Ašgi, **Lisin** and Lil). The tradition is at odds with the Sumerian myth in which it is **Enki** who is the consort of Ninhursaĝa. Šul-pa-e remained a minor god, whose character is not certain. In one Sumerian poem offerings are made to Šul-pa-e in the **underworld**, and in later tradition he was included among the **demons**. Astronomically, Šul-pa-e was one of many names of the planet Jupiter.

tablet of destinies

The tablet of destinies, along with the **me** and his crown and throne, was one of the objects whose possession guaranteed **Enlil** his supreme position as ruler of the universe and controller of the affairs of men and **gods**. It was envisaged as a tablet of cuneiform writing, impressed also with cylinder seals, in other words as an unalterable legal document or authorised treaty. The god is described as 'holding it in his hand' or 'clutching it to his breast'. The tablet invested its holder with the power to determine the destinies of the world, and not for nothing was it described as a cosmic bond linking heaven and the **underworld**.

In the Sumerian poem '**Ninurta** and the Turtle', it is **Enki** who holds the tablet. Both this and the Akkadian Anzû poem concern the theft of the tablet by the bird Anzû (**Imdugud**). In the Babylonian Epic of Creation, it is **Tiāmat** who gives the tablet to **Qingu**.

taboos

The term taboo, meaning set apart or consecrated to a god and hence forbidden to general use, is used as an approximate translation of Sumerian *ni-gig*, Akkadian *ikkibu*; *azag* (Akkadian *asakku*) has a similar meaning.

The sense of this idea is that of a thing, place or action forbidden to the generality because it is sacred to a particular god; or a thing, place or position, or activity reserved for a god or king. For instance, one should not eat a certain meat, fish or vegetable on a particular day of the month because it is the *ikkibu* of a particular god, e.g. eating game might be an *ikkibu* of the god Sumuqan (Šakkan). Similarly one should not mention certain subjects or perform certain actions on a particular occasion or during a particular ritual, for the same reasons. The name of the god concerned is always specified. A certain place might be an *ikkibu* of the king, and denied to everyone else.

The common usage, referring to any form of infringement, of the phrases 'to eat the *ikkibu*' and 'to take or steal the *asakku*' may give some idea of the original application of the concepts: likewise 'to step on the *anzillu*' (a synonymous word). Later these words all became little more than synonyms for 'sin'.

See **magic and sorcery**; **purification**.

talismans: see **amulets**.

Tammuz: see **Dumuzi**.

Tašmētu: see **Nabû**.

temple prostitution: see **prostitution and ritual sex**.

temples and temple architecture

Mesopotamians might worship in open-air sanctuaries, private chapels in domestic houses or small separate chapels in the residential quarters of town. The heart of religious life, however, was the temple.

As the words for a temple in Mesopotamian languages suggest, the temple was nothing more or less than the god's personal abode on earth (Sumerian *e*; Akkadian *bītu*, 'house'), and the deity normally 'lived' in his or her temple in the form of a **cult statue** standing in the main shrine. In the historic periods, at least, the temples of the various gods had their own names, such as the **E-kur** ('Mountain House') of **Enlil** at Nippur or the **E-abzu** ('Abzu House') of **Enki** at Eridu (similarly **E-ana**, **Esagil**, **Ezida**).

According to Sumerian tradition, **Eridu** was the oldest city of southern Mesopotamia. There archaeologists have unearthed a sequence of mud-brick temples repeatedly rebuilt during the late fifth and early fourth millennia BC. The earliest is only a small shrine, about three metres square. Yet this structure already shows important elements which continued in the temple form of later times: an **altar** in a niche set opposite the doorway and a small offering table in front of it. In later periods the plan was elaborated but retained its essentials. The shrine was lengthened and numbers of rooms added on either side.

As each successive rebuilding of the Eridu temple was constructed upon the ruins of its predecessors, it eventually came to stand upon its own mound, making an impressive image on the skyline and towering above the surrounding buildings. According to one theory, this development gave rise to the construction of **ziggurats**, or temple towers. The external appearance of the temple was also improved by series of alternating buttresses and recesses, possibly in imitation of the vertical reed bundles that supported the walls in reed houses. In later periods this form of buttressed façade became the most characteristic feature 148 of Mesopotamian temple building, and was also copied in temple construction in Egypt.

By early historic times (late fourth millennium BC) we can see some greater diversity in adaptations of the basic temple plan. In the E-ana precinct at Uruk some half dozen temples, though no longer built at any great height, preserve the earlier arrangement with a main sanctuary, lateral rooms and an axially placed altar. The sanctuary is now occasionally of cruciform design, as also is that of the contemporary temple at Tell Brak in northern Syria (see **eye and eye-idols**). In all other respects the plan continues that of the prehistoric temples. However, some temples, such as the so-called White Temple at Uruk, continued to be built on raised ground. Although again simply the ruins of earlier buildings, the platform was now faced with sloping brick panels, similar to ziggurat construction. The walls of the temple itself were again heavily buttressed, with evidence of original wooden decoration within the alcoves. In such temples the long sanctuary and side-rooms remain, with entry for the worshippers through one of the side-rooms. At either end of the sanctuary, however, are also major doorways, so that the shrine stands as a kind of portal. So that it does not intrude upon this thoroughfare, the altar is displaced from its axial position.

Some archaeologists have postulated a division of these temples by function. In ground-level or 'low' temples the deity normally resided and received worship, as represented by a **cult statue**. In contrast, 'high' or platform temples are thought to have been used as a portal by a god on his visits to earth.

Representations of temples are shown on early historic seals before we ever have the depiction of any god. The temple is characterised by its rectangular shape. Its identity as a temple is shown by the frequent association of processions of men approaching the building carrying offerings of various kinds. Buildings of this type may also be shown flanked by divine emblems, usually the **ring-post** or **ring-staff** (although both of these can also be seen on byres, presumably as divine protection for the animals). Similar rectangular buildings are shown on seal designs which associate them with groups of quadrupeds, usually goats. It has been suggested that we have here represented a different kind of temple, a rural shrine constructed not of brick but of timber poles and reed matting.

From the Early Dynastic Period we have the remains of two 'high' temples, or rather of the temple platforms only, since in neither case has the building itself survived. One is at Tutub (modern Khafajah), the other at al-'Ubaid close to Ur. In both cases the platform is surrounded by an oval-shaped outer wall, enclosing a sacred area with certain smaller buildings. The temple platform at al-'Ubaid was faced with baked brick walls, approach to the temple being by a projecting stone stairway. In the angle between the two was found a cache of objects which provide unique information about the external decoration of an Early Dynastic temple. Early Dynastic temples of the 'low' type are perhaps best represented at sites excavated in the Diyala River valley. They all retain the same basic arrangements as the early historic 'low' temples, and all, in fact, were founded at that earlier time. There are, however, some elaborations, creating a kind of temple complex. The temple of Sîn (**Nanna-Suen**) at Tutub acquired a forecourt with surrounding dependent buildings, while the temple at Tell Agrab became a complicated unit comprising a number of sanctuaries in addition to the principal shrine.

Little is known of any type of architecture in the Akkadian Period, and the site of the capital city Agade is unknown. It seems, however, that in this period the Sumerian temples continued in use and were restored.

Much of the religious architecture of the subsequent Third Dynasty of Ur is little understood. From the central precinct at Ur have been recovered the ground-plans of two large square buildings, each of which seems to be a combined temple and palace. From the same period comes a great mausoleum of the Third Dynasty kings and associated mortuary chapels. At Ešnunna (modern Tell Asmar), excavations have unearthed an interesting building complex combining a temple of the deified Šu-Suen, king of Ur, and the ruler's residence (see **deification of kings**). The temple is constructed on a central axis, leading from a main gateway flanked by towers through a central courtyard to the sanctuary itself, its niche equipped with altar and cult statue. Since the temple had been dedicated to a god-king of Ur, after the fall of Ur it was incorporated into the palace.

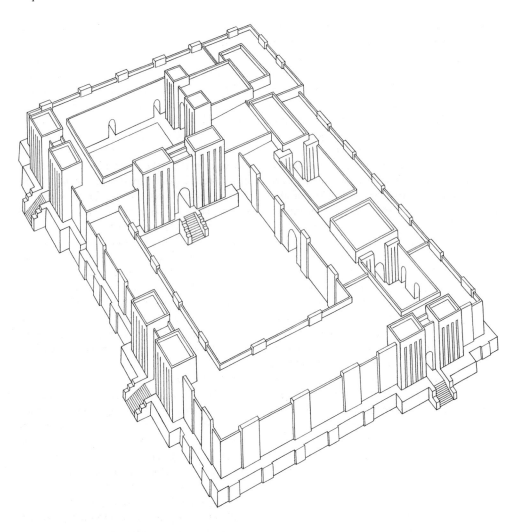

148 A reconstruction, based on the University of Chicago excavations, of the temple of the local goddess Ištar-Kitītum at Nērebtum (modern Ishchali) in the city-state of Ešnunna. The building measured approximately 100 × 60 m. Isin-Larsa Period.

148   From the beginning of the second millennium BC, there is a large temple complex at the town of Nērebtum (modern Ishchali in the Diyala region), associated with a local goddess Ištar-Kitītum (Ištar (**Inana**) of Kiti, probably a local village). It was really three separate temples, each with its own self-contained area and associated buildings. One of these temples, dedicated to Ištar herself, was built at a higher level, with a large treasury behind it. Each of the gateways to the temple was guarded by a pair of towers.

For the most part the religious architecture of the Kassites seems to have followed the existing Sumerian style. A high ziggurat with associated temples was built at the new capital Dūr-Kurigalzu (modern 'Aqar Quf near Baghdad). A temple at Uruk, however, introduces a new feature: relief figures modelled in the brickwork of the façades. Probably the figures were magically protective.

At official level, the Assyrians perhaps placed a greater emphasis than hitherto upon secular architecture – in particular the palaces of the Assyrian kings. However, heavy programmes of state religious building also flourished. The Middle Assyrian temple of Ištar at Aššur was built on the foundations of an earlier Sumerian temple of **Inana**, originally a single shrine like the temples of the south. By the thirteenth century BC, side chambers and a subsidiary shrine at the corner had been added. A purely Assyrian element was the separation of the goddesses' sanctuary from the area of worship, with the altar placed in a niche at the top of a wide stairway. Representations on seals show that the corner and gateway towers of Middle Assyrian and Neo-Assyrian temples were built to a greater height than the rest of the building, and were provided with windows. The façades were decorated with series of often elaborately decorated columns, probably a development from the buttressed façades of Sumerian temples, and the tops of the walls and towers had crenellated parapets. The remains of vaulted roofs have been found in some temples. The interiors of the temples were earlier decorated with painted panels and glazed bricks, later with monumental stone reliefs.

See **boats**; **building rites and deposits**; **ĝipar**.

Tešup: see **Tišpak**.

three: see **numbers**.

Tiāmat

In the unique version of the **creation** of the gods preserved in the Babylonian Epic of Creation, after the separation of heaven and earth the only entities in existence were Apsû (see **abzu**) and Tiāmat. Apsû personified the fresh subterranean waters and Tiāmat the salt waters: the name is a form of the word *tiamtum*, 'sea'. Apsû and Tiāmat were envisaged as a male-female pair, although it is said that 'their waters mingled together'. They engendered a line of gods including Anu (**An**), Anu's son Ea (**Enki**) and (apparently) other deities, whose activities so disturbed Apsû that he planned to exterminate them (despite Tiāmat's protests). When Ea slew Apsû, Tiāmat determined to be avenged and created eleven monsters (see **Tiāmat's creatures**) with, as her champion, the god **Qingu**, described as her 'lover'. Eventually, after a heroic contest, **Marduk**, champion of the younger gods (in the Assyrian version his name is substituted with that of **Aššur**), defeated the monsters and Qingu and destroyed Tiāmat by splitting her skull with his **mace**, while standing on her 'lower parts'. He broke her in two 'like a dried fish', using one half to roof the heavens and the other to surface the earth: her breasts formed mountains, Tigris and Euphrates flowed from her eyes, her spittle formed clouds. While in some respects Tiāmat, like other deities, is described in anthropomorphic terms, it is difficult to form a precise picture of how the author of the Epic envisaged her. In other passages it seems to be implied that the salt sea waters were inside her.

Tiāmat's creatures

In the Babylonian Epic of Creation, in order to avenge herself on the younger gods, **Tiāmat** gives birth to eleven monsters, or groups of monsters (bearing some resemblance to the **Slain Heroes** defeated by **Ninĝirsu** or **Ninurta** in a story of earlier origin). The eleven are the *mušmahhu*, *ušumgallu* and *bašmu* (three types of horned **snake**), the *mušhuššu* (a **snake-dragon**), the *lahamu* (possibly identical to **Lahmu**, the long-haired 'hero' figure), the *ugallu* ('great storm-beast', the **lion-demon**), the *uridimmu* ('raging lion', the **lion-humanoid**), the *girtablullû* ('scorpion-man': see **scorpion-people**), *ūmu dabrūtu* ('fierce storms'), *kulullû* ('fish-man': see **merman and mermaid**), and *kusarikku* (a mythical beast probably derived from the **bison**: see **bull-man**). All of these are defeated by **Marduk** (in the Assyrian edition, **Aššur**) in a great battle. Images of them were placed by Marduk in the *apsû* (**abzu**) as a monument to the victory.

The creatures of Tiāmat were sometimes invoked in magical incantations (see **magic and sorcery**), and **figurines** of some of them were

149 'The Tower of Babel' by Pieter Breughel the Elder, painted in AD 1563. The biblical story of Babylon's tower has provided a favourite theme for artists from the Middle Ages to the present day.

among those used in Neo-Assyrian protective magic, as a consequence of which their distinctive iconography can in most cases be determined (see **demons and monsters**).

Tišpak

It seems very likely that the Mesopotamian deity Tišpak was in origin identical with the Hurrian storm god Tešup. At any rate he replaced **Ninazu** as **local god** of the city of Eš-nunna in the Akkadian Period or early in the Old Babylonian Period. The city of Ešnunna (modern Tell Asmar), situated to the north-east of Babylonia near the Diyala River, lay at the southernmost extent of the area inhabited by the Hurrian people.

Tišpak was a warrior god, as implied by his epithet 'Lord of Armies'. In a Babylonian myth, Tišpak is instructed by Sîn (**Nanna-Suen**) to kill the monster Labbu. An ancient description of an artistic representation of the god has him carrying bow, arrows and **mace**.

The animal symbol of Tišpak (see **beasts of** 138 the gods) was probably the **snake-dragon**.

Tower of Babel

According to the Book of Genesis (11:1–9), the 149 Babylonians wanted to build a mighty city and a tower 'with its top in the heavens'. The completion of the project was frustrated by Yahweh, who scrambled the speech of the workers to the point where they could no longer understand one another. The people were then dispersed throughout the world.

On one level the story seems to be a myth to explain the presence of diverse human languages. In an earlier Sumerian poem, **Enki** created all the languages from one original tongue. The Biblical imagery, however, was probably inspired by the **ziggurat** or temple tower at Babylon, in Hebrew *Babel*. The metaphor of the tower for world language was suggested by a pun on Hebrew *bālal* (to confuse): 'Therefore its name was called Babel, because the Lord confused the language of all the earth'.

The ziggurat of **Marduk** at Babylon was known as E-temen-an-ki ('Foundation of heaven and earth'). It had a base 100 metres square, and reached 91 metres in height, in seven stages, the uppermost being a temple described as built in blue-glazed brick. After the partial demolition of the ziggurat in the Hellenistic Period and its subsequent decay, for many centuries visitors to Mesopotamia sought the location of the Tower of Babel at a variety of neighbouring sites.

'tree of life': see **stylised tree and its 'rituals'**.

trident: see **fork**.

turtle
In the Sumerian poem 'Ninurta and the Turtle', when **Ninurta** has recovered the **tablet of destinies**, the **me** and the divine plans, which had been stolen from **Enki** by the bird **Imdugud**, he seems unwilling to return

150 A turtle as symbol of the water god Ea. One of the emblems carved on a *kudurru* of the Kassite Period.

them to their rightful owner. Enki accordingly makes a clay turtle which he brings to life. The turtle digs a hole in the ground and covers it over, and Ninurta falls into the hole. The turtle pays no attention to the hero shouting 'Let me get out!', and Enki rounds on Ninurta: 'What success did your strength bring you? Where is your heroism now?' Presumably the *me*, the plans and the tablet of destinies were returned to Enki.

Represented in art from prehistoric times onwards, the turtle apparently first became associated with the god Ea (**Enki**) in the art of the Akkadian Period. On **kudurrus** it can 90,150 stand as a symbol of Ea, as an alternative to the **goat-fish** with ram-headed staff (see **standards, staves and sceptres of the gods**). Sometimes the turtle itself is placed on the back of a goat-fish instead of the staff. The device no doubt seemed appropriate for a god of the fresh-water **abzu**, and already had a mythological basis in the Sumerian Imdugud story.

ub-šu-ukkina: see **assembly of the gods**; **E-kur**.

udug (utukku)
Udug (Akkadian *utukku*) was a term for a particular type of **demon**, and like many such words it was originally neutral as regards the beneficial or baleful influence of the beings. Gudea, ruler of Lagaš, asks a goddess for the protection of a 'good *udug*' and a 'good **lama**' to guide him. In a large collection of magical incantations intended for use against a wide range of malevolent demons, we read both of a specific 'evil *udug*' and in general terms of evil '*udug*s' (where the term seems to include other demons as well).

See **Seven (demons)**.

Ulmašītum: see Anunītu.

ūmu dabrūtu
Ūmu dabrūtu, meaning in Babylonian 'violent storms', is the name of one, or of one of the species, of eleven monsters created by **Tiāmat** in her conflict against the younger gods (see

Tiămat's creatures). It is not known in what physical form this particular species was imagined.

underworld

What happens to people when they die? What is the nature of death? These eternal questions troubled the Mesopotamians as they have, and still do, all other peoples. Because of **disease** and man's lesser control over his environment in ancient times, the average lifespan may have been no more than thirty years, and those who did live into old age acquired experience and wisdom commanding great respect. Death is final, and there is no return from it. The dead 'bite the dust' in a very real sense when their bodies are covered with earth.

These observations found mythic expression in the idea that there is another 'world', where all the dead are together, in the ground (beneath the surface of the earth), where they continue to live some residual form of life altogether inferior to life on this earth. The Sumerians had quite a number of different names for this other world: *arali, irkalla, kukku, ekur, kigal, ganzir*, all of which were borrowed into Akkadian as well. Otherwise it was known simply as the 'earth' or 'ground' (Sumerian *ki, kur*; Akkadian *erṣetu*), the 'land of no return' or, occasionally, the 'desert', or else the 'lower world'. This last name makes clear the location of this *underworld*, and from various sources we learn that there was a stairway down to its gate (for which the name *ganzir* was used); that it was possible to open up a hole in the ground which would give access to the underworld; and that the underworld was situated even lower than the **abzu**, the fresh-water ocean beneath the earth. The last point is clearly an attempt to reconcile two conflicting cosmological ideas, and it is interesting that there are traces of other beliefs about the location of the 'underworld'. The name 'desert' sometimes used to refer to it, and the designation of the **river of the underworld** by the names of actual rivers distant from Sumer, perhaps suggest a rival belief that the world of the dead was located in a remote and inaccessible area of the earth's surface, perhaps far in the west. Although the word **kur** referring to the underworld means 'earth', there seems also to have been some confusion with *kur* meaning 'mountain(s)', and hence possibly another trace of this belief.

The underworld is always described as in complete darkness, dusty and unpleasant. All the dead, without exception, wander there, thirsting for water and having only dust to eat. Sometimes they are described as naked, or clothed with feathered wings like birds. Apart from these spirits of the dead (**gidim**), the underworld is also the home of the **dead gods**, of some **demons** (who are described as the 'offspring of *arali*' and who issue from the underworld to bring tribulation to mankind), and of a number of deities, principally **Ereš-kigal**, queen of the underworld, and her husband **Nergal**. In the Mesopotamian conception, unlike that of the Egyptians, there was no judgement or evaluation of the moral qualities of the dead. They stood before Ereškigal, who merely pronounced the sentence of death upon them while their names were recorded on a tablet by **Ĝeštinana**, scribe of the underworld, as if they were labourers turning up for work. The god **Ningišzida** functioned as majordomo of Ereškigal's household, **Pabil-saĝ** was her administrator, **Namtar** her minister or messenger, and Neti was the **gate-keeper**. The god **Enmešarra** and other gods are at times associated with the underworld, and in later Babylonian texts 600 Anunnakkū (**Anuna**) gods are assigned to the underworld. This reflects the development of a more precise picture of the nether regions.

A number of literary works from one and a half millennia reflect imaginatively the changing conceptions of the underworld. The Sumerian poem 'Gilgameš, Enkidu and the Nether World' (a version of part of which was incorporated into the Babylonian Epic of Gilgameš) describes a conversation between **Gilgameš** and the ghost of his dead servant **Enkidu** which makes it clear that while life in the underworld is most unattractive, it can be made slightly more tolerable if surviving relatives make regular offerings to the dead of food and drink, so that it is desirable to leave as many descendants as possible. Those who have no children have a hard time indeed after death, while those who do not even receive proper burial are worst off: the person who died in a fire or whose body lies in the desert does not even have a *gidim* in the underworld.

frontis.   The Sumerian poem 'The Descent of **Inana** to the Underworld' (also preserved in an Akkadian version, 'Ištar's Descent') and the myth '**Enlil** and **Ninlil**' both deal with the excep-

tional circumstances of gods who overcome the laws of nature by making a visit to the underworld from which they succeed in returning. In both cases this is only achieved by the provision of a substitute who takes their place or is left behind in the underworld so that they may return.

The Babylonian Epic of Gilgameš includes an account of a **dream** dreamed by Enkidu before his death (separate from his description of the underworld after his death), in which

151 A Neo-Babylonian cast copper or bronze plaque, apparently used as a magical protection against evil demons. Originally it probably hung in a wooden frame. Looking over the top is the god Pazuzu. The uppermost register shows emblems of the main gods, thereby probably invoking the protection of the deities symbolised. Next, a row of seven animal-headed beings, probably also magically protective. The third register shows a sick man lying in bed and flanked by fish-garbed figures (perhaps priests), accompanied by supernatural protective beings. Below, the evil goddess Lamaštu returns along the river of the underworld to her infernal home, driven on by Pazuzu and tempted by various offerings. Ht. of plaque 133 mm.

those who were kings in life are reduced to the same ghastly state as all the other dead. This emphasis on the levelling aspect of existence in the underworld is not usual. The retelling of this dream has an appropriate dramatic effect on Gilgameš.

An unusual Neo-Assyrian poem describes a vision of the underworld experienced by a prince named Kummaya, in which the prince is nearly prevented from returning to the world of the living by Nergal, who berates him for having the temerity to enter his wife's domains. The god **Išum** intercedes on his behalf and he is allowed to return – in fact to wake up, since the grim vision turns out to have been a dream. It is very detailed, but perhaps idiosyncratic. The prince has been thought to be Assurbanipal, later king of Assyria (ruled 668–*c.*627 BC).

See **afterlife; death and funerary practices; galla; kur; Lugal-irra and Meslamta-ea; night; Ninazu; Nungal; river of the underworld; Šakkan; Šul-pa-e**.

Urarṭian gods

The state of Van, better known by the name Urarṭu applied to it by the Assyrians (and appearing in the Bible in the form Ararat), lay in the mountainous area around and to the south of Lake Van in what is now south-east Turkey and the neighbouring areas of north-west Iran and Armenia. The oldest definite evidence for the kingdom is from the third quarter of the ninth century BC. Urarṭu, which rose to become a powerful influence in the international politics of its day and a thorn in the flesh of Assyrian kings, was finally overthrown by the Scythians and absorbed into the Median, then into the Persian empire. The people of Urarṭu spoke a late form of the Hurrian language and preserved some aspects of Hurrian culture. Among their deities were:

Haldi, the national god of Urarṭu;

Bagbarti, the wife of Haldi;

Tešeba, a storm god (corresponding to Hurrian Tešup);

Šiwini, a sun god (corresponding to Hurrian Šimigi);

Šelardi, a moon god.

Uraš (god)

The god Uraš was the local deity of the northern Babylonian city of Dilbat. He is mentioned in connection with the city in the Prologue to the Laws of Hammurabi of Babylon. In one tradition, he was regarded as an ancestor of **An**. In later periods he was even identified with An, or with **Ninurta**. He was among the gods worshipped in the city of Aššur. The Uraš Gate at Babylon was named probably from the direction of Dilbat, to the south of Babylon.

Uraš (goddess)

Uraš is the name of a goddess who in some traditions is the wife of **An**. In ancient commentaries, the name Uraš is explained as meaning 'earth', and according to other traditions the wife of An is **Ki** ('earth' in Sumerian). Uraš was said to be the mother of the goddesses **Ninisina** and **Nisaba**. It has been suggested that the element -urta in the name of the god **Ninurta** (where Nin- means 'lord') is the same as the word *uraš*, but this cannot be definitely shown.

Usmû: see **Isimud**.

Uttu

Uttu was the name of the Sumerian goddess associated with weaving. Since the same sign is also used sometimes to write the word for 'spider', it is possible that she was envisaged in the form of a spider spinning a web.

Utu (Šamaš)

Utu was the Sumerian sun god, whose Akkadian name was Šamaš. He represents the brilliant light of the sun, which returns every day to illuminate the life of mankind, as well as giving beneficial warmth, which causes plants to grow. In the Sumerian tradition, Utu was the son of **Nanna**, the moon god, and twin brother of **Inana**. In Akkadian traditions he

31, 152

152 Aspects of Šamaš, from cylinder seals of the Akkadian Period. The god is shown as the rising sun, emerging through the open gates of the eastern mountains; at his court receiving worshippers; and as dispenser of divine justice. He is distinguished by the rays emanating from his shoulders and by his pruning-saw (*šaššaru*).

was sometimes made the son of Anu (**An**) or of **Enlil**. His wife was **Šerida** or (in Akkadian) Aya. The two principal temples of Utu, both called E-babbar ('White House') were at Sippar in Akkad, and Larsa in southern Sumer. In the Assyrian Period, there was a joint temple of Šamaš and Sîn (**Nanna-Suen**) at Aššur. The principal minister of Utu, his charioteer and, according to some traditions, his son, was the minor deity Bunene, worshipped from the Old Babylonian Period at Sippar and Uruk, and later at Aššur.

The cult of Utu is attested from the earliest 82 times. Described as bearded and 'long-armed', Utu emerged from the doors of heaven at dawn and made a daily journey across the skies to enter the 'interior of heaven' once again at dusk by the parallel set of doors on the western hori-152 zon. Cylinder seals show two gods opening the doors of heaven for Utu to come forth (see **gatekeepers**): the god brandishes his emblem the pruning-saw, typical of such saws still used in the Near East, with an arc-shaped blade and large, jagged teeth. In the Babylonian Epic of Gilgameš, the twin-peaked mountain Mašu is located near the eastern doors of heaven.

Presumably because the sun, in its path across the skies, sees everything, Utu/Šamaš came to be regarded as a god of truth, justice and right. Šamaš, together with Adad (see **Iškur**), is invoked during Babylonian extispicy rituals. As a protector of right and destroyer of evil, he also had a warrior aspect to his personality.

A third aspect of Utu was his direct interest in the affairs of mankind. One of the early legendary kings of Uruk is described as a 'son of Utu' in the composition called the 'Sumerian King List', and Utu acted as a special protector of some of the later heroic kings of the city, for instance **Gilgameš**. In the Babylonian Epic of Gilgameš, Šamaš helps the hero against the monstrous guardian of the Cedar Forest, Humbaba (**Huwawa**). In the Sumerian poem 'Dumuzi's Dream', Utu helps **Dumuzi** to escape from the **galla**-demons who have come to take him to the **underworld**. Babylonian Šamaš also acts as a just advisor in the legend of **Etana**, when the eagle, who has been cruelly tricked into a pit by the serpent, implores the god's help. Šamaš brings along Etana, who has been praying to Šamaš for the 'plant of giving birth' (see **'plant of life'**), and Etana and the eagle are able to assist each other: subsequently Etana rides on the eagle's back to heaven.

A completely different rôle is assumed by Utu in a typically irreverent Sumerian poem when he tries to seduce his twin sister Inana by getting her drunk. The goddess of love responds by pretending complete ignorance of sexual intercourse or even kissing.

See **Arabian gods; bull-man; cross; horse; lion-humanoid; night; ring-staff; rod and ring; Sacred Marriage; solar disc; Ṣalmu; scorpion-people; winged disc**.

utukku: see **udug**.

vase with streams
The device known as the 'flowing vase' or 'fertility vase' is a round-bodied, short-necked, flared-rim jar with streams issuing from its mouth. Sometimes **fish** are shown swimming along the streams, or replacing the streams but implying their presence. The vase can be held by figures of various kinds. It is a common element in art from early historic to Achaemenid 16,63 times. The Akkadian name for the vessel was apparently *hegallu*, 'abundance'.

In the Akkadian and Neo-Sumerian Periods, the vase is sometimes held by the water god **Enki** (Ea), but at this time, as in later 115 periods, it is most often held by figures of **Lahmu**. Apparently the motif was associated 153 with Ea and the creatures of the **abzu**, among whom Lahmu was sometimes to be counted. The vase was not, however, a divine symbol in the sense that it represented a particular deity, but was a general attribute of certain divine and semi-divine figures, perhaps signifying **fertility** and abundance.

Venus: see **Inana**.

visions: see **dreams and visions**.

153 Naked Lahmu gods hold vases with flowing streams, to which the water-buffalo come to drink. From the cylinder seal of Ibni-šarrum, scribe to King Šar-kali-šarrī of Agade. Akkadian Period.

wedge

154
151 A wedge-shaped implement is depicted as a divine symbol or attribute in art from the Old Babylonian down to the Neo-Babylonian Period. It probably represents not so much the basic element of cuneiform writing as the
2,5 actual stylus used to produce this script on leather-hard clay. In practice a reed was used, but gods' styli might be of gold or silver. On seals and sealings of the Old Babylonian Period, this wedge is held by a number of

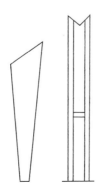

154 A wedge-shaped stylus and tablet or writing board, symbolising the scribal god Nabû. A common device among the symbols of the gods on Neo-Babylonian monuments.

apparently different male deities, including the water god Ea (**Enki**); a god who stands on a **bull**, so probably Adad (see **Iškur**); and a god who stands on a **snake-dragon**, probably **Nabû**. From Middle Babylonian and Middle Assyrian times we find the wedge not only as an attribute of the scribal god Nabû, but also as his 10 independent symbol. It may be shown vertical or horizontal, single or double, sometimes next 90 to (or replaced by) another piece of writing 20 apparatus, which has been interpreted as a tablet or writing board. Sometimes, especially on Neo-Babylonian seals, the symbol is shown on the back of Nabû's snake-dragon, or the god, holding his wedge, himself stands upon 110 the dragon.

Some temple slaves were branded with the symbol of a wedge (see **dedication**).

wine: see **alcohol**; **food and drink of the gods**; **libation**.

winged disc

Both the origins and meaning of the winged solar disc are matters of controversy. Probably its ultimate origins were in Egypt, from where it passed via the Syrians and the Hittites to Mesopotamia. It first appears there in the glyptic art of the Mitannian kingdom, and was then transmitted to Assyrian and Babylonian art. 21,155 Taken over by the Achaemenid Persians, it remained an important emblem in Iran until

155 Assurnasirpal II, king of Assyria (883–859 BC), rides into battle, firing at the enemy. From the sky he receives more than symbolic support from a god flying in a winged disc. Monumental stone relief from the royal palace at Kalhu (modern Nimrud). Ht. 0.93 m.

modern times. Often in Assyria, and normally in Achaemenid art, the figure of a god is shown 131,144 above the central disc, in Assyria sometimes with the heads of two facing figures, perhaps 82 **scorpion-people**, set at the ends of the wings.

The disc in Assyria was a symbol of Šamaš (**Utu**), though it has been attributed by some scholars to **Aššur** or **Ninurta**. The disc is often supported by supernatural creatures, 82 such as a pair of **bull-men**, a pair of scorpion-men or a figure of **Lahmu**.

See Ṣalmu; stylised tree and its 'rituals'.

'winged gate': see **bull and 'winged gate'**.

witchcraft

Witchcraft, or sorcery, is the term used for the less attractive aspects of magic, which played a prominent part in everyday life in ancient Mesopotamia. Witchcraft was officially disap-proved of because of its harmful effects and was punishable under the law, although its techniques were probably not very different from those of acceptable white magic. The practitioners of witchcraft seem to have been more often female than male. According to the laws of Hammurabi of Babylon (reigned 1848–1806 3 BC), a person accused of witchcraft had to submit to the **river ordeal**, and if proved guilty forfeited all property to the accuser. However, if they were proved innocent, the accuser was put to death.

See: **magic and sorcery**.

word

The idea of the power of a god's word as an instrument of **creation** is less common in Mesopotamia than, for instance, in the Hebrew literature of the Bible. However, just as kings command and things happen, so the Mesopotamian **gods** had only to utter for actuality to follow. The Sumerian *balaĝ* poems (long religious lyric poems) abound in meditations on the 'Word' of particular gods, dwelling as much on the terrifying and potentially destructive aspects of this attribute as on its beneficial, creative side: the Word of **An** or **Enlil** can cause floods, destruction and **diseases** just as much as it can bring new life to the people.

In magical practice, it was extremely important to pronounce the words of an incantation clearly and exactly. Incantations are usually in Sumerian or Akkadian, occasionally in the Elamite language and only rarely are they complete mumbo jumbo, although some words of the 'abracadabra' type are used.

See **magic and sorcery**.

wrestlers

156 Wrestling seems to have been a favourite sport among the Sumerians and Babylonians. **Gilgameš** and **Enkidu** wrestle when they first meet: it has been suggested that the passage in the Old Babylonian version of the Epic of Gilgameš describes what is called belt-wrestling, where each contestant grapples the other by the belt while trying to floor his opponent.

In some magical protective rituals, images or **figurines** of wrestlers were used. 'You make two bitumen figurines of wrestlers linked together and place them on the threshold'; 'You draw twin wrestlers in whitewash on the gate; you place bitumen figurines of twin wrestlers on the threshold, left and right.' Boxers as well as wrestlers are depicted in Babylonian art.

See **magic and sorcery**.

Xisouthros: see **Ziusura**.

Zababa

Zababa was the **local god** of the important city of Kiš in northern Babylonia. His cult is attested already from the Early Dynastic Period. In the local tradition of Kiš, his wife was **Inana/ Ištar**, and the worship of Inana of Kiš was an important secondary cult of the goddess. The personality of Zababa appears to have been that of a god of war, and from the Old Babylonian Period he was identified with **Ninĝirsu** or **Ninurta**. In a **list of gods** he is described as the '**Marduk** of battle'. The principal cult centre of Zababa was the temple E-mete-ursaĝ at Kiš. An eagle-headed staff (see **standards, staves and sceptres of the gods**) was his symbol.

ziggurats

Ziqqurrātu (usually anglicised as 'ziggurats') were pyramidal, stepped temple towers constructed at many of the cities of southern Mesopotamia from about 2200 until 550 BC, and imitated in the north by the Assyrians. They were built of solid brick, without internal rooms or spaces (save for drainage shafts). On the summit was constructed one or more shrines, usually to the principal god of the city, and sometimes including the bedchamber used for **Sacred Marriage** ceremonies. Access to the summit, when there is evidence, was by an exterior triple stairway or by spiral ramp. In

156 A wrestling bout depicted on a limestone plaque of the Early Dynastic Period, from the temple of the goddess Nintu at Tutub (modern Khafajah). W.240 mm.

other cases, if there was access at all, it may have been from the roof-tops of neighbouring buildings. Usually the structures were square or rectangular, averaging about 40 × 50 metres at base. No example is preserved to its full original height. The largest surviving ziggurat is at Al-Untaš-Napiriša (modern Choga Zanbil), in Elam, built in the thirteenth century BC, 100 metres square and preserved to 24 metres high (which is estimated at slightly less than half its original height). Uniquely, access was via internal stairways.

157 The best-preserved example is that of the moon god **Nanna** at Ur. The lower part of the structure, built by Ur-Nammu, founder of the Third Dynasty, is substantially intact, and enough of the upper part survives for reliable reconstruction. The monument is 64 × 46 metres at base and originally about 12 metres in height with three storeys (increased to seven by Nabonidus in the sixth century BC). The corners are oriented to the cardinal points of the compass. The walls, sheer on three sides but relieved by shallow buttresses, curve slightly outwards from corner to corner and slope steadily inwards towards the summit, where the shrine stood. This was reached by a great stairway on the northern side, dividing into three separate stairways, each of a hundred steps, from the level of the lowest terrace to the ground. Two of these stairways lean against the walls, while the third projects at right angles at the middle of the structure, focusing attention on the central axis, and so on the summit and shrine. The approach on all four sides was through a broad courtyard with gateways flanked by towers. The core of the ziggurat is sun-dried brick, faced with more than two metres of baked bricks set in bitumen.

The ziggurat at Ur shares some features with ziggurats in general, throughout the long history of their construction. Horizontal layers of reeds or reed matting were usually placed at intervals between the courses of brick, and external weep-holes and internal vertical shafts were intended to release moisture and rainwater.

The development of the ziggurat should probably be seen as an extension of the principles of 'high' temple construction (see **temples and temple architecture**). There is evidence for the existence of models of ziggurats. On seals the association of ziggurats 158 with symbols of gods may suggest that such

157 The ziggurat tower at Ur, in present-day southern Iraq, partially reconstructed.

158 A worshipper stands before a censer, an altar with offerings, a symbol and a (model ?) ziggurat. From a cylinder seal of the Neo-Babylonian Period.

models were placed in shrines. In late Babylonian times it is likely that instead of, or in addition to, their original function as temple towers, the ziggurats were employed as astronomical observation posts (see **astrology and astronomy**).

See **Tower of Babel**.

Ziusura (Ūt-napišti)

Ziusura is the hero of the story of the **Flood** in a Sumerian version probably dating from the late Old Babylonian Period. The **gods** decide to send a flood 'to destroy the seed of the human race'. A certain god takes pity on mankind and instructs the king of Šuruppag, Ziusura, to build a great boat, in which he is able to survive the waters. After his salvation, he makes an offering of thanks and eventually receives an 'eternal inspiration', going to live in the country of **Dilmun**.

A version in Akkadian of the Flood Story, incorporating the creation of mankind, may be of slightly earlier date; part of a later Standard Babylonian version also survives. In these, the protagonist is called Atra-hasīs, 'the very wise'. The best known account of the Flood, however, is that incorporated into the Standard Babylonian Epic of **Gilgameš**. In search of immortality, Gilgameš journeys to visit one Ūt-napišti (probably *Ūta-napištam*, 'He found life'), remembering that this man had received

eternal life after surviving the Flood. Ūt-napišti's story is then related. This time the initial setting is the city of Šuruppag, and it is Ea (**Enki**) himself who instructs his protégé on the construction of a vessel, by which his family, together with artisans, animals and precious metals can be saved. After seven days of riding the storms, the ship runs aground on Mount Nimuš (probably in the Judi Dagh in south-east Turkey). After another seven days a pigeon, a swallow and a raven are sent out. The last finds a place to perch and so does not return, indicating that the waters are receding. The survivors then leave the ship and make sacrifices to heaven. Repenting the entire business, **Enlil** rewards Ūt-napišti for saving human and animal life by the grant of immortality: 'Until now Ūt-napišti has been only human, but from now on Ūt-napišti and his wife shall be like us gods.'

When Gilgameš requests Ūt-napišti to show him the secret of immortality, the hero of the Flood challenges him to stay awake and conquer sleep. In this Gilgameš fails: he can never be immortal. Ūt-napišti does tell Gilgameš, however, of a plant that has rejuvenating properties for mortals. Gilgameš acquires the plant but loses it to a passing snake, who eats it up, shedding its old skin for a new one (see '**plant of life**').

The latest version of the story is one written in Greek in about 275 BC by **Berossos**, priest of Bēl (**Marduk**) at Babylon. The hero is now called Xisouthros, clearly echoing the original Sumerian name. At the command of the god Kronos, Xisouthros saves his family, friends and the animals in a ship which he has constructed. When the Flood subsides, he releases birds in order to test the recession of the waves; the third group do not return. Xisouthros disembarks with his wife, daughter and pilot, who make sacrifices to the gods. They disappear. The rest of the company also disembark and proceed to Babylonia on foot, the vessel coming to rest on the Cordaean mountains of Armenia.

The Biblical narrative of Noah and the Flood in Genesis shows many similarities to the story of Ziusura in the Mesopotamian tradition.

See **Dilmun**.

zodiac

The association of certain constellations with the months of the year was first made by the Babylonians. By about 1000 BC they recognised eighteen zodiacal constellations (constellations through whose path the moon and planets appeared to move): the Hired Man (corresponding to our Aries), the Stars (the Pleiades, see **seven dots; Seven (gods)**), the **Bull of Heaven** (Taurus), the True Shepherd of Anu (**An**) (Orion), the Old Man (Perseus), the **Crook** (Auriga), the Great Twins (Gemini, see **Lugal-irra and Meslamta-ea**), the Crab (Cancer), the **Lion** (Leo), the Furrow (Virgo, see **Šala**), the Scales (Libra), the **Scorpion** (Scorpius), **Pabilsaǧ** (Sagittarius), the **Goat-fish** (Capricornus), the Great One

(Aquarius), the Tail, the Swallow and **Anunītu** (these last three forming together Pisces). Later the constellation the Field (Pegasus) was added.

By 600–500 BC these were systematised in such a way that they were distributed among the twelve months, singly or sometimes in pairs. For instance, the second month of the Babylonian year (corresponding to mid-April to mid-May) had both Taurus and the Pleiades; the third month Gemini and Orion; and the twelfth month Pisces and Pegasus. By about 400 BC the number of zodiacal constellations was reduced to the twelve that we are familiar with today, each covering 30° of the sky, and beginning with Aries for the first month (corresponding to mid-March to mid-April).

All these constellations are illustrated on astronomical tablets and on stamp-seals of the Hellenistic Period. Some of them may also be depicted on earlier **kudurrus**. 147,1

See **astrology and astronomy**.

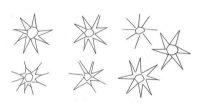

159 Signs for constellations, including the Pleiades, Leo and Taurus, drawn on a clay tablet with an astronomical text, found at Uruk (modern Warka) and dating from the Seleucid Period.

Recommended further reading in English

Georges Roux, *Ancient Iraq*, 3rd ed., Penguin Books, Harmondsworth, 1992.
[Undoubtedly the best general introduction.]

Nicholas Postgate, *Early Mesopotamia: Society and Economy at the Dawn of History*,
paperback ed., Routledge, London, 1994.

Susan Pollock, *Ancient Mesopotamia: The Eden that Never Was* (Case Studies in Early
Societies series), Cambridge University Press, 1999.

Julian Reade, *Mesopotamia*, revised ed., British Museum Press, London, 2000.
[Covers the period down to the early second millennium BC.]

Joan Oates, *Babylon*, revised ed., Thames and Hudson, London, 1986.

H.W.F. Saggs, *The Greatness that was Babylon*, revised ed., Sidgwick and Jackson,
London, 1988.

H.W.F. Saggs, *The Might that was Assyria*, Sidgwick and Jackson, London, 1984.

Amélie Kuhrt, *The Ancient Near East, c. 3000-330 BC*, 2 vols, Routledge, London, 1995.

Marc Van De Mieroop, *A History of the Ancient Near East c. 3000-323 BC*, Blackwell,
Oxford, 2003. [These two works complement one another very satisfactorily: Kuhrt is
detailed, with many further references, while Van De Mieroop's narrative is very
readable, with a strong forward thrust.]

P.R.S. Moorey, *The Ancient Near East*, Ashmolean Museum Publications, Oxford, 1987.

Michael Roaf, *Cultural Atlas of Mesopotamia and the Ancient Near East*, Facts on File,
New York and Oxford, 1990.

Piotr Bienkowski and Alan Millard (eds), *Dictionary of the Ancient Near East*, British
Museum Press, London, 2000.

Eric M. Meyers (ed.), *The Oxford Encyclopedia of Archaeology in the Near East*, 5 vols,
New York and Oxford, 1997. [Poorly edited but includes some excellent individual
articles.]

Jack M. Sasson (ed.), *Civilizations of the Ancient Near East*, 4 vols, Charles Scribner's
Sons, New York, 1985. [Valuable collection of essays on various aspects of history and
society in the ancient Near East, including Egypt.]

Gwendolyn Leick, *A Dictionary of Ancient Near Eastern Mythology*, Routledge, London
and New York, 1991.

Stephanie Dalley, *Myths from Mesopotamia* (The World's Classics series), paperback ed.,
Oxford University Press, 1991. [Up-to-date translations of the myths in Akkadian.]

Erica Reiner, *'Your thwarts in pieces, your mooring rope cut': Poetry from Babylonia and
Assyria*, University of Michigan, Ann Arbor, 1985.

James B. Pritchard (ed.), *Ancient Near Eastern Texts relating to the Old Testament*, 3rd ed. with Supplement, Princeton University Press, 1969.

James B. Pritchard (ed.), *The Ancient Near East in Pictures relating to the Old Testament*, 2nd ed. with Supplement, Princeton University Press, 1969.

E. Strommenger, *The Art of Ancient Mesopotamia*, Thames and Hudson, London, 1964. [Excellent photographs by M. Hirmer.]

J.E. Curtis and J.E. Reade (eds), *Art and Empire: Treasures from Assyria in the British Museum*, British Museum Press, London, 1995. [Numerous full-colour photographic illustrations.]

Julian Reade, *Assyrian Sculpture*, revised ed., British Museum Press, London, 1998.

Beatrice Teissier, *Ancient Near Eastern Cylinder Seals from the Marcopoli Collection*, University of California Press, Berkeley, 1984. [Valuable especially for its outstanding introduction on the history of cylinder seals.]

D. Collon, *First Impressions: Cylinder Seals in the Ancient Near East*, British Museum Publications, London, 1987. [Extensively illustrated.]

C.B.F. Walker, *Cuneiform* (Reading the Past series), British Museum Publications, London, 1987.

The Oriental Institute, University of Oxford, The Electronic Text Corpus of Sumerian Literature (www–etcsl.orient.ox.ac.uk).